Literary Criticism and Cultural Theory

*Edit*ed by
William E. Cain
Professor of English
Wellesley College

A Routledge Series

Literary Criticism and Cultural Theory

William E. Cain, *General Editor*

The Imperial Quest and Modern Memory from Conrad to Greene
J. M. Rawa

The Ethics of Exile
Colonialism in the Fictions of Charles Brockden Brown and J. M. Coetzee
Timothy Francis Strode

The Romantic Sublime and Middle-Class Subjectivity in the Victorian Novel
Stephen Hancock

Vital Contact
Downclassing Journeys in American Literature from Herman Melville to Richard Wright
Patrick Chura

Cosmopolitan Fictions
Ethics, Politics, and Global Change in the Works of Kazuo Ishiguro, Michael Ondaatje, Jamaica Kincaid, and J. M. Coetzee
Katherine Stanton

Outsider Citizens
The Remaking of Postwar Identity in Wright, Beauvoir, and Baldwin
Sarah Relyea

An Ethics of Becoming
Configurations of Feminine Subjectivity in Jane Austen, Charlotte Brontë, and George Eliot
Sonjeong Cho

Narrative Desire and Historical Reparations
A. S. Byatt, Ian McEwan, Salman Rushdie
Tim S. Gauthier

Nihilism and the Sublime Postmodern
The (Hi)Story of a Difficult Relationship from Romanticism to Postmodernism
Will Slocombe

Depression Glass
Documentary Photography and the Medium of the Camera Eye in Charles Reznikoff, George Oppen, and William Carlos Williams
Monique Claire Vescia

Fatal News
Reading and Information Overload in Early Eighteenth-Century Literature
Katherine E. Ellison

Negotiating Copyright
Authorship and the Discourse of Literary Property Rights in Nineteenth-Century America
Martin T. Buinicki

"Foreign Bodies"
Trauma, Corporeality, and Textuality in Contemporary American Culture
Laura Di Prete

Overheard Voices
Address and Subjectivity in Postmodern American Poetry
Ann Keniston

Museum Mediations
Reframing Ekphrasis in Contemporary American Poetry
Barbara K. Fischer

The Politics of Melancholy from Spenser to Milton
Adam H. Kitzes

Urban Revelations
Images of Ruin in the American City, 1790-1860
Donald J. McNutt

Postmodernism and Its Others
The Fiction of Ishmael Reed, Kathy Acker, and Don DeLillo
Jeffrey Ebbesen

Postmodernism and Its Others
The Fiction of Ishmael Reed, Kathy Acker, and Don DeLillo

Jeffrey Ebbesen

Routledge
New York & London

Published in 2006 by
Routledge
Taylor & Francis Group
270 Madison Ave,
New York NY 10016

Published in Great Britain by
Routledge
Taylor & Francis Group
2 Park Square,
Milton Park, Abingdon,
Oxon, OX14 4RN

© 2006 by Taylor & Francis Group, LLC
Routledge is an imprint of Taylor & Francis Group

Transferred to Digital Printing 2010

International Standard Book Number-10: 0-415-97544-1 (Hardcover)
International Standard Book Number-13: 978-0-415-97544-5 (Hardcover)
Library of Congress Card Number 2005031226

No part of this book may be reprinted, reproduced, transmitted, or utilized in any form by any electronic, mechanical, or other means, now known or hereafter invented, including photocopying, microfilming, and recording, or in any information storage or retrieval system, without written permission from the publishers.

Trademark Notice: Product or corporate names may be trademarks or registered trademarks, and are used only for identification and explanation without intent to infringe.

Library of Congress Cataloging-in-Publication Data

Ebbesen, Jeffrey, 1961-
    Postmodernism and its others : the fiction of Ishmael Reed, Kathy Acker, and Don DeLillo / by Jeffrey Ebbesen.
         p. cm. -- (Literary criticism and cultural theory)
    Includes bibliographical references (p.   ) and index.
    ISBN 0-415-97544-1 (acid-free paper)
    1. American fiction--20th century--History and criticism. 2. Postmodernism (Literature)--United States. 3. Reed, Ishmael, 1938--Technique. 4. Acker, Kathy, 1948--Technique. 5. DeLillo, Don--Technique. I. Title. II. Series.

PS374.P64E22 2005
813'.5409113--dc22   2005031226

ISBN10: 0-415-97544-1 (hbk)
ISBN10: 0-415-80292-X (pbk)

ISBN13: 978-0-415-97544-5 (hbk)
ISBN13: 978-0-415-80292-5 (pbk)

Taylor & Francis Group
is the Academic Division of Informa plc.

Visit the Taylor & Francis Web site at
http://www.taylorandfrancis.com

and the Routledge Web site at
http://www.routledge-ny.com

Publisher's Note
The publisher has gone to great lengths to ensure the quality of this reprint but points out that some imperfections in the original may be apparent.

Permissions

Excerpts from *Conjure: Selected Poems, 1963–1970,* copyright by Ishmael Reed, reprinted by permission of the Lowenstein-Yost Associates

Excerpts from *Mumbo Jumbo* by Ishmael Reed, copyright 1972 by Ishmael Reed, reprinted by permission of Lowenstein-Yost Associates and Scribner, an imprint of Simon & Schuster Adult Publishing Group

Excerpts from *The Adult Life of Henri Toulouse Lautrec,* by Kathy Acker, reprinted by permission of Grove Atlantic, Inc.

Excerpts from *Divine Horsemen: The Living Gods of Haiti,* copyright 1953 by Maya Deren, reprinted courtesy of McPherson and Company.

Excerpts from *White Noise,* by Don DeLillo, copyright 1984, 1985 by Don DeLillo, used by permission of Viking Penguin, a division of Penguin Group (USA) Inc.

To Annie and Jules, for everything.

Contents

Acknowledgments	xi
Introduction What is Postmodernism, and What Difference Does It Make?	1
Chapter One Politicizing Authority, Authorship, and Identity in Ishmael Reed's *Mumbo Jumbo*	15
Chapter Two Combative Textualities: Kathy Acker's *The Adult Life of Toulouse Lautrec by Henri Toulouse Lautrec*	67
Chapter Three Don DeLillo's *White Noise:* Reading Consumers and the Politics of Commodified Education	113
Chapter Four Repoliticizing Depoliticized Categories: Literary Inheritance, Textual Activism, and the Space of Reading	163
Notes	203
Bibliography	229
Index	243

Acknowledgments

Like many graduate students, I spent years trying complete my dissertation while simultaneously cobbling together a livelihood through numerous low paying adjunct positions. While the process was painful and deeply depressing at times, my committee members at University of Connecticut unflaggingly supported my project; without their generous advice, critique, and council, this book—which is a revised version of that dissertation—would most likely never have been completed. As my primary advisor, Patrick Hogan encouraged theoretical and argumentative rigor but also offered invaluable practical advice on writing. In addition, he deserves thanks for his generosity in matters intellectual and otherwise. Another member, Clare Eby, helped me avoid the linguistic pomposity which so often makes academic writing inaccessible, removing it from the public sphere. She also offered sound commentary and advice on American and African-American literature. On a more personal level, Clare provided consoling words in my bleaker moments. I am indebted to Jerry Phillips for our conversations and arguments about Marxism.

Other scholars also contributed to this book's content. Conversations with Paul Maltby at West Chester University inform my discussions of modernism and postmodernism, as well as my analysis of Don DeLillo's *White Noise*. Mike McColl deserves special thanks for reading numerous versions of the manuscript, providing critique and insight. Pete Puchek also provided writing advice and intellectual support, as did Bronwyn Lepore.

Bruce McPherson of McPherson & Company deserves recognition for his generous and accommodating treatment of a first time author. Mercedes Marx from Lowenstein-Yost went beyond the call of duty in her assistance with the Reed material. Max Novick of Routledge offered valuable editorial advice and demonstrated enormous patience. Production editor Robert Sims displayed a similar forbearance. Carey Nershi of IBT was enormously gracious and accommodating regarding last minute manuscript revisions.

I also owe thanks to Ishmael Reed who, in April 2002, allowed a graduate student to lunch with him and discuss his work.

Finally, I am indebted to my wife, Anne, for her financial and moral support, as well as her tireless work on manuscript formatting and editing. Without her, this work would never have been possible.

Introduction
What is Postmodernism, and What Difference Does It Make?

Many current theorists and writers claim that the most representative cultural artifacts of our time are "postmodern" and fit within the aesthetic-historical category frequently termed "postmodernism." As the prefix "post" and its companion (i.e. "modernism") suggest, the term "postmodernism" bears some relation to that which has come before it, presumably, "modernism." But as Rudolf Beck, Hildegard Kuester and Mark Kuester suggest, the term covers widely disparate phenomena and is by no means universally defined, applied, or agreed upon. Their outline of the word's myriad usage succinctly describes this battlefield of contending ideas:

> While some critics define it [postmodernism] as a counter movement challenging modernism, others prefer to see it as a continuation of modernist endeavors. Sometimes critics do not even agree on whether certain artists should be counted as moderns or postmoderns, for postmodernism is far from being a homogeneous movement. For example, there is a spectrum of quite different definitions in various cultural fields such as literature, art, history, architecture and music, and these definitions were created at different points in history stretching from the beginning of the twentieth century to the 1960s, 70s, and 80s. (Beck, Kuester, and Kuester 3)

Obviously, these divergent construals render the term "postmodernism" highly problematic, often making it an all purpose descriptor for whatever cultural product one pleases.[1] Although scholars have produced significant works attempting to define "postmodernism" and apply it to cultural-material phenomena (e.g. Jameson 1983, 1997; Hutcheon 1988), writers continue to debate postmodernism's character and categorical legitimacy.

Far less debatable, however, is poststructuralism's historically central role in theorizing postmodernism. Indeed, critics have discussed poststructuralism and its connection to postmodernism since at least the nineteen-seventies. In the early eighties Jürgen Habermas even equated poststructural theory with postmodernism (Habermas 1981; Huyssen 205). Habermas' equation of theory and practice may have been overly simplistic.[2] But if one considers the primary exegetic methods critics frequently use to define and analyze "postmodern" literary works, they inevitably derive from the poststructural theories of Jacques Derrida and a handful of other writers (e.g. Roland Barthes, Jean Baudrillard, Jean François Lyotard, Michel Foucault, Julia Kristeva, Jacques Lacan). This small group of foundational theories I loosely term "poststructural postmodernism." While the theories of poststructural-postmodernism possess their own unique insights, they share one essential feature. That feature is extreme epistemological skepticism, and it exceeds—if not in kind, then at least in degree—that usually associated with modernism.[3] This thoroughgoing disbelief is traceable to the poststructuralist assumptions "that the subject is constituted in language" and "that there is nothing outside the text. . . ." (Huyssen 208)

Although many poststructural critics claim this textualizing gesture represents a theoretical advance beyond modernism, Andreas Huyssen observes that it ultimately entails a postmodern aestheticism similar to the modernist one it rejects; to demonstrate the point, he points to the qualitative literary elements often used to define both modernism and postmodernism (as figured in poststructuralism). For example, modernism and poststructural-postmodernism "emphatically privilege aesthetic innovation and experiment," as well as thoroughgoing textual "self-reflexiveness" (Huyssen 208). In this sense, two rather obvious points deserve emphasis. First, poststructural theorists of postmodern literature usually believe this formal experimentation and radical reflexivity—both of which are inextricably tied to content—reflect the aforementioned epistemological-linguistic reading of self and world. Moreover, and related to this, they hold that extensive literary deployment of such techniques enacts a progressive politics by undermining the repressive logic of Enlightenment reason. According to this view, reason is responsible for past and present class, race, and gender oppression.

The books I consider in the following chapters, Ishmael Reed's *Mumbo Jumbo* (1972), Kathy Acker's *The Adult Life of Toulouse Lautrec by Henri Toulouse Lautrec* (1978; hereafter *A.L.T.L.*), and Don DeLillo's *White Noise* (1985), are typically placed within the postmodern category according to the above qualitative markers and are thus said to embody the epistemological skepticism just noted. But poststructuralism's emphasis on textuality, with its concomitant rejection of all foundational assumptions, renders this simplistic categorization highly suspect. Specifically, the aforementioned novels critique dominant cultural ideology from a modernist political perspective, namely, one committed to ethical and historical truths. Poststructural-postmodernism rejects this ontological commitment, replacing it with an idealistic anti-foundational philosophy which reduces material reality to infinitely interpretable texts. This textual view necessarily scatters reality and self interminably, rendering state, politics and political critique impossible because they have no foundation. Even the simple notion of "consent" loses legitimacy because there is no reason to choose it over, say, totalitarianism. In this sense characterizing Reed, Acker, and DeLillo as poststructurally postmodern requires one ignore their grounded politics in favor of this groundless and relativistic textualism. This conflict between the three authors' modernist political grounding and poststructural-postmodernism's rejection constitutes an important thematic in this book's general problematizing of the postmodern category.

Poststructuralism's refiguration of the literary-social sphere constitutes the stage for this conflict in so far as it defines postmodern literature largely according to formal experimentation, radical reflexivity, and other related narrative techniques and content. These features reflect poststructuralism's radical reinterpretion of "authorship," text," and "reader." This refiguration follows from the epistemological-linguistic premises noted above, and results, again, in an aporetic rejection of truth and grounded politics. Accordingly, it dismantles traditional notions of self, be it an authoring or reading self, as well as text, and world. A brief reconsideration of several poststructural founders already mentioned illustrates various particulars regarding this radical textualization. As their theories overlap and impinge on all three categories, I list them in no particular order. Jean Baudrillard, one influential figure on the list, offers a textualism which reduces reality to pure simulation. According to his view, inescapable and coercive capitalist media replaces world and self with endlessly repetitive images and meanings having no external reference. Here, as in many of the accounts which follow, the authorial self and the reading subject devolve to mere textual representations, though in this case they become mere copies of the consumer identities and lifestyles which have no reference outside their media representation. In the case of Jean François Lyotard, another central theorist in poststructural-postmodernism, we have a thinker who renounces the truth of grand narratives in favor of micronarratives, a scheme wherein all narratives carry equal validity. In this respect, Lyotard holds that a "text" and its interpretation—like George Bush's reading of WMDs—is "true if I say so." Jacques Derrida's deconstruction and dissemination envision self and world as inhabited by infinite textual traces which effectively undermine their identities. A similar operation occurs in Julia Kristeva's notion of "intertextuality." For its part,

New Historicism reduces material history to a series of readings or texts. The foundational theories of Michel Foucault and Jacques Lacan also deserve mention here. They disperse the autonomous subject, as well as the subject who writes, into so many discourses or displacements.

These and earlier observations demonstrate that "author," "text," and "reader" are central battlefields in fights about political possibilities and the status of reality. It is therefore all the more significant that Reed, Acker, and DeLillo's political critiques, while ontologically grounded, nevertheless evince clear affinities with poststructuralism's conceptual refigurations. Indeed, ostensible similarities between poststructuralism's rereading of these concepts and their narrative treatment in Reed, Acker, and DeLillo partly explain the critics' placement of the three within the postmodern category. Each novel manifests—in a particularly germane fashion—one of the three elements in poststructuralism's problematized matrix of author, text, and reader. As a group, the works deploy formal and content driven strategies ostensibly similar to those of poststructuralism, and designed to dismantle these three concepts. At the same time, each novel offers an ethically grounded political critique that resonates with poststructural critics' progressive politics, but which is logically incompatible with poststructural-postmodern tenets.

The critics' tendency to disregard this incompatibility and equate these novelists' epistemology with that of poststructuralism is often the result of populating the postmodern category in a highly selective manner. When approaching literature, they isolate only those textual elements their chosen theory deems "postmodern," eliding elements which do not fit their chosen paradigm. As concerns the novels of Reed, Acker, and DeLillo, critics tend to suppress the modernist ethical-political grounding that secures and fuels these authors' critiques of dominant ideology.

The suppression of grounded ethics appears particularly ironic, given that postmodern theory is intimately related to the revolutionary politics of the nineteen sixties. That political drive survives within the heart of many academics and motivates their postmodern analyses. But frequently the same scholars who hold these political beliefs neglect their theory's assumptions, practicing a kind of bad faith wherein they support a writer's political agenda but simultaneously suppress the agenda's foundation. Their literary analyses then fetishize supposed postmodern qualities. Theoretical assumptions then disappear from consciousness, replaced by a zeal to find said qualities in the literary work.

So, for example, critics analyzing Reed sympathize with his anti-racism and support his intertextual political critique of ethnocentric white history. This ideological sympathy motivates their analyses of *Mumbo Jumbo*. However,

Introduction 5

as already noted, postmodern theoretical conviction equally motivates their analysis; so, they scan Reed's text for "intertextuality"—a supposed postmodern quality—and isolate his anti-racist use of historical intertexts. But this forecloses the selection process, limiting it to one element ("intertextuality") in a stable of postmodern qualities. The critic suppresses what remains, including the ethical foundation implicit within Reed's historical-material critique of dominant culture. Similar problems arise when these same critics address Acker and DeLillo. Critics sympathize with Acker's political-textual attack on patriarchy and capitalism, so they dutifully explore *The Adult Life of Toulouse Lautrec by Henri Toulouse Lautrec* for its systematic undermining of the "readable text," Acker's literary accomplice to patriarchy and capitalism, but also one of postmodern theory's favorite targets. However, this neglects Acker's own convictions regarding actual historical oppression of women and the poor. Applications to DeLillo are much the same. DeLillo attacks consumerism and the consumer lifestyle as political ideology. Academics equally abhor Hummers and JCrew, but retranslate his social-material attack on ideology into postmodern concepts like Jean Baudrillard's "simulation," which Baudrillard does not articulate as ideology, but rather as a concept bearing no relation to reality, except in so far as it references the non-existent, or, to paraphrase the theorist himself, except in so far as it refers to a copy without an original.

In an attempt to examine these issues and problematize the postmodern category more generally, this book centers discussion around the problematized matrix of authorship, text, and reader. As already noted, this matrix is not just a matter of passing literary interest, but one with deeper social-political implications. With this in mind, Chapters One through Three address how these writers' political critiques deploy altered visions of author, text, or reader in manners akin to poststructuralism. As Reed, Acker, and DeLillo's political critiques each highlight one of the three conceptual spheres, I have allowed the texts to dictate the category and author addressed. While these authors' grounded political critiques inherently conflict with the ungrounded theory they resemble, this contradiction remains mostly unspoken in Chapters One through Three. In Chapter Four, however, I address this matter directly, explicating the inherent conflicts between the authors' grounded politics and poststructural-postmodernism's ungrounded denial of the same. Such observations, combined with analyses from previous chapters, aim to problematize the postmodern catetgory more generally.

Ishmael Reed's *Mumbo Jumbo,* the first chapter's focus, highlights authorship, since Reed's interest, in large part, is the authorship of African-American identity and that identity which writes. Reed reworks the concept by combining traditional Haitian voodoo—aspects inherited by African American culture—with elements of the black jazz tradition. Reed borrows many of his voodoo concepts from Maya Deren's *The Divine Horsemen: The Living Gods of Haiti* (1953), a key study of Haitian voodoo practices. Reed blends these practices with the improvisational writing methodology he finds in great African-American jazz artists (e.g. John Coltrane). As a final move in his reconstruction, he adds dance and cooking. With voodoo as its structural centerpiece, these elements form a series of tropes which refigure authorship in a less singular, more communal, way. But such an authorial vision is also distinctly emblematic of African-American syncretism. Put another way, authorship becomes a never ending process of building upon the borrowed and referenced material of black culture past and present. In fact, it could even be said to borrow from past and present American culture more generally. Its connection with the past, then, strongly resembles communal historical memory. For all these reasons this authorial practice acts out the "Neo-HooDoo" aesthetic, Reed's response to issues confronting African-American writers as they seek to reconnect and invigorate African ideas within an African-American tradition and history quashed by western ideals.

It is not hard to see echoes of postmodern theorists like Foucault, Derrida, and Kristeva in the above observations. In Reed's removal of singular authorship—namely, his refiguring of it as borrowing/referencing from other authors—he seems similar to Foucault, who makes the author a function of discourses past and present. Like Derrida and Kristeva, Reed also sees an author's text not as a singular work, but as one inhabited by other texts, whose reality is evident in traces of her/his work. Here, we may think of Kristeva's "intertextuality" or Derrida's "dissemination" and "trace." In a related sense, Reed seems similarly informed by New Historicism in his stressing the need for reinterpreting given historical texts for the present.

But as I have stated, we must appreciate Reed's reconstruction of authorship as political critique. Again, we may consult the aforementioned political climate of the sixties, recalling Reed's membership in the experimental Umbra poetry group, as well as his affiliation with Amiri Baraka and Ron Karenga. In the nineteen seventies Reed—like black writers Clarence Major and Toni Cade Bambara—continued his political-artistic work by taking an almost Althusserian approach to language and dominant writing conventions, seeing them not as natural, but as "products of the dominant ideological apparatus"; in a major genre like the novel, such techniques merely reproduce forms of consciousness that maintain status quo material relations (Hogue 1986, 57). Hence the three writers sought to discern "other kinds of intelligences . . . that lay beyond the discursive formation of the ideological apparatus" (Hogue 57). Their subsequent experimentations with form were the result of this search.

Reed's *Mumbo Jumbo* (1972) represents one stellar example of his own search. While the book develops an alternative "intelligence" in its reworking of authorship, its construction simultaneously undercuts dominant ideology as it appears in numerous cultural practices. Reed's book can be loosely defined as a detective story, but with a parodic mismanagement of that genre's conventionally tight linkage between question and answer, cause and effect; thus, for Reed the detective formula stands in for the dominating logic of western reason and falls accordingly. Here, again, he echoes Derrida, though somewhat differently, as he uses right and left voodoo spirits to delineate a non-western, non-binary logic of "*différance.*" All this accounts for his plot's appropriately baggy structure, as PaPa LaBas—Reed's Americanized voodoo-inspired detective—searches for the Text of Jes Grew (the African-American spirit) and fights for its possession against the forces of the Wallflower Order, which roughly represents dominant white western ideology. Along the way the book takes advantage of the above theoretical concepts to introduce ideological voices of all kinds, as Reed attempts to author a new vision of African-American culture and identity. Here, especially, we see Reed employ intertextuality in a New Historicist vein. He presents myriad texts and discourse, but juxtaposes them so as to force reinterpretation of heretofore given facts. This act simultaneously unmasks the ideological grounding of dominant discourses while also reinterpreting African-American identity and culture. But as we shall see, Reed's reconstructed vision of African-American identity and culture will refuse dogmatism. It is thus at odds with other popular visions that strictly curtail notions of African-American identity (e.g. New Black Aesthetic).

Interrogating Kathy Acker's *The Adult Life of Toulouse Lautrec by Henri Toulouse Lautrec* (1978), Chapter Two shifts investigative focus from postmodern authorship to the postmodern text. Acker's novel, like many others in the postmodern category, foregrounds textuality. Her text reflects upon the ideological nature of all narratives, but in doing so it also challenges dominant ideology through the textual form itself. She holds form partially accountable for gender oppression and oppression of the poor. In form, she sees a fundamental thought process which structures all of life. Indeed, this attack on narrative form is a paradigmatic feature of her oeuvre. It's politically charged dismantling of form plays out over and over again in her work.

Acker's history is important for understanding her work. As an undergraduate she studied under Herbert Marcuse and continued to do so even after his famous move to California. In subsequent years she worked in sex shows to support herself while she also wrote extensively. Experiences like those she had as a sex worker and as a twenty something in sixties California deeply affected her writing and politics. In fact, one could say that Acker's texts formally enact her politics.

Like Reed, Acker uses detection to structure her work. But she conducts a more pointed attack on detective fiction than Reed, though there is a similar disdain for its strict conventions (e.g. tight linkages between cause and effect). The pointedness of her attack is partly indicated by her use of a secondary character, appropriately named Hercule Poirot, after Agatha Christe's famous detective. Acker as constructor of the story tirelessly frustrates this detective's logical attempts to solve the murder of a young girl. In fact, the character Poirot never solves the murder, and Acker's narrative simply ends, never successfully closing the traditional hermeneutic process of question and answer. Thus the story frustrates the logic entailed within the detective genre, but also the more general logic of traditional western story telling (e.g. the novel).

For Acker, this constant frustration of formula is her assault on western reason and elements she believes are inextricably tied to it. In particular, following the poststructural ideas of Derrida, Kristeva, and others, Acker finds a complex relationship between reason, gender, patriarchy, and capitalism; like many poststructuralists, Acker locates this relationship squarely within language, in what Derrida calls "logocentrism." Logocentrism is western reason's belief in identity and binary hierarchy (e.g. identity/non-identity). But, importantly, this binary logic is far from innocent in its very ideological confirmation and isolation of subjective gendered identity (male/female). It also entails a negative and thoroughgoing "phallocentrism" wherein one gender—the female—must take up an inferior right hand position in the hierarchy (i.e. male/female). The relationship of the two logics, logocentrism and phallocentrism, Derrida phrases "phallogocentrism."

As is common in some types of poststuctural analysis, Acker also equates the marginalized—in our case the poor in capitalist society—with the derided or oppressed term; hence, women have oppression in common with the poor. For Acker there is no escaping the logic of all this within current consciousness; the logic is thoroughgoing and inescapable. All male and female relationships will fall into forms of domination, just as all relationships within capitalism will.

Acker's anti-detective tale attempts to formally subvert this logic. Her method is primarily defamiliarization, much like Brecht's. Here, Acker consciously employs intertextualized texts to violate boundaries of identity and gender, but also to rehistoricize a dehistoricized past and to make visible class relations. In terms of rehistoricizing the dehistoricized, she intertextually inserts actual historical reports—much like newspaper reports—into the novel's story, disrupting the reader's usual passive habit of taking in a clean, linear story. The result makes readers see the text anew, and appreciate history long since forgotten. At the same time, the experience of individual subjects is not lost in her book, as we see Toulouse—the ostensible protagonist of uncertain gender—and other "working girls" in her Montmartre brothel—one dominant locale of the book's action—suffer in squalid lower class conditions of Paris. As we will see, Acker's ubiquitous profanity serves, in part, to speak their pain.

Defamiliarization also serves to break down the numerous and interrelated binaries noted earlier (e.g. identity/nonidentity, self/other). Again, the method has affinities with Kristevean intertextuality, and the defamilarizing method works similar to Derrida's deconstruction. In fact, Acker's similarity to Derrida can be said to extend to the aforementioned subversion of the detective tale, to the extent that such subversion represents a general subversion of genre itself. And genre, according to Derrida and Acker, is the perfect example of a commanding law, namely, one which constructs inviolable boundaries, much like the sacred boundaries between the poles male/female. But again, for both Acker and Derrida, any such claim of identity—with its requisite boundaries—entails what is outside of it, namely, the other derided pole (e.g. male implies the absent female pole).

At the same time, I hope to show that Acker's work is informed by her own idiosyncratic amalgamation of these theories. Nowhere is this more plain than in her joining of Derridean and Kristevean theory with Lacanian psychoanalysis. In particular, Acker joins Kristeva and Derrida's critique of identities with Lacan's attempts to de-reify unified subjectivity. These appear especially evident in Acker's movement of the speaking subject Toulouse, as often evinced by shifting proper names and pronouns. For Acker this serves again to problematize the ideological notion of the "I," whose construction takes place at the moment one enters phallogocentric language.

As such theoretical issues are complex and sometimes quite confusing, the Acker chapter will employ various other theoretical perspectives designed to render Acker's formal experimentation more understandable. Besides the methods noted above, I will also use numerous insights gleaned from narratology, especially as they are explicated in Mieke Bal's perceptive book, *Narratology: Introduction to the Theory of Narrative* (1997). The use of Bal's narratological tools enables us see more precisely how a text may be manipulated to accomplish certain goals, in this case Acker's. In addition, I have found various structuralist observations helpful in discerning related formal aspects within Acker's text. Finally, Catherine Belsey's essay "Constructing the Subject: deconstructing the text" (1997) proves most instructive for matters concerning the ideological nature of the subject and its constitution within language and literature.

The third chapter will discuss Don DeLillo's *White Noise* (1985). This book appears especially appropriate for the reader category because it remains accessible to many kinds of readers. Such accessibility is due partly to the book's clever referencing of quotidian experience in contemporary America. At the same time, the book addresses troubling issues concerning political agency and the place of the university in public life. DeLillo's book does not disembowel like Reed and Acker, but rather discomforts. It gives readers the pleasure of laughing at a contemporary academic's profession, but it also offers subtle hints regarding the profession's present state. While presented humorously, these hints might discomfort readers. Equally attractive and unsettling to contemporary readers is their own identification with the protagonist and his family, all of whom are awash in a world of consumable products, so much so that one family member even speaks a product's name as a mantra in her sleep. Indeed, part of the book's appeal is its surreal depiction of contemporary experience in consumer society, its reference to the inescapable commercialism of readers' everyday lives.

At the same time, this appeal should also be seen as a function of formal accessibility. DeLillo's work, unlike Acker and Reed's, seems reader friendly, if by that one means fiction giving an audience a fairly straightforward plot and relatively coherent characters. Acker and Reed's work represent fairly radical interventions at the level of form (e.g. intertextual or interdiscursive interruptions) which can make for tougher reading. DeLillo's novel, on the other hand, has a surface more like the traditional novel with a fairly clear beginning, middle, and end. But DeLillo has in common with Acker and Reed the rough form of a detective tale, as we see his protagonist, professor Jack Gladney of Hitler studies, search for his wife Babette's drug dealer, a man who distributes a substance which makes its users forget death.

In the process, one element of DeLillo's novel parodies the college novel and its mystery sub-genre to call readers' attention to the contemporary crisis of faith in the university's mission, as well as how that crisis is intimately related to certain social-economic developments—including consumerism—within postmodernity. While the genres (college novel and college mystery) may not appeal to all audiences, DeLillo's references to other contemporary issues in education would appeal to many people, as our nightly news presents myriad symptoms of its imperiled condition. Political leaders pass funding cuts for universities; thus, schools announce tuition increases; the media announces beneficial and altruistic corporate investment in universities, with an accompanying forgetfulness of the deleterious effects such investment poses to the university's enlightenment mission; political conservatives on news-talk decry supposed prejudicial admission policies, blaming the liberal left university for it and our increasingly depraved American culture.

Putting such observations in Jürgen Habermas' terminology, we might say DeLillo's parody references contemporary capitalist America's "legitimation crisis" (Habermas 1975). DeLillo's cast of academic characters, including his narrating protagonist, Professor Jack Gladney, symptomatically exemplify this crisis within the social-cultural realm of education. While education has traditionally been self-legitimating because of cultural heritage (e.g. the historically presumed belief in the humanities' value for society generally), this belief has increasingly lost legitimacy in great part because of the instrumental capitalist logic accompanying the corporatizing of the university. Habermas suggests that such loss of legitimacy imperils not only the university's legitimacy, but also the legitimacy of the larger society. Examining DeLillo's text through Habermas helps us see not only the novel's appeal to readers' contemporary experience, but also how the author launches a political critique of present social-economic conditions.

Accessibility plays a role here as well, because DeLillo's appeal to many audiences means his political critique reaches a wide variety of readers. The breadth of his audience one can gauge by looking at the Book of the Month Club. In particular, this chapter will investigate the motivation and methodology behind the club's inclusion of *White Noise* as selection of the month. Using Janice Radway's examination of club readership and methodology (Radway 1989), I will refigure DeLillo's critique as a sort of tool bag for readers, intended for their everyday lives. This tool bag is basically diagnostic, illuminating contemporary social reality for readers; readers may use these observations as they will; the hope, of course, is political action on their part and thus social change.

Importantly, during the course of investigation we will see how readers' individual aesthetic preferences condition their acquisition of the tool bag. This is made especially clear as DeLillo's book explores the fragmented nature of contemporary life as seen through Jack Gladney, his family, and colleagues. Their lives, like most people in the middle class, are caught up in a consumer society of purchasable identities. In this sense the novel presents phenomena familiar to many American readers experiencing life within postmodernity. Viewing these aspects through Fredric Jameson's distinctions of molar and molecular elements (Jameson 1979) allows us to see how some readers are attracted to coherent plotting and character (molar elements), while others prefer linguistic experimentation, or pushing language to its limits of comprehensibility (molecular elements). While the analysis clarifies different reader appeals, it also shows how different readers may come to similar—if disturbing—conclusions about consumer driven society in late capitalism. Interestingly, different readerships will come to see this shared reality as a kind of Baudrillardian simulation, wherein the real has disappeared, replaced and refashioned as a plethora of consumable goods. But unlike Baudrillard's simulation, DeLillo seems to contend that reference still exists, that the surreal social conditions exemplified in the novel are matters of ideology and economics. In fact, the horrific specter of Jack's bread and butter, Adolph Hitler, reminds us of the all too real referent.

Finally, Chapter Four will look at how these three novels, while bearing strong affiliations with much art labeled postmodern, are in fact not so postmodern at all, in either an aesthetic or political sense. While postmodernism is stereotyped as pure surface by writers like Jameson (1983, 1997)—and thus lacking in the depth and political conviction of modernism—we will discover that the works discussed herein are anything but that. In fact, all these novels contain elements of political and ideological critique, which are fueled by modernist ethical beliefs to a greater or lesser degree. Moreover, all of them are overflowing with the very historical reference much postmodern theory denies. In this sense, the texts I examine possess a referential depth opposed to the unreflective surface critics like Jameson report as dominant in postmodernity. This chapter, then, purposefully disturbs overly reassuring conceptions of postmodernism, but while doing so reinserts a politics most (grand) postmodern theory denies, even as it disavows its own grandiloquence.

Starting with Reed, this section of the book will refigure these authors, taking politics, history, and critique into account. I will demonstrate Reed's constant use of historical reference in his critiques, and discuss his relation to the African-American writing tradition and that tradition's goal of political change. In some sense, the chapter makes Reed very traditional in this respect. Equally, however, this part of the analysis will problematize and situate his work in relation to some famous poststructural-postmodern theories, most notably that of Henry Louis Gates, who defines African-American literary tradition as infinitely disseminating non-identity. Such non-identity is related to the poststructural notion of "hybridity," a conceptual assertion which supposedly breaks down unified identities of all sorts (e.g. ethnic-cultural and gendered identities). While Gates perhaps phrases it differently, he nevertheless interprets Reed's novels as part of an indeterminable African-American literary tradition, which makes them strongly resemble such hybrids. But as I hope to show, hybrids do not avoid identity claims, but merely substitute other identity claims. The same is true of African-American literary tradition as hybrid. In fact, in this section I hope to show–following the work of Patrick Hogan (2004)–that literary tradition, and thus African-American literary tradition, is ultimately idiolectal. Gates' reading of tradition is no exception. Such is also the case with Reed's refiguring of African-American tradition and identity, brilliant as it is.

This chapter's discussion of Acker will consult a number of postmodern theories with an eye to understanding Acker's evident ethical-political grounding and aims. As the chapter will show, Acker's manifestly ethical stance is itself precluded by the very poststructural theories she idiosyncratically adopts. This examination in no way lessens her art's value, but serves to indicate political inadequacies of many poststructural postmodern theories. While I will consult a number of theorists here, prominent on the list are Jean Baudrillard and Michel Foucault, as well as Gilles Deleuze and Félix Guattari.

My discussion of DeLillo's *White Noise* is equally critical and problematizes the novel's supposed postmodern status. Fredric Jameson's diagnostic of postmodernism is central in this respect, though I will argue against his global claims examining among other things the real world power of a political critique which reaches numerous sorts of readers and on a large scale. This is particularly evident from the Book of the Month Club's inclusion of *White Noise* as a recommended selection for its readership. Such findings would, of course, dispute the often claimed inevitability of the postmodern condition, namely, one in which politics on a large scale becomes impossible. I will also highlight the issue of reference, since DeLillo's work, despite claims to the contrary, remains concerned with real world reference, politics, and history.

The book will close with a number of remarks concerning a "poststructural postmodernism" and its relation to political rhetoric within the contemporary world, noting the striking similarity between theory's dictates and real political speech.

Chapter One
Politicizing Authority, Authorship, and Identity in Ishmael Reed's *Mumbo Jumbo*

Ishmael Reed's work, like that of other writers addressed in this book, is fueled by deep political commitment. Reed's novels frequently evince this resolve through his trademarked satire, which is scathing and politically ruthless. In perhaps his most famous novel, *Mumbo Jumbo,* Reed uses this trademark to present his own deeply personal but nevertheless socially critical authorial vision. Reed's book interweaves this vision with a systematic undermining of white-western constructions of black identity and history. In so doing, Reed offers a version of authorship based on a personal reading of African-American tradition, but one which also has numerous affinities with poststructuralism's reconstruction of the concept.

His political project and kinship to postmodernism are visible through strategic maneuvers which undercut traditional *unitary* authorship by dispersing individual authorial voice and its authority. Probing African-American cultural inheritance, Reed unearths its historical-social connections to African and Voodoo tradition. He uses this rich inheritance to enact authorial dispersal, but it also grants him the power to reimagine self and author.[1] In this respect, Reed's goals are bold. He actually wants to rethink the west's whole notion of unity, be it unity of self, unitary authorship, textual unity, or some version of racial identity which encourages conformity, repressing both difference and multiplicity. Reed believes such notions mark the (white) west's victorious erasure of blackness from history. Likewise, attempts by black thinkers to devise a unitary African-American identity—authorial and otherwise—are equally doomed, for they merely repeat the original (western) error.

As one remedy for this Reed consciously draws on historical *voices* issuing from African religious tradition, as well as the transported diaspora voices of Haitian Voodoo, and remnants of these within African-American tales, writing, dance, and music (especially jazz). As an author

Reed employs these inherited voices within the novel, making them speak through various characters and references; but in so doing their speech does not reside simply in the past; rather, they are the sum of African-American identity up to the present but also its open departure point for the future.

At the same time, his method of employing these voices seems equally indebted to Africa, Haiti, and Voodoo. Evidence indicating this includes Reed's Voodoo structures and terminology, which are largely drawn from Maya Deren's *Divine Horseman: The Living Gods of Haiti* (1953), an exhaustive study of Haitian Voodoo practices credited in *Mumbo Jumbo*'s bibliography. That same bibliography also cites Milo Rigaud's *Secrets of Voodoo* (1969), another work on Voodoo practices. If one requires further evidence of influence, one need only peruse Reed's *Shrovetide in Old New Orleans* (1977), or examine his poetry (e.g. *Conjure* 1972), and numerous interviews (e.g. Gover 1978).

This influence seems particularly important for understanding Reed's refiguring of authority, authorship, and identity. Specifically, one must appreciate his methodical adoption of Voodoo's syncretic practices.[2] "Syncretism" loosely means a particular culture's ability to include within itself numerous different signs and practices from other cultures (e.g. Voodoo's absorption of Catholic "saints" as "loas" [Voodoo spirits]). Reed's writing method and authorial vision follow this "syncretic" model. That is, Reed consciously borrows sources and includes them within his writing; he borrows voices, manipulates them, and allows them to speak according to his wishes. He captures these voices in numerous ways, borrowing at once from the quotidian language of twenties black jazz culture (seen in words like "Boogie Woogie," "Pep," "ragged," and "jazzed up" *Mumbo Jumbo* 114–115) but also from the language of various academic discourses (e.g. psychological discourse as seen in excerpts from Jung, or Freudian terminology like "hysteria" *Mumbo Jumbo* 62, 169), as well as from photographs and drawings.

At the same time, such characteristics also appear similar to those found in poststructural-postmodernism. Reed's dispersal of authorship through syncretic compositional technique—a technique closely resembling Fredric Jameson's "pastiche" (Jameson 1983;1997)—would seem to establish him as a "postmodern" writer. Indeed, Jameson cites Reed as exactly this sort of postmodern artist in both his short essay ("Postmodernism and Consumer Society" 1983, 18) and his widely read book *(Postmodernism, or The Cultural Logic of Late Capitalism* 1997, 26). Moreover, Jameson's linkage between postmodern artistic form—art as disjointed pastiche—and poststructuralism's refiguring of subjectivity—the individual as schizophrenic, psychically fragmented—would seem to justify such categorical claims, at least insofar as Reed's syncretic form disseminates authorial unity. At the same time, it is also interesting to note that Reed's collage-like compositional technique bears a certain resemblance to the older work of Brecht and Walter Benjamin. While this chapter is concerned to demonstrate Reed's more postmodern aspects, such resemblances are central for understanding Reed's attitude toward both authorship and African-American identity. As part of this I hope to indicate a certain tension within Reed's work between an apparently postmodern desire for authorial dispersal and a seemingly modernist desire for a uniquely individual authorial voice. Such tension is evidenced here in moments of irony and in sections when the artist contends with the community, past writers, and history itself.

Reed's satire a persistent practice in his fiction, is especially useful for investigating such issues. In the case of Mumbo Jumbo this satire both critiques and constructs. Specifically, it critiques unitary visions of textual authorship, as well as authorship of history, culture, and racial identity. At the same time, it is constructive, offering an alternative authorial vision directly tied to Voodoo and African notions of polytheism and syncretism. Moreover, it produces a series of tropes—jazz, dance, and cooking—which embody the African-Americanization of these Voodoo and African conceptions. These tropes announce the African-American writer's location and activity within our culture; in this sense they enact Reed's "Neo-HooDoo" aesthetic, his response to issues confronting African-American writers as they seek to reconnect and invigorate African ideas within an African-American tradition and history quashed by western ideals.

Satire: Critical and Constructive Functions

According to M. H. Abrams,

> "Satire," can be described as the literary art of diminishing of derogating a subject by making it ridiculous andevoking towards it attitudes of amusement, contempt, scorn, or indignation. It differs from the *comic* in that comedy evokes laughter mainly as an end in itself, while satire "derides"; that is, it uses laughter as a weapon, and against a butt that exists outside the work itself. That butt may be an individual . . . , or a type of person, a class, an institution, a nation or even . . . the whole human race. (187)

In terms of Reed's work, however, we may connect this definition of "satire" to a further definition of the term offered in Michael Jarrett's brilliant book *Drifting on a Read: Jazz as a Model for Writing* (1999). As his book's title suggests by the words "[d]rifting" and "read," Jarrett's text concerns the ways jazz can be used as a model for writing off of what one has read.[4] But in the process of discussing how one writer may play off of the writing of another writer, Jarrett gives a further definition of satire. Specifically, Jarrett observes an historical connection between food and satire. In its literal meaning, "*Satura,* the Latin term from which we derive the English word 'satire,'" signifies "'mixed dish,' 'farrago,' 'hodgepodge,' or 'medley'" (Jarrett 24). In connection with this Petronius' *Satyricon*—the first (complete) usage of *satura* as a writing trope—displays a first chapter clearly affiliating "literary composition with food preparation,"[5] while the book itself represents the first literary invocation of *satura* "as a generative device or trope for writing" (Jarrett 25–26). I will save discussion of satire's relationship to food for later, when I comment on Reed's compositional technique as "gumbo." For now, it seems important simply to remember Abrams' definition of "satire" (*satura*) as a "derogating" technique designed to evoke "attitudes of amusement" or "contempt," and its association with "mixed dish" or "farrago" as productive figures for writing. Thus, satire is both *critical* ("derogating") and *constructive* (preparing a "mixed dish" of different literary forms, such as Petronius' Menippean mixture of verse and prose forms).[6] With this in mind, we can look at how Reed satirically critiques unitary authorships of all kinds.[7]

The Basic Mumbo Jumbo *and Reed's Critical Satire*

In terms of plot, Reed's *Mumbo Jumbo* follows two basic tracks, although it interrupts these in the middle of the book to narrate an alternative cultural, religious, and racial history. One track follows Hinckle Von Vampton, a Knights Templar, as he tries to translate The Text or The Book of Toth. This book is subsequently lost when the Muslim Abdul Hamid, hired by Von Vampton to translate the work, burns it for its lewd descriptions and narrative. Von Vampton and his group, the fanatical white Christian "Knights Templar," want to translate The Text/The Book of Toth, but they also desire to destroy it, or at the very least, conceal its contents. Their desire stems from the book's content, which is nothing less than an alternative historical account of civilization, one that runs counter to (white) western Christianity's narrative of culture, race, and history.

Opposed to Von Vampton is PaPa LaBas and his Voodoo group. The novel's second track follows the detective PaPa LaBas as he searches for that same Text as the cause of the "Jes Grew epidemic."[8] This Jes Grew we might loosely term the African-American spirit,[9] whose definition remains highly contested not only during the period of the novel's action, the Harlem Renaissance, but also today. LaBas, for his part, is a Voodoo houngan (priest) taking part in this battle of definitions. He worships many loas (spirits), which makes him a polytheist akin to Osiris, the ancient mythological king of Egypt. Hinckle and his band of Knights Templar goons are strict monotheists akin to Set, the rather nasty brother of Osiris. The two sides—LaBas' and Hinckle Von Vampton's—spend the novel locking horns over who will possess The Text/The Book of Toth. In the end, neither side achieves both possession and translation of the text. This is due in part to Hamid's action and because Reed—as author—refuses the possibility of a final or last word, namely, definitive texts of any kind. In this respect, the interruption of the two tracks just noted indicates Reed's attempt to rewrite the Bible—as well as customary western interpretations of historical cultural influence—by having his main character, the houngan (priest) PaPa LaBas, relate an alternative history of religion from a distinctly non-western and non-Christian perspective.

Here, however, an important point deserves emphasis. *Mumbo Jumbo* does, indeed, tell another version of history, and it does offer numerous oppositional discourses to those of dominant (white) western culture. We may list a number of strategies here, including the refiguring of meaning through intertextual reference (e.g. pictures, historical or other texts), and Reed's employment of fictional speakers to characterize texts, historical figures, or cultural material. Significantly, however, these characterizations are not always trustworthy. His protagonist and sometime narrator, LaBas, for instance, can speak truth, but he can just as easily commit hyperbole, or worse yet, make entirely false statements. What, as readers, should we make of this? One possibility is that the sliding scale of communicative truthfulness is deliberate on Reed's part. It injects a sense of irony, which is especially evident in the more outlandish claims by LaBas, and serves to undermine even the alternative historical-cultural constructions of African-American HooDoo; this, in turn, troubles formation of *one* absolute authoritative voice, even that of HooDoo.[10] Preventing absolute authority in these matters does not necessarily mean an endorsement of absolute relativism on Reed's part, but rather suggests a reintroduction of central issues regarding history and cultural identity; in particular, Reed appears to believe that all constructions of history and cultural identity involve ideology and power relations. The critical questions for Reed would seem to concern the ideological beliefs lurking behind these constructions, and who has the power to make them in the first place. If taken in this way, Reed's mission is not to tell the true history and cultural identity of African-Americans; rather, his vision is but one assemblage, an alternative to the time worn hegemonic constructions offered by dominant (white) western culture. Such an interpretation would consider the ironic and outlandish claims of his African-American characters (e.g. LaBas) not as correctives in the absolute. The claims are equally ideological. But on the whole they might give voice to a previously silenced position while also indicating history and cultural identity are matters of contestation.

Returning to Reed's narrative of this alternative history, one may observe that he isolates the beginning of religion in Egypt, and in the person of the black African Prince Osiris. Osiris is associated with nature both because he marries his sister Isis (goddess of nature) and because "people began to circulate stories that his mother was the sky Nut and the earth his father Geb" (*Mumbo Jumbo* 162). He practices worship of the many gods within nature through dance and music. The beauty of Osiris' dance and its divine connections are recorded in The Text or The Book of Toth by his "faithful Birdman Toth" (*Mumbo Jumbo* 165). The Text or Book of Toth constitutes "[a] Book of Litanies to which people . . . could add their own variations" (*Mumbo Jumbo* 164).

Set, Osiris' brother, "hated agriculture and nature, which he saw as soiled dirty grimy etc." and "[h]e considered music 'loud' and 'boisterous'" (*Mumbo Jumbo* 163). He believed music and dancing were a waste of time, and that people should be more disciplined and regimented. In addition, Set hated his brother. So, he killed him and installed himself as king to be worshiped. For Reed, Set's belief system—one based on monotheism, regimentation, hatred of nature and all things carnal—is the root of Atonism, which precedes but also structures Christianity's belief system in the future.

Tracing this Christian lineage is part of Reed's rewriting or authoring of religious and cultural history. Thus Reed draws a genealogy of Atonism that extends from Set to Moses, the latter sneaking into the room where Isis guards Osiris' precious book of dances (The Text or Book of Toth). To steal this book, Moses seduces Isis but does so when she is in "the Petro aspect of herself," the Haitian Voodoo term for "left hand" or "aggressive" loas (spirits) (*Mumbo Jumbo* 180; Deren 62, 295. This results in Moses knowing only one side of The Text or Book of Toth, namely, the "aggressive" or "right side." Thus, Moses' knowledge of the book is "mangled" and "partial." Here, Reed uses Haitian Voodoo to depict The Text or Book of Toth as having two distinct sides (i.e. a left hand, or "Petro" hand and a right hand, or "Rada" hand). Both sides have loas (spirits), but as Maya Deren notes, the more noble "houngans [priests] and mambos [priestesses] 'serve with both hands'" (Deren 68). As Moses possesses only one hand, the "Petro" ("left") hand, he cannot possibly "serve with both hands"; his knowledge and practical powers remain incomplete. In the end, Reed paints a heritage that extends from Set to Moses to Jesus, and ultimately to the Atonist Knights Templar and their military arm, The Wallflower Order.

Especially revealing for this essay's concerns is how The Text or The Book of Toth—an embodiment of the African-American spirit indebted to the Voodoo conception of religion as consisting of both the "right" and "left" hands—does not involve a condemnation of either side, left ("Petro") or right ("Rada"). The scheme does not appear to have, as Atonist-Christianity does, a manichean vision, which is to say, "a doctrine of . . . two contending principles of good (light, God, the soul) and evil (darkness, Satan, the body)" (*Webster's New World Dictionary* 892). As Maya Deren's work indicates, it would be a cultural misunderstanding to conceive of the right ("Rada") and left ("Petro") hands "on a moral plane, as an opposition between good and evil . . ." (61) "Rada" ("right") rites remain essentially "benevolent, paternal and passive," while the "Petro" ("left") rites represent "aggressive action" or "rage," but "not evil" (Deren 61–62). There is no moral equation made. In *Mumbo Jumbo* Reed even states as much: "The rites, principally Rada and Petro, are not inherently good or evil . . ." (213) Thus, we can see Reed's redrawing of religious authority as directly opposed to Atonism and Christianity. There exists no condemnation of "difference"—Christian or otherwise—along the lines seen in Set and exhibited further in the Christian Knights Templar.

This makes Reed's religious conception similar to poststructural attitudes concerning binary oppositions. That is, Reed does not favor "left" ("Petro") or "right" ("Rada") but sees them as implied by one another; each is the present absence of the other. As we shall see in the discussion of Reed's writing tropes, this embracing of difference comes directly from Voodoo, which envisions an entirely different scheme of authorship, authority, and cultural identity. But it is interesting here simply to note how Reed's Voodoo position conforms to postmodern poststructuralism's belief that each pole of a binary opposition is implicated with its opposite in a relation of presence/absence, or what deconstructionist Jacques Derrida terms a matrix of "*différance*" (Derrida, *Of Grammatology* (1976), *Margins of Philosophy* (1982)).

Continuing with Reed's redrawing of history and religion, it is necessary to note that Osiris and previous (black) Egyptian religious divinities are transmogrified and integrated into Christianity as The Text or The Book of

Toth passes from generation to generation. That is, the characters of the deities are purposefully disfigured so that Christianity can steal them. You might say, they are both plagiarized and bowdlerized. Reed addresses this integration and wiping away of the black face of history throughout *Mumbo Jumbo*. In one place he has Buddy Jackson say, "The white man will never admit his real references. He will steal everything you have and still call you those names" (*Mumbo Jumbo* 194). In another place Reed's sometime narrator, LaBas, talks of "Atonist scholars" in the "*Daily Heliopolitan*" who practice "yellow journalism" by representing, which is to say authoring, "Osiris as Pluto, a castrated god of the underworld (remember Taurus?) But they kept on Isis as Virgin Mary . . . Mary was the mother of the Atonist compromise Jesus Christ. They made him do everything that Osiris does, sow like a farmer, be a fisherman among men but he is still a *bokor* [a self-serving priest], a sorcerer, an early Faust" (*Mumbo Jumbo* 170). Reed's simultaneous and sarcastic mixing of past and present through the "Daily Heliopolitan"— a clear reference to both contemporary mass produced "Daily" newspapers and the city "Heliopolis," center of ancient Egyptian sun worship—serves to show that such "yellow journalism" continues into the present, as (white) contemporary mass newspapers persistently misrepresent or author versions of black identity and black culture.

However, Reed saves special venom for the Christian theft and perversion of ancient Greek beliefs, though he also has some animosity for the Greeks themselves. There are several reasons for this. On the one hand, Reed desires to punish Greek philosophy—specifically its notions of "rationality" as adopted by Christianity—because of its subsequent use by Christians to dismiss the beliefs of other religions. Here, we may think of the Christian contention that its practices are "sound" or "reasonable," while those of Voodoo—or any other non-western religious tradition—are "superstitious." Thus, a practice like Christian "mass" is reasonable, while Voodoo worship of loas (spirits) is "mumbo jumbo" and "superstition." In addition, Reed finds in the Greeks, as well as in the Christian culture which adopts Greek "philosophy," a philosophical separation of the human from nature and a reduction of the physical or carnal to a lesser or lowly position. Here, we can think of the Christian and Greek philosophical notion that the "body" is somehow less than "mind," often exhibited in the idea that carnal pleasure or physical activity (e.g. dance) represents a lesser or degraded activity than those using mind (e.g. employing intellection in abstract philosophical thought). But Christianity's use of Greek thought, its attempt to author and coopt it as part of Christian tradition, is Reed's real target. Specifically, he wants to satirize how Christianity did to the

Greeks—and Greek philosophy—what it did to Egyptian (black) culture and religion, namely, steal and contort its beliefs for the betterment of the Christian system. In this sense Christian tradition sought, again, to author a cultural narrative, erasing traces of influence and difference.

We can look to *Mumbo Jumbo*'s title to see how the (white) west—under Greek influence—authors and authorizes ways of thinking, or legitimizes a particular organization of the phenomenal world. While Reed offers up a definition of the term "mumbo jumbo" early in the novel as a "magician who makes the troubled spirits of ancestors go away" (7), the western reader is no doubt more aware of the term's other meanings, namely, "mumbo jumbo" as "meaningless ritual, unintelligible expression, gibberish, etc." (*Webster's New World Dictionary* 967) Hence, in *Mumbo Jumbo* we see Hubert "Safecracker" Gould—an agent for the racist Atonist Knights Templar who has painted his face black to pass as an African-American writer-critic—"writing down the 'nigger mumbo jumbo words' he is hearing from the surrounding tables" (101). Here, Gould acts on the second and third definitions of "mumbo jumbo," "meaningless ritual" and "gibberish." He writes down what he hears for two reasons. First, Gould writes it down because he understands neither the rituals used by African-Americans nor their language. Second, though Gould understands neither, he still wants to use the ritual and language within the Templar's sham New Negro magazine to manipulate visions of African-American identity, thereby solidifying white western cultural hegemonic representations.

Two examples make clear the difference between Gould's Knights Templar vision of reality and that of Reed's African-American Voodoo tradition. In the first instance Benoit Battraville talks with PaPa LaBas and Black Herman (LaBas' assistant). LaBas wonders, "What is the American fetish about highways?" (*Mumbo Jumbo* 135) Battraville replies, "They [Americans] are after themselves. They call it destiny. Progress. We call it Haints. Haints of their victims rising from the soil of Africa, South America, Asia" (*Mumbo Jumbo* 135). In the second example PaPa LaBas argues with his daughter, Earline, who claims that his "conspiratorial hypothesis about some secret society [Knights Templar] molding the consciousness of the West" is wrong, because he has no "empirical evidence for it" but only his "knockings" (his Voodoo sensibilities) (*Mumbo Jumbo* 25).

Bringing these two examples together, we may observe that both illustrate two completely different narratives of reality. In the first example, we have LaBas announcing that Americans have a "fetish about highways." For Voodoo, the "fetish" signifies "loas" (spirits, gods). With Battraville's reply, it makes sense to interpret this as saying Americans worship the spirit of "highways." If we add to this that the American self finds itself in "destiny" and "Progress," then it seems legitimate to claim that what the American self worships is the spirit behind "highways," namely, that Enlightenment spirit of inevitable Progress ("destiny") through reason. The capital "P" in "Progress" is Reed's sarcastic jab at a western belief system that equates all technological and social developments with inevitability and "progress." The capital "P" indicates an idea that has been entirely mystified. Personification of America as a self ("after themselves") furthers the comparison, as it refers to Enlightenment "reason" as an individual activity for individual betterment. The costs of that betterment are registered in Battraville's "Haints" ("haunt[s], ghost[s], or spirit[s]"), which speak of the cultures destroyed by that western Enlightenment spirit (its "victims rising from the soil of Africa, South America, and Asia"). Earline's attack on LaBas for his irrational "knockings"—which do not constitute "empirical evidence"—merely serves to delegitimize the Voodoo part of African-American inheritance since its version of cause and effect differs from that of the west. That the attack comes from LaBas' own daughter, who merely mimics her boyfriend's words, shows Reed's disdain for the New Negro habit of throwing away aspects of African-American tradition in the name of bettering the race. Nathan Huggins' *Harlem Renaissance* (1971) discusses this New Negro abandonment of a cultural past and attempts to author a new one. Huggins cites Malcolm Cowley's *Exile's Return* (1962) as evidence for this loss and New Negro attempts to author a new racial and cultural identity:

> In its [*Exile's Return*'s] early pages Cowley explains why a group of young intellectuals around World War I felt no sense of value in their own experience and past. All of their education, as Cowley remembers, pointed them to some other place than home. They were trained out of their regional dialects and into a colorless, school-learned Ameri-English which all of their teachers had dutifully acquired. The stuff of imagination, art, and literature was never pulled from the mysteries of their own country and the experiences of their own people. Rather, they were asked to dream of medieval European castles and English country life. . . . Culture to the educated American had nothing to do with folk roots—one's past or one's life—rather, it was clothes that one could wear after a long process of divestment of the familial, the regional, the natural. (60–61)

Therefore, these young intellectuals, or New Negroes, "went searching for some roots in European civilization grafting themselves on to the only culture America had taught them to respect" (Huggins 61). But American culture, as Huggins points out, holds up for veneration things like "self-reliance" and "individual freedom"; as blacks were at one time the enslaved and still cut off from their past, it was difficult for them—as the once enslaved and culturally disinherited—to find and author a uniquely American and black self (Huggins 61). The result was an alienation and shame at the black past, which led to the adoption of "white" notions of "culture"and "success." This "shame about their past," observes Huggins, "was a measure of how much they had drunk up the values of the white American world around them" (Huggins 61). In essence, in drinking up this white version of self necessitated a certain repression: Those things reminiscent of the former condition [of blacks]—unskilled and field labor, enthusiastic religion—were to be denied. The professions (medicine, dentistry, law, the ministry, teaching, and undertaking) and business were to be embraced. One was to joint the more sober Protestant denominations" (Huggins 62). This, to LaBas, is the less pleasant side of the celebrated New Negro and the Harlem Renaissance. It is also part of what makes whites and New Negros think alike. For both of these groups, LaBas and blacks using older non-western belief systems speak "mumbo jumbo." In this sense the (white) west—assisted by aspects of the New Negro—authors a singular vision of reality and delegitimizes a reality authored by another, namely any non-western vision, but specifically that of Voodoo.

It is important, however, to temper these remarks by emphasizing Reed's irony via the narrator, LaBas. In this particular case LaBas neglects Earline's perfectly legitimate criticism of his thought (i.e. its lack of empirical support) and her valid demand a few lines later for a black intelligencia of "scientists," "engineers," and "lawyers" to challenge white dominated society (*Mumbo Jumbo* 26). On this view, LaBas' condemnation of the New Negro amounts to an almost rabid anti-intellectualism, which Reed might want readers to take ironically. Tinging criticism of the New Negro phenomenon with irony perhaps presents a more generous view of the movement; or, put another way, to criticize certain elements of the New Negro is not to condemn the notion altogether.

But the ironic presentation does not end here. Irony accumulates further in LaBas' over-the-top description of another instance of western authoring of cultural ideas and identity. In this case it is Reed's depiction of Atonist-Christianity's adoption of Greek philosophical attitudes toward the body and mind. In one episode of *Mumbo Jumbo,* Reed's narrator, LaBas, simultaneously goes after both the Greeks and Christians. LaBas speaks about Thermuthis, a Pharaoh's daughter, who is both an avid fan of Greek philosophy and the person responsible for rescuing Moses—an Atonist who will ultimately destroy Egypt's pantheon of gods in favor of a single monotheistic one—from death. Here is Reed's description—via LaBas—of Thermuthis' fixation with Greece: "Thermuthis had had her 'been to': her expatriate fling in Europe. Hadn't she hung out in the cafés and listened to Greek, the language of 'civilization'? Hadn't she learned how to be vague? To flim flam?" (*Mumbo Jumbo* 175). Here, we have an indictment against the western authored narrative that Greece alone possessed the "language" of "'civilization.'" Equally, however, we have an indictment against Platonic rhetoric as simply learning "how to be vague," or worse yet, committing "flim flam." This critique continues as the arrogant daughter of the Pharaoh (Thermuthis) personally goes to inspect the dying Osirian rites of her own people. In so doing, the portrayal indicts Greek philosophy's hatred of the body and valorization of the mind:

> Thermuthis and some of her Greek friends went down to these places at night and were appalled at the frankness of these rituals; the Pussies and Dicks on the wall as decoration, the low-down gut bucket music. They were snobs. . . . All day they [Thermuthis and her Greek friends] sat around discussing such things as 'if I stand in the water today am I the same person who stood there yesterday etc. etc.' you know. Jiving the citizens of Egypt. (*Mumbo Jumbo* 175)

The denigration of the bodily seems clear enough through the narrator's description of the Osirian "rituals" and decorations ("Pussies and Dicks on the wall") as "frank." But Reed's LaBas also critiques highly esteemed Greek philosophy, depicting its philosophical ponderings as simple snobbery and inconsequential ("'if I stand in the water today am I the same person who stood there yesterday etc. etc.'"), or as a way of deceiving other people ("Jiving the citizens of Egypt").

Elsewhere, we see this denigration of the bodily connected up with authorship. Here, the novel appears to critique the Greek theft of Egyptian ideas and the conscious plagiarizing of them within Greek tradition. Speaking of Dionysus' ("God of Nysa"), the character LaBas observes how the Greek Homer expurgates sections of his [Dionysus'] work involving dance—a carnal activity—and then shamelessly plagiarizes the left over bits: "Dionysus traveled to Greece where the Dance 'spread like wildfire' although Homer doesn't mention it. He nevertheless helped himself to the stories Dionysus brought concerning Osiris . . ." (*Mumbo Jumbo* 168).

At the same time, Reed also critiques the way Atonist-Christianity authored Greek philosophy and thought. That is, Reed uncovers how Christianity authored and authorized a particular version of Greek thought bowdlerizing aspects of its contents, specifically, its pantheistic contents. Here, Reed intertextually utilizes Roman emperor Julian, a key whipping post for early Cappadocian Christian theology in its attempts to integrate and coopt Greek philosophy. Julian's views of theology, as Jaroslav Pelikan has observed, fought against the Cappadocians, attempting a "reinstatement of polytheism" through "conscious and systematic borrowing of elements of both belief and practice from other religious traditions . . . [which] marked it [Julian's theology] as, strictly speaking, syncretistic rather than simply polytheistic" (79). Reed's use of Julian shows a remarkable sense of religious history which works well in his critique of monotheism and Christianity's attempt to portray Greek ideas as its own. In this sense Reed uses Julian—via the narrating LaBas—to do several things. On the one hand, he quotes Julian to delegitimize Christianity: "Jesus. . . . accomplished nothing worth hearing of . . ." (Julian qtd. in *Mumbo Jumbo* 171). But he also uses him to bring up the historical fact that Greece was polytheistic, a fact which Cappadocian Christians sought to cover up by way of resorting to the Greek belief in some first mover, a belief that in truth did *not* make ancient Greeks any less polytheistic. The death rattle of Greek polytheism and its associations with Osirian mysteries comes when, in LaBas' words, "the Atonists in the late 4th century B.C. convinced the Emperor Constantine to co-sign for the Cross" (*Mumbo Jumbo* 168). Of course, as with earlier instances of ironic over the top rhetoric, LaBas' description here is untrustworthy; by definition, "4th century B.C." is some three hundred years before "the Cross" and Christianity as we customarily think of it.

Interestingly, intertextual moments like those of Julian above show Reed's critical project as *not simply critical,* but also *constructive*. The very act of inserting Emperor Julian's text into Reed's own reauthoring of cultural history—the book *Mumbo Jumbo*—makes Reed satirical in the "mixed dish" sense. That is, from different sources (e.g. Julian's text) he *constructs* a whole (i.e. *Mumbo Jumbo*), even if part of that whole's end aims to criticize a particular form of authorship and narrative. As we shall see in the next few examples, Reed's book continues this critical but constructive satire by attacking the western *social scientific* appraisal and *literary authorship* of black identity and culture.[11]

In the instance of social anthropology, Reed takes Sir James Frazer's *The Golden Bough* as an instance of authoring ancient Egyptian and African cultural identity. First, Reed discusses how Osiris attended a university in Nysa, which existed in "a land of dates coffee goats sheep wheat barley corn and livestock" (*Mumbo Jumbo* 161). Then, he describes Osiris' journey to other lands and his effort to educate people in agriculture: "Across the Red Sea were Ethiopia and the Sudan where the young man [Osiris] would commute bringing his knowledge of agriculture and comparing notes with the agriculturalists of these lands" (*Mumbo Jumbo* 161).

As these cultures relied heavily on agriculture, they celebrated and honored it. It was a celebration of nature and life, in all its aspects. But this is precisely what the Victorian Frazer cannot tolerate. Here, it is worth quoting Reed at length, both because it illustrates again the western denigration of the body and because Reed intertextually utilizes Frazer's own words to condemn him:

> There were agricultural celebrations; dancing and singing,. . . . At this time in history those who influenced the growth of crops and coaxed the cocks into procreation were seen as sorcerers. The theater accompanying these rites, the agriculturalists' rites, was a theater of fecundation generation and proliferation, a theater that Victorian Sir James Frazer of The Golden Bough calls "lewd and profligate." (*Mumbo Jumbo* 161)

Thus, Reed indicts the western tradition of anthropology for placing its own mind centered, body hating, cultural template over the African and Egyptian cultures. Words like "profligate"—meaning, among other things, "abandoned to vice,"—betray Frazer's ideology and that of his Victorian compatriots.

But Reed is not done with western social science and its authorship of other cultural identities. He also shamelessly attacks Freud, while embracing—at least in part—Jung, who Reed sees as holding ideas closer to the African-American spirit. The attacks on Freud are peppered throughout *Mumbo Jumbo*. In one place Reed addresses Freud's concept of "hysteria." Here, Reed implicitly accuses Christians of erasing Greek culture but also simultaneously announces how "Egyptian-derived mysteries"—and their celebration through possession—were turned into the psychological concepts of neurosis and mental illness in Freud's "hysteria" (*Mumbo Jumbo* 168):

> The Greeks established temples to these Egyptian-derived mysteries where peoplewould go out of their heads so that the gods could take them over. (About the 10th century the Atonist priests will call this diabolical possession or corrupt the Greek word *daimon* so as to have evil

connotations. Freud, the later Atonist [according to 1 biographer, a big fan of Moses, Cromwell and other militarists], is to term this "hysteria." (*Mumbo Jumbo* 169)

Reed refers here to the Christian erasure of Greek polytheism by rendering the term "*daimon*" inaccurately, so as to make it equated with the more manichean concept of "demon." The original concept refers in Greek mythology to lower divinities who held positions between humanity and the gods. But Freud has also transformed a cultural and religious practice of worship (possession) into a mental illness ("hysteria"). Reed believes that Freud, like Frazer, has superimposed his own beliefs and ideology like all purpose template over the cultural and religious practices of others.

This and other elements critical of western ideology are rendered through intertextual moments. The diagnosis itself is seconded within *Mumbo Jumbo* by the white American culture which fears the "Jes Grew epidemic." It is evidenced in Reed's intertextual insertions of "situation reports"—shortened to "SR" in the novel—which constantly evoke fear of the "Jes Grew epidemic" and encourage all people to turn in those who carry or conceal it (e.g. jazz bands) to the "PSYCHIC DEPARTMENT OF PUBLIC HEALTH" (*Mumbo Jumbo* 77). Furthermore, intertextual reference occurs in the earlier cited reference to a biographer's comments on Freud: "[A]ccording to 1 biographer, [Freud was] a big fan of Moses, Cromwell and other militarists . . ." (*Mumbo Jumbo* 169). While most obviously this refers to observations made within Ernest Jones' biography of Freud (1953),[12] it is also interesting to note that Reed uses references to Moses and Cromwell as a point of attack upon Freud's own worship of the strong father figure, itself a stand in for an omnipotent and singular God. The critique, I suppose, is based on a story from Freud's childhood and what LaBas sees as its lingering effects within the psychologist's own theories. As concerns the childhood incident, Freud's own *Interpretation of Dreams* indicates he was once very humiliated by what he perceived as his father's cowardice in the face of a cruel anti-Semite; as a result, Freud decided to model himself after heroic warrior figures (e.g. Hannibal) (Breger 27). This tendency to worship heroic father substitutes even led him to name his own son after the aforementioned Oliver Cromwell (Breger 27).

In another place we see another sort of intertextual play wherein Reed blends a mixture of historical fact with his own reading of both Freud and Jung. The result is a general condemnation of the former analyst's ideology. Here, *Mumbo Jumbo* depicts Freud's own personal confrontation with Jes Grew (the African-American spirit) when he visits America with Jung. In this instance "Freud. . . . pushes into the hinterland of the American soul and here in this astral Bear country he sees the festering packing Germ [Jes Grew]. Freud faints. What he saw must have been unsettling to this man accustomed to the gay Waltzing circles of Austria, the respectable clean-cut family, the protocol, the formalities of 'civilization'" (*Mumbo Jumbo* 208). Freud, according to our narrative, was shocked by the "symptoms" of Jes Grew (jazz and jazz dance as expressions of the African-American spirit), and so fainted.

The actual historical reference point of all this is Freud and Jung's visit to America in 1909, which also marks the birth of Freud's hatred of America (Breger 188–190). Interestingly, however, Reed takes great liberties not only with the historical facts surrounding this visit, but also with the physical maladies Freud attributed to America, as well as analyst's well known fainting history. Reed—via the narrator—constructs a reverse stereotype, wherein Freud becomes part of the "gay Waltzing circles of Austria," themselves representative of (white) European civilization. This, he sets against a vision of a specifically African-American sprit (Jes Grew) which is—at least to a large degree—Reed's or the narrator's own idiosyncratic reading of Freud's anti-Americanism read as symptom (i.e. fainting). Certainly, that Freud fainted frequently is not in doubt; moreover, he did have fainting spells in America, as well as a good deal of indigestion, diarrhea, and some incontinence (Breger 188–189; Ferris 257, 260). But Reed, at least through his narrator, uses this to paint a picture of a white European rationalist who faints at the sight of cultural difference.

This representation is supplemented one page later with a narrative commentary on the sight which precipitated the fainting; following it is an amusing question and answer session at a news conference which ostensibly announces a psychoanalytic meeting of the minds between Jung, Freud, and presumably Ferenczi—something that did in fact take place in New York in nineteen hundred and nine (Breger 200; Ferris 1997). While both instances prove revealing, let us first look at the narrative commentary:

> What did this clear-headed, rational 'prudish' and 'chaste' man see? 'The Black Tide of Mud,' he was to call it. 'We must make a dogma . . . an unshakable bulwark against the Black Tide of Mud,' uttered this man who as a child returned from church and imitated the minister and repeated his sermons in a 'self-righteous manner.' (*Mumbo Jumbo* 209)

Reed, via his narrator, seems determined here to paint a negative picture of Freud. The narrator accomplishes this by intertextually citing remarks not necessarily coming from Freud himself, but rather attributed to him by his one time follower, C.G. Jung. The remarks are thus open to an ironic reading, since the narrator's viewpoint is clearly skewed. The intertextual moment itself comes from Jung's *Memories, Dreams, and Reflections* (1963), wherein he recounts Freud saying, "My dear Jung, promise me never to abandon the sexual theory. That is the most essential thing of all. You see, *we must make a dogma* of it, *an unshakable bulwark*" (150; italics mine). Then, "in some astonishment," Jung asks, "A bulwark—against what?" (Jung 150). Freud supposedly replied, "*Against the black tide of mud* . . . of occultism" (Jung 150; italics mine). Aside from the obvious intertextual moments I have put in italics here, it is central also to note Jung's characterization of Freud's comments, namely, that they were delivered to Jung "with great emotion, in the tone of a father saying, 'And promise me this one thing, my dear son: that you will go to church every Sunday'" (Jung 150). This reference equates Freud's theory and its sexual base with a religion and its dogma. As such it would seem to account for Reed's above depiction of Freud as "a child returned from church," who "imitated the minister and repeated his sermons in a 'self-righteous manner'" (*Mumbo Jumbo* 209). Interestingly, our earlier critical comments about "hysteria" and "*daimon*" return on the next page of Jung's text, but this time in terms of Freud's own dogmatic conviction: "Just as the psychically stronger agency is given 'divine' or 'daemonic' attributes, so the 'sexual libido' took over the role of a *deus absconditus,* a hidden or concealed god" (Jung 151).

As already remarked, Jung and Freud did in fact meet in New York in the early nineteen hundreds. The comical news conference which follows the narrative commentary just examined parodies that meeting and its announcement to the media. Here Reed's narrator uses Freud's own methods against him. Someone, presumably a reporter, asks Jung what Freud meant by "The Black Tide of Mud . . ."; Jung responds, "He meant occultism," but then another reporter objects firmly, "Why, then, did he employ the language of the Churchman: 'Dogma'?" (*Mumbo Jumbo* 209). Jung, playing straight man for Reed, retorts, "It was merely a figure of speech"; Reed then makes his reporter deliver the comic coup de grace via a question: "But according to his own theories, don't figures of speech have latent significance?" (*Mumbo Jumbo* 209). This, of course, drives home the earlier point—however ironized—of Freud's own repressions and fixations.

Obviously, in order to poke fun at Freud, Reed's narrator conflates "The Black Tide of Mud" with black African (and African-American) heritage, as uncivilized, an almost polymorphous perverse sort of culture. The dancing, the music, and the generally uproarious behavior Freud cannot tolerate, at least according to Reed's narrator. He is a "respectable" white man familiar the "Waltzing circles of Vienna," with "the protocol, the formalities of 'civilization.'" Jazz and jazz dance—and those who do it—are representative of primitive civilization and its all consuming "Black Tide of Mud." In this sense Reed uses Jung to condemn Freud's supposedly "scientific" thought as mere racist ideology. Furthermore, Reed impugns Freud's call for a "dogma . . . an unshakable bulwark against The Black Tide of Mud" by making Jung remark that "dogma" cannot simply be read as a "figure of speech," but must itself be read more deeply as an expression of latent content ("latent significance"). As such, Freud's own histrionic pleadings (his call for a "dogma" against "The Black Tide of Mud") must be read as a symptom of a psychological illness. Thus, Reed turns the tables on Freud himself, and tops it off by observing—again, through Freud's own words—that the lack is not in the African or African-American, but in Freud: "He [Freud] admitted once that he could not discover 'this 'oceanic' feeling in himself'" (*Mumbo Jumbo* 209). This reversal exploits Freud's own comments about himself in *Civilization and Its Discontents* (1961). In that book Freud remarks, "I cannot discover this 'oceanic feeling' in myself" (12). While the critical reversal is less than even handed with its source (Freud), Reed nevertheless works it to his counter-narrative's advantage, as Freud becomes the one lacking.

Critical work like this clearly seems similar to poststructuralism as postmodernism. For one, his critique of Frazer and Freud—one which tries to destroy these positions as it builds or authors an alternative—resembles the New Historicist recognition that texts cannot be read as autonomous wholes. Instead, they must be reread, or interpreted, within their historical contexts, where they will be seen to evince ideologies inherent in the times of their production. These ideologies are reflected in representations (e.g. Jung's description of Freud's "The Black Mud"; Frazer's characterization of "lewd and profligate" African Egyptian behaviors) authored by historians and others in social scientific fields. Moreover, Reed's use of intertextuality—namely, his quotation and manipulation of Jung to characterize Freud—represents a clear example of postmodern literary technique. In fact, Reed's authoring of this critical vision of Freud seems to follow exactly along lines noted by Hutcheon (1988), who says that true postmodern writing is "historiographic metafiction" (fiction which parodies, or uses bits of historical narrative). Freud's and Frazer's narratives are precisely the sorts of canonized texts or sources appropriate for such an metafictional endeavor.

Though I have mostly cited examples of Reed's indictment against the Christian west's singular authorship of cultural identity, one could just as easily note other instances. For example, *Mumbo Jumbo* also takes a swipe at

Islamic monotheism and equates its intolerance for multiplicity with Christianity's. One example of this in *Mumbo Jumbo* begins with Abdul Hamid warning PaPa LaBas and his assistant, Black Herman, that their critique of a singular God could land them in hell: "You'd better be careful with your critique PaPa LaBas, Abdul replies. Remember 'He that worships other gods besides Allah shall be forbidden to Paradise and shall be cast into the fires of Hell" (*Mumbo Jumbo* 35). In response Black Herman shoots back: "Precisely, . . . intolerant just as the Christians are" (*Mumbo Jumbo* 35). In this regard Hamid's Islamic religious position appears just as repressive as Atonist Christianity. Thus PaPa LaBas draws some parallels between Hamid's Islamic hardline monotheism and Christianity's quashing of other belief systems. Here, LaBas directly accuses Abdul Hamid of affiliation with repressive Puritan and Pilgrim attitudes saying, "Sounds as if you've picked up the old Plymouth Rock bug and are calling it Mecca" (*Mumbo Jumbo* 36). He further remarks to Hamid, "You are no different from the Christians you imitate. Atonists, Christians and Muslims don't tolerate those who refuse to accept their modes. . . . They [Christianity and Islam] are very similar, 1 having derived from the other" (*Mumbo Jumbo* 35). To prove his case LaBas then launches an attack linking the history of the Muslim religion to Christianity while simultaneously enumerating their mutual repressive practices:

> Muhammed seems to have wanted to impress Christian critics with his knowledge of the bible, . . . They agree on the ultimate wickedness of women, even using feminine genders to describe disasters that beset mankind.
>
> Terming women cattle, unclean. The Koran was revealed to Muhammed by Gabriel the angel of the Christian apocalypse. Prophets in the Koran: Abraham Isaac and Moses were Christian prophets; each condemns the Jewish people for abandoning the faith; realizing that there has always been a pantheistic contingent among the 'chosen people' not reluctant to revere other gods. (*Mumbo Jumbo* 35)

However, regardless of particular variant, notions of singular authorship and singular narrative extend down from a belief in monotheism to a belief in a particular and dogmatic aesthetic. This monotheistic aesthetic Reed equates with Atonism, after "Akhnaton (devoted to Aton)," who believed in the God of the "Sun's flaming disc," and who is commonly called "'the burner of growing things'" (*Mumbo Jumbo* 174). It is Atonism's dogmatic belief in the singular authorship of the world (monotheism) that leads it to be "the burner of growing things," namely, of other visions of authorship, be it authorship of an culture, identity, or an aesthetics (*Mumbo Jumbo* 132). In Reed's *Mumbo Jumbo*, Atonism is represented predominantly by its nineteen twenties incarnation, the Knights Templar, whose enemy is the "Jes Grew epidemic"—a play on "Just Grew"—which is Reed's vision of the African-American jazz spirit in music and dance during the "Harlem Renaissance," a spirit he believes intimately related to African and Haitian Voodoo spirits. For the Templars, "Jes Grew is the boll weevil eating away at the fabric of our forms our technique our aesthetic integrity" (*Mumbo Jumbo* 17) Since this new African-American aesthetics represents itself in a wide variety of "carriers" with different styles—from artists like "Louis Armstrong," "Bessie Smith," "Josephine Baker,"to "Jelly Roll Morton"—Atonists see it in the plural, as "growing things," which must all be destroyed (*Mumbo Jumbo* 50; 152;162). Furthermore, as the metaphor "carriers" suggests, Atonists see the African-American jazz spirit as a "a disease," though for Reed it is a positive one, a kind of "anti-plague" (*Mumbo Jumbo* 6; 64). Atonists perceive this "disease" as infecting language, effectively destroying its essence. This sentiment is embodied in Atonist thug Biff Musclewhite's pleading words as he attempts to convert young revolutionary Thor Wintergreen:

> Son, these niggers writing. Profaning our sacred words. Taking them from us and beating them on the anvil of BoogieWoogie, putting their black hands on them so that they shine like burnished amulets. Taking our words, son, these filthy niggersand using them like they were their god-given pussy. Why . . . why 1 of them dared to interpret, critically mind you, the great Herman Melville's *Moby Dick*!
> . . . . They're the 1s who must change, not us, they . . . they must adopt our ways, producing Elizabethan poets; they should have Stravinskys and Mozarts in the wings, they must become Civilized!!!! (*Mumbo Jumbo* 114)[13]

Musclewhite's speech makes Atonist destructive intentions clear enough, but it also brings together different aspects of this emerging aesthetic by noting both the medium of jazz ("Taking our words" and "beating them on the anvil of BoogieWoogie") and that of prose writing (through references to "words," as well as "Melville's *Moby Dick*" and black writers commenting on it).[14]

But again, Reed does not just single out Atonist-Christianity as the solitary perpetrator of unitary aesthetics, authorship, and identity. He also throws his critical net wider to indict Atonisms of all kinds, including those writers—black or white—who would envision one unitary version of African-American identity or one unitary form of African-American writing. Of special interest here is Reed's depiction of the dogmatic black Muslim Abdul Hamid. At one level Hamid serves as a general representation of the Atonist view of authorship. However, Hamid is black, indicating Reed's insistence that Atonism is a mind set that any member of any race can hold. Here, I believe, Reed uses Hamid as a representative of certain writers and theorists associated with the "New Black Aesthetic" movement. He uses Hamid to critically parody or satirize these theorists and their positions on what constitutes authentic "black" writing (i.e. the one "True" African-American aesthetic with a capital "T"). Furthermore, this parody or satire constitutes Reed's critique of any position—"New Black Aesthetic" movement or otherwise—which would isolate one and only one absolute vision of African-American identity. First, let us see how Reed uses Hamid to critique unitary authorship generally. Then, we can turn to his critique of the "New Black Aesthetic" and its vision of aesthetics and unitary African-American identity.

Reed's character Abdul Hamid, a Muslim magazine editor and overzealous follower of Islam, is frequently read as Jes Grew's enemy because he burns The Book of Thoth (Jes Grew's ostensible "Text," a freestyle "how to" manual of African-American identity). Certainly, Hamid's actions would appear to support this contention. He does indeed burn The Text, and his vitriolic hand written note to PaPa LaBas—an interesting bit of intertextual play—announces the fact and clearly states his motivations. For Hamid The Text inaccurately accounts for African American identity and history:

> I have decided that black people could never have been involved in such a lewd, nasty, decadent thing as is depicted in here. This material is obviously a fabrication by the infernal fiend himself!!! So, into the fire she goes!! It is our duty to smite the evil serpent of carnality. I am going to sell the beautiful, precious box, the Book of Toth arrived in, from the proceeds I will build a great mosque in whose reading room, only clean and decent books shall be kept. (*Mumbo Jumbo* 202)

Yet we should observe that Hamid does not simply *correct* a falsehood; rather, he *expurgates*—censors through incineration—aspects of African/Carribean/American history which appear offensive to his Islamic tastes. Like Umberto Eco's venerable monk Jorge, whose pious distaste for laughter and all things carnal leads him to destroy Aristotle's text in the postmodernist *The Name of the Rose* (1983), so Hamid's fundamentalist Islamic contempt for the bodily impels him to destroy unsavory textual evidence from the African-American past. In this way he is also like his New Negro brethren (e.g. Alain Locke) who, under Christian influence, forget "the side-splitting, bellyaching, satirical ways" of traditional African art and "only appreciate heavy, serious works" (*Mumbo Jumbo* 96). Thus, both Eco's Jorge and Reed's Abdul Hamid enact revisionary histories which eliminate offensive particulars. Certainly this reading seems additionally supported by Hamid's own hasty editorial correction symbol, "u," which adds the word "carnality" as if it were an essential aspect of his objection.

In sum, then, Hamid's true motivations appear rather suspect. His intentions, it would seem, extend beyond simple correction of supposed inaccuracies. Rather, his burning of The Text combined with his note's content betray a man intent on *authoring*, one who believes African American history and identity depend on thinkers like himself to parcel out "correct" knowledge, determining the shape and content of African American identity, history, and future—or their text(s)—so to speak. Indeed, the texts available in Hamid's "reading room" will contain "only clean and decent books," renderings of African-American history and identity to his liking. Additional remarks from Hamid's note would seem to support this point:

> They [the publishers] seem only interested in our experience's seamy side. But this is necessary now. Works of reform. Works, which will assist these backward, untogether niggers in getting themselves together. We must change these niggers! Change niggers! niggers, change! Change! Change! Niggers! Make them backward niggers!
> . . . for now we need a strong man, someone to 'whip these coons into line.' Let the freedom of culture come later! I Know this sounds contradictory but I don't have God's mind, yet! (*Mumbo Jumbo* 201)

This overwrought harangue demanding reform under dictatorial guidance expresses not only Hamid's desire to shape African-American identity, but his final word ("yet!") also appears to announce that although he presently remains somewhat uncertain of divine intentions, he will have grasped those intentions soon enough. Then, he and other Islamic cognoscenti will know exactly what must be said or written and how.

Hamid's words and actions are interesting for another reason as well. We may discover within his authoritative actions and language an essential function some postmodern theorists attribute to traditional authorship, and one which these same theorists wish to abolish. This aspect we may call "the principle of thrift," a notion Michel Foucault first explicated in "What is an Author" (1984), his pivotal essay hastening the (postmodern) theoretical erosion of unitary authorship. In this essay Foucault remarks that authorship has, among other things, a specifically "ideological" function.

Here, he opens the issue with a kind of rhetorical dialectic: "How can one reduce the great peril, the great danger with which fiction threatens our world? The answer is: one can reduce it with the author" (118). Well, even if we presume Foucault correct in this matter, how, exactly, do fictions—or in this case readings/writings of African-American identity and history—represent a "great peril" or "danger" to the present world? Foucault offers an answer. He holds that what our culture fears is myriad and multiplying significations—unstoppable trains of meaning—launched by fiction. The author represents an answer to this endless multiplication. "The author," remarks Foucault,

> allows a limitation of the cancerous and dangerous proliferation of significations within a world where one is thrifty not only with one's resources and riches, but also with one's discourses and their significations. The author is the principle of thrift in the proliferation of meaning.
> .... [H]e is a certain functional principle by which, in our culture, one limits, excludes, and chooses; in short, by which one impedes the free circulation, the free manipulation, the free composition, decomposition, and recomposition of fiction. ("What is an Author" 118–119)

It is important to remark here that Foucault finds the authorial "principle of thrift" ideological. It is ideological in character precisely because it "inverts" the way we consciously—and typically—think of authorship. That is, "we are accustomed to presenting the author as a genius, as a perpetual surging of invention," but this position proves ironic since, "in reality, we make him function in exactly the opposite fashion" (Foucault, "What is an Author" 119). The author, claims Foucault, must therefore be viewed as "an ideological product" because "we represent him as the opposite of his historically real function" (119). Indeed, Foucault's remarks prove especially illuminating in Abdul Hamid's case. More explicitly, they unveil his violent foreclosure of meaning for exactly what it is, namely, ideology. Hamid can give up neither his conception of God's unitary voice nor his stoic and monolithic vision of African-American personality and history.

Abdul Hamid's censorial disavowal of The Text or The Book of Toth resembles closely the censorship Reed finds in some black aesthetic authorial visions, specifically, demands made by those aligned with the New Black Aesthetic. These writers include Amiri Baraka, Houston Baker, and Addison Gayle, who feel Reed's negative portrayal of black characters is tantamount to race betrayal (e.g. Abdul Hamid and the Negro Android in *Mumbo Jumbo*, the Moochers in *The Last Days of Louisiana Red*).

Gayle, for instance, has remarked on the necessities of this New Black Aesthetic in his book *The Way of the New World* (1976). Among these necessities is an avoidance of the aforementioned negative portrayal of American blacks, and replacing that with "what is noble and beautiful in a race of [black] people . . ." (Gayle qtd. in Martin 28). Thus, when referring to Reed's *The Last Days of Louisiana Red* at the Second Annual National Conference of Afro-American Writers, Gayle commented that the work did nothing to raise the image of African-Americans in a country already awash in negative stereotypes (Martin 1988, 36–37). Similarly, Houston Baker's *Black Literature in America* (1971) set strict guidelines for "proper" African-American writing. But perhaps the most vitriolic in his criticism of Reed was Amiri Baraka during his Black Nationalist and Marxist phase. Baraka specifically accuses Reed of being a "capitulationist," one who, like Booker T. Washington before him, merely gives in to the images and values of white America. Regardless of the form, in all three cases the African-American author's task in this vision remains similar to a loyal party propagandist who merely mouths the party definitions of reality and individuality.

Looking at Reed's early writing career with the Umbra poetry group, we can find the roots of the split between Reed's vision and the more unitary vision of writers like Baraka. Both Baraka and Reed were part of the group at one time. According to Reed, one reason for the group's break up was because he saw Baraka "promoting a form of 'cultural nationalism'" (Reed qtd. in Oren 203), promoting he later gave up for a socialist hardline. While Reed was at one time a promoter of this nationalism early in his career, by 1970—before publication of either *Mumbo Jumbo* or *Conjure*, the two primary texts I use in this essay—he was very much opposed to the idea (Oren 203).

If we connect this Umbra period to an anecdote about Reed and Baraka, some clues appear about Reed's satirical character constructions. These clues have much to say about Reed's portrayal of unitary authors. As Oren has remarked, Reed drew characters in his novels from real life (Oren 209). These characters have real historical roots, according to Oren, in Reed's short stint as a room mate with Baraka. Joe Johnson, also a room mate and member of the group, says Baraka and his nationalist buddies would constantly complain to Reed that his poetry employed "the white man's language and references" because it sometimes made reference to a "big word" or contained "some Greek references" (Johnson qtd. in Oren 209). Of course, Baraka's objections also included Reed's portrayal of less than likable black characters. As regards the construction of these characters, Oren describes them as drawn from Reed's life. Baraka, as it turns out, is one of these satirical character types. According Johnson, these characters "have a pretense at being nationalists, they seldom have a job, they are like moochers, they go around and feed off of other people and the first chance they get, they rip the person off" (Johnson qtd. in Oren 209). This, according to Johnson is a direct play on Baraka and his friends, and while I would not disagree with either Johnson's observations or Oren's seconding of them, I would add another aspect to all this, namely, Reed's desire to critique visions of unitary authorship of texts and cultural identity, be those visions nationalistic or whatever. On this point we may return to the figure of Hamid in *Mumbo Jumbo*. In an obviously hyperbolic fashion, Reed's narrative offers Muslim editor Abdul Hamid as a figure for the New Black Aesthetic critic. While it is true that Hamid's staunch Islamic viewpoint would seem to ally him more with a group like the Nation of Islam, it is his singular drive to construct only *one* vision of African-American cultural identity that associates him with the New Black Aesthetic. That is, he is an "editor" who refuses to include within African-American identity certain carnal aspects because they are "lewd," "nasty" or "decadent" (*Mumbo Jumbo* 202). For Hamid any representation which violates that "proper" mode must be destroyed. Though his vision is driven by religious zeal, it is no less singular than the African Nationalist vision driving segments of the New Black Aesthetic, which not only prescribed proper portrayal of blacks, but also delineated real from false blacks.[15] Reed himself has said Hamid is modeled on the Nationalists (Martin interview 1981, 183), though certainly his critique of Hamid's censorial vision could and should be read more generally. At the same time, it seems unwise to dismiss the fact that New Black Aesthetic critics like Baraka, Gayle, and Baker did attack Reed for painting less than favorable black characters. Indeed, their politically driven aesthetic supported *only* positive and unified images of blackness; to paint any other picture meant failure to support authentic African-American identity.

Reed, not surprisingly, sees such unitary vision as myopic and driven by vague academic terminology. Here, he comments on this tendency:

> The West's Afro-American aesthetic is multi-cultural—it's not black. That's what they don't understand. This black aesthetic thing is a northern, urban, academic movement—that's why you have a fancy word like 'aesthetic,' which nobody figures out. When you come to talk about standards of taste, everyone differs. It's a vague enough word so that they can get away with it. And even though they try to make it sound like it's really important—that's the black intellectual pastime—discussing all these phantoms and things. You look at all these conferences for a hundred years, same questions. (Martin Interview 1981, 180)

Later in this same interview, Reed continues and makes the point that aesthetic endeavors like those of Baraka, Baker, and Gayle which try to pinpoint authentic and singular identity are non-scientific, riddled with vagueness, and may even constitute a racist take on identity:

> Blacks are probably more American than any other group here. I know that a lot of blacks have Native American ancestry—I know I do, and it's something to be paid more attention to. You see, this black aesthetic thing was not scientific, as I guess a lot of the things which come from the English department are not. Social sciences are not—but this black aesthetic was a classic example of imprecision. Because Africans do not consider Afro-Americans in this country to be really black, because their ancestry is so mixed up—you know, Indian, European, African—so actually one could say that by singling out one part of your ancestry and labeling that might be considered racist. So that's why I was always intrigued that these professors who are supposed to be scientists would try to peddle that. (Martin Interview 1981,182)

This myopic view, namely, one which Reed thinks disallows other viewpoints (e.g. Voodoo and other influences) the power to author and authorize texts and cultural history, is no better than its white western counterpart, which remains equally closed minded. Reed, however, offers an alternative; that alternative is the Voodoo notion of syncretism—which represents an open minded alternative in its inclusiveness—and applies it as an authoring technique. This syncretic technique, it will become apparent, has postmodern affinities.

But before turning to this syncretic view, we should bear in mind a point which further ironizes Reed's own counter-narrative of syncretic Voodoo. In particular, I refer to Reed's earlier remark to Reginald Martin that the "black aesthetic . . . is not scientific." Juxtaposing this remark with *Mumbo Jumbo*'s Voodoo counter-claims would seem to ironize Reed's own syncretic alternative; such a reading would, of course, jibe with Earline's earlier noted critique of LaBas' irrationality. It would also appear to correspond with a view of authority, authorship, and identity which sees itself as one option among many. This possibility should therefore be kept in mind as we approach Reed's syncretic vision of authorship.

Reed's Constructive Satire: Syncretism as Postmodern Technique

As my earlier remarks suggest, we find the origin of Reed's authorial vision in the African and Voodoo religious tradition of "syncretism," a cultural tradition of openness, but one which also marks the terrible exigencies of blacks forced—via the slave trade—from Africa to Haiti, and eventually America. In the abstract, "syncretism" is basically the ability to integrate or absorb signs and practices from other sources. This has some special implications for authorship, since an author could be syncretic and "integrate" or "absorb" other sources (e.g. texts) and practices (e.g. writing style). Such an authorial practice might produce a text containing intertextual pastiche (a text constructed of other absorbed texts), a tendency many have equated with postmodern writing (e.g. Hutcheon 1988; Jameson 1983). But before exploring this possible implication, it seems essential to understand the depth of tradition Reed draws upon here because it acts as an evidentiary counterweight to the sort of postmodern syncretic authorship just noted. Specifically, I refer to syncretism in the concrete; namely, how in reference to African cultures and Haitian Voodoo, syncretism represents the ability of the many African cultures—under the exigencies of slavery and forced diaspora—to integrate and absorb parts of one another to form the amalgam of cultures which is Haitian Voodoo.

The length and depth of this tradition is indicated by Maya Deren, who notes that while the dispersal and fragmentation of African tribes throughout Haiti was accomplished to the benefit of colonists—after all, if you are going to subjugate a majority, you best destroy their unity—there remained untouched a number of core beliefs, some of which are the belief in possession by Gods; religious rituals involving drums, dancing, and song; as well as a belief in ancestor worship (Deren 58). The result was a religion with "overlapping" beliefs; for example, "In some cases, the deity of the numerically dominant group absorbed the similar deities of the others; or the emphatic character of one tribe, such as the warlike quality of the Nagos, gave their deity of war, Ogoun, preeminence over all other representatives of that principle" (Deren 59). At the same time, "because Voudoun was a collective creation, it did not exact the abandonment of one tribal deity in favor of another. On the contrary, it seemed rather to delight in as generous an inclusion as possible" (Deren 59). In this sense it was "tolerant rather than absolutistic and exclusive" (Deren 66).

This magnanimous spirit of inclusion extends even to the retention and identification of (African) places within Voodoo ritual. Thus, "Voudoun" (which is the Fons word for god) includes the loa (the Congo word for the spirits) of many nations; they are invoked as stemming from their various homes" (Deren 60). In the end, however, the precise place names indicated by loas become not so much geographical references—since that would not mean that much to contemporary Voodoo worshipers—as "adjectival characterization[s]" designed to "indicate a special quality of benevolence, respected authority, and prestige" (Deren 60).

This syncretic tendency did not just involve African concepts. On the contrary, as the case of Haitian Voodoo makes clear, the traditional syncretic practice of absorption and integration of sources also included certain colonial Christian aspects. Deren clearly indicates that western efforts to christianize Voodoo devotees proved fruitless. This, was because the subjugated people of Haiti, with their syncretic tradition, accepted catholic icons all too readily, though not at all in the sense intended. Instead, voodoo worshipers welcomed the new spirits (e.g. saints) in their voodoo cosmology. Specifically, catholic icons became other loas (spirits) *equal* to those already found in the voodoo pantheon (Deren 54–57). As a result Christian icons contained in innumerable Sobagui (alters) peppered Haiti's landscape, but the desired overthrow of heathen religion proved useless.

These observations about African and Voodoo syncretic practice clearly illustrate it as creative and *constructive,* namely, in its absorption of different sources to construct itself. If we were to describe it in terms of authorship, we might say that African peoples—forced from their homeland to Haiti—authored their Haitian Voodoo cultural identity from numerous cultures available to them. We could therefore also maintain that they practiced satire in two of its senses. They practiced "satire" as a "mixed dish," referring to the identity they constructed from numerous sources, and they practiced "satire" as a "generative device or trope"—a strategy, if you will—for constructing cultural and racial identity, as well as texts (e.g. novel).

As regards Reed's use of this syncretic tradition, there appears a kind of paradox. On the one hand his syncretic method of authoring appears traditional and inherited from African voices, which are mixed to form the Haitian Voodoo culture; Reed will make this into the specifically American HooDoo. But this traditional syncretism in the hands of Reed as author appears somewhat similar to both satire and postmodern "blank parody" or "pastiche" (e.g Jameson 1983; 1997). If we begin with the term "satire," Jarrett notes, within modern times "one name given for the writing [authoring] . . . with the trope of *satura* [satire] is collage" (26). Regardless of medium, "collage," often referred to as "montage," can be defined generally as "juxtaposition of two more or less distant realities" (P. Reverdy qtd. in Hebdige 105). Obviously, the "distant realities juxtaposed could be, in the case of literature, different genres (e.g. historical narrative, social scientific narrative).

Reed does exactly this by mixing the aforementioned anthropological narratives (Frazer's *Golden Bough*) and psychological narrative (Freud's psychoanalytic concepts). Furthermore, he introduces newspapers into the "mixed dish" by inserting examples of the hegemonic white capitalist press during the nineteen twenties. In one example, Reed gives us a headline:

"MUSCLEWHITE BAGS COON" (*Mumbo Jumbo* 123). The newspaper article then continues: "Biff Musclewhite, fearless curator of the Center of Art Detention and consultant to Yorktown Police, shot and killed Berbelang the bad, cute black bandit, and leader of a gang of dope-sniffing self-styled Mu'tafikah" (*Mumbo Jumbo* 123). Ostensibly, the content of this mass produced newspaper is truthful; however, Reed reveals it as anything but that since its "facts" do not match the reality of the scene represented, namely, the real facts of the shooting and the real characters of individuals involved. The real facts appear before Reed's intertextual insertion of the newspaper excerpt. In truth Musclewhite is not a "curator" but a hired killer for the Atonists. As for Berbelang and the Mu'tafikah—that group devoted to returning artefacts in museums to their places of origin and whose name is a play on "motherfucker" as well as a number of other words—they are never portrayed as "dope-sniffing."[16] Rather, depictions of them as "dope-sniffing," and Berbelang as a "bad, cute bandit" represent Reed's textual parody of the hegemonic white news. Here Reed's text displays the language of that news machine. In so doing, the novel reveals it as just another ideological tool for manipulation by the white Atonists.

Similarly, in Reed's "Situation Reports" (represented as "SR" in *Mumbo Jumbo*), we have short pieces of prose in all capital letters and without quotation marks. These appear throughout Reed's text and seem almost like newspaper or radio reports, sometimes issuing from an ideological source similar to white Atonist tabloids, other times simply sounding like a spiritual audio version of Dos Pasos' "Newsreels." Reed presents an example of the former type through a skewed view of Haitians fighting for liberation against American forces:

> A LATE BREAKING DEVELOPMENT IN HAITI. RUMORS CIRCULATE THAT A SOUTHERN MARINE IS VICTIM OF CANNIBALISM. THE ACTION IS TERMED BARBAROUS, GHASTLY, HEINOUS, AN AFFRONT TO THE ENTIRE 'CIVILIZED' WORLD. (*Mumbo Jumbo* 59–60).

Here is an instance of the spiritual audio version:

> THE LOCATION MAY SHIFT BUT THE FUNCTION REMAINS THE SAME. CREOLE BANDS CONCEAL JES GREW FROM CHICAGO'S PSYCHIC DEPARTMENT OF PUBLIC HEALTH. ERZULIE WITH HER FAST SELF IS SHELTERED IN A 'VOCALIZING' TRUMPET WHICH SINGS FROM MUTE TO GROWL. (*Mumbo Jumbo* 77)

In this last case, it seems as though Reed simply wants to represent the spirit of the time he writes about, namely, the jazz age of the nineteen twenties. That the version sounds, when read out loud, like a radio broadcast seems natural, since jazz and the jazz age was communicated to a great degree through the mass market of radio. Reed's use of "SR"'s without quotation marks—elements also missing from the newspaper entries—helps produce a fragmentary narrative

Reed adds to this cacophonous collage of speakers the voices of other loas, which he summons through photos or drawings dispersed throughout the narrative. Examples include a photograph of a black power march, sketches depicting America's conquest of the west, and narratives from history books, including an historical narrative about the Harding administration. Such parodic technical interventions suggest strong affinities with modernism and poststructural-postmodernism. Specifically, the fragmentary and multimedia aspects of *Mumbo Jumbo* look very much like modernist narrative experimentation and collage as advocated (in the west) by Dadaism and Surrealism, but also by Brecht and his philosophical supporter Benjamin. These same features also seem to coincide with Fredric Jameson's definition of "postmodernism." According to Jameson, "blank parody"—parody without material-historical reference or critique—is a defining features of postmodernism, and it is directly connected to the insights of poststructuralism (Jameson 1983; 1997). In this respect, Jameson reduces Ishmael Reed's politically driven parodic attacks to the politically vacuous reiterations of previous forms. According to this interpretation, Reed's syncretism or collage embodies poststructuralism's linguistic insights regarding the dissolution of identity and subjectivity. His formal practices (i.e. syncretism or collage) dissolve individual authorship and identities much like Julia Kristeva's "intertextuality" (Kristeva 1980, 1984). Though Kristeva actually prefers the term "transposition" to "intertextuality"—mostly because she believes the latter word can so easily be confused with a "banal . . . study of sources'"—the concept's deconstructive effects on the singular text and identity operate similarly; that is, "intertextuality," which is "transposition of one (or several) sign systems into another . . . [,]" operates in all works, so every work's identity is threatened from within by the "other" of its embedded intertexts (Kristeva, *Revolution in Poetic Language* 59–60).

While such evidence would seem to indicate Reed's writing is poststructurally postmodern, Reed's own comments suggest that his parodic syncretism and collage are rooted in Voodoo practice. Speaking about his Voodoo inspired vision in an interview, Reed notes that "Voodoo rites" become conversations among contending loas (spirits), each with its own viewpoint (Gover Interview 15). Such conversations can even result in boisterous and emotional arguments. As he puts it, contending "loas show up at the same time, sometimes, and they start quarreling, everybody talking at the same time" (Gover Interview 15).[17] The attending narrative fragmentation produced through such parodic collage offers an alternative, and possibly politically informed, explanation of Reed's compositional method. Taken in this sense, Reed's aforementioned use of photographs, drawings, and narratives from history books reintroduces the evacuated critical content and historical reference seen in Jameson's reading.

If we set aside these concerns and return to Reed's use of this inherited syncretic—or collage—model of authoring, we should understand that he adapts it for authoring and authorizing a specifically *American* incarnation of African-*American* identity. Furthermore, he mixes with the traditional syncretic model another aspect of "satire," namely its "derogating" aspect. Doing this gives Reed the freedom to create—or author—a vision of African-American identity, but also the chance to "derogate" and challenge authorship of dominant (white) western narratives of history, cultural influence, and identity.

Monotheistic Authorship and Reed's Polytheistic Tropic Response:
Voodoo Loas, Houngans, and Syncretism as Roots of Dispersed Authorship

Reed constructs his multi-voiced authorial vision largely through African religious inheritance. The heritage of Polytheism and Voodoo are the most significant in this respect. Here, polytheistic Voodoo becomes both an inspirational authorial model and a combative foil. In this combative role Reed sets polytheism's pluralistic vision against Christianity's demand for a singular and absolute God. Specifically, Voodoo's polytheistic system allows for many gods and many voices. Christianity's monotheistic God, on the other hand, demands obedience to his singular authority and viewpoint. The Bible states the singular and authoritative nature of the Christian view: "I am the first, and hereafter am I, and no god was before me . . ." (Isaiah qtd. in Pelikan 82). He is the author who created the universe "ex nihilo" ("from nothing"), and the God who authors and authorizes scripture. In short, this Christian God represents an exemplary instance of the singular and unitary author; only his words and creation remain original and sacred, and as such, only he deserves worship. Thus in *Mumbo Jumbo* monotheistic Christianity and it formative precursor—what Reed calls "Atonism"—are represented as eliminating all competing deities. In Reed's words, "All of the gods who were rivals of the 1 they called Jehovah (the cover-up for the Flaming Disc God) were driven underground and the many were reduced to one" (*Mumbo Jumbo* 170).

For Reed, this monotheism is equally evident in authorship. For example, Reed portrays Moses as a model of the unitary author. Moses says, "I'm the 1. For once music wouldn't just be used as a background to dancing but he would be a *soloist* and no 1 in the audience would be allowed to play a whistle or beat a drum or rattle a tambourine" (*Mumbo Jumbo* 182 [italics mine]). Reed's use of the term "soloist" and the number "1" have significance here. As Reed states in his poem "Neo-HooDoo Manifesto," "Neo-HooDoo is not a church for egotripping" *(Conjure* 21). The specific "egotripping" is that of the singular author who believes she or he alone creates without outside influence or help. That is, this author believes s/he, like a little god, creates the text "ex-nihilo." Similarly, Moses, as one of the many thieves of The Text/The Book of Toth in *Mumbo Jumbo* believes he alone creates its meaning, can speak its spirit in a singular fashion. As author, Reed's employment of "1" serves two purposes. At once it is an attempt to get away from the pronominal sense of "one" as singular entity, exchanging for it a mere number in a sequence ("1"). At the same time, Reed's use of mathematics refers back to the body, thereby reversing the binary favoritism of mind over body. Counting, as part of mathematics, has its roots in body parts (fingers, toes) as they once signified for the user the things being counted; this, at least, seems strongly suggested by writers in mathematics (e.g. Clawson 1996, Ebbinghair 1990). This practice, of using numbers instead of words, occurs throughout Reed's *Mumbo Jumbo* to similar effect. Namely, it serves to call attention to the myth of the "egotripping" author who see him or herself as sole creator of a text.

On the other hand, Reed's vision of divinity and authorship is directly opposed to the western monotheistic tradition. In particular, Reed finds his divinity—or, more appropriately, his divinit*ies*—within the inherited religious traditions of Africa and the Carribean. These traditions are not monotheistic, but polytheistic. For Reed polytheism acts as a very general model of identity for African-American culture, the individual writer, and aesthetics. This identity's more specific aspects come from the inherited Carribean religious tradition of Voodoo, a tradition historically linked to the slave trade and the black diaspora which resulted as Africans were forced to places like Haiti and the United States. These Voodoo ideas act as general tropes for Reed's vision of authorship. Once we understand the general structure of this tropic vision, we may then connect it to some specific tropes Reed uses to represent the author's location and writing activity.

To begin, Voodoo is a polytheistic religion which does not worship the god of (first) creation ("*le gran' maître*"), but rather spirits called "loas" (Deren 54–55). Though a loa can sometimes be the spiritual concentration of a direct familial ancestor, it often represents a manifestation of the nanchon's ("nation" or "tribe's") spiritual accumulation of history, knowledge, or way of thinking (Deren 27; 70–71; 86–92; 334). When the loa is a person, she or he must be one "who has been distinguished for . . . wisdom or power, love or therapies, disciplines or skills—who has perhaps reached the rank of houngan (priest),[18] with all the accomplishments that such a rank signified," and "is reclaimed with elaborate care, so that his special virtues may not be lost" (Deren 28). This elaborate method of reclamation Voodoo worshipers call "*retirer d'en bas de l'eau*" (loosely translated "reclamation from the water below") (Deren 27; 336). After this ceremony any given loa may return to materiality through a process of "possession" whereby the spirit or god "mounts" a living human being—much like a rider "mounts" a horse—and temporarily displaces that human being's "*gros-bon-ange*," or "soul" (Deren 29; 330). "The function and purpose of such divine manifestation" as possession "is the reassurance and the instruction of the community" (Deren 30). Thus, it would be reasonable to say "[t]he living do not serve the dead; it is the dead who are made to serve the living" (Deren 28). Or, if you like, the spirits of the dead (loas) return to serve those who are alive.

Some additional aspects of Voodoo loa and the nature of the houngan deserve emphasis here if we are to understand Reed's take on African-American identity and authorship. Firstly, these loas are numerous and may possess ("mount") anyone. Secondly, loas have power to "modify" material circumstances, but they are powerless to "create" anything new; so, for example, a loa "can help a garden grow and can bring rain," but it cannot "create either the seed or the water" (Deren 55). Thirdly, we may in certain instances envision loas not so much as personal spirits, but as specific ways of thinking, believing, or valuing. In this sense they may be considered somewhat like Foucault's "discourses," though the particulars of a Voodoo version would have to be specified.[19] An example of this sort of loa possession might be a white or African-American writer who composes according to a strict agenda. As an example, we might think of an African-American writer who is "mounted" (possessed) by a "loa" (spirit) who makes her write according to a specific aesthetic theory, one which includes specific demands for character portrayal, say the aesthetic theory of an Amiri Baraka. Or, as an equal possibility, we might find an African-American writer's *maît-tête* (his or her "master of the head" loa, what might otherwise be called the psyche's dominant way of thinking)[20] is strongly allied to Amiri Baraka's way of viewing the world.

Furthermore, we can discern another type of possession that might occur. In this instance we could imagine the following scenario: A past writer exhibits such a high degree of skill and wisdom that his community deems him a (literary) "houngan."[21] In fact, this community so venerates this literary houngan that—after his death—it performs the rite of *retirer* to preserve his skills and wisdom as a loa. We might then imagine this loa of the dead writer possessing ("mounting") another writer many years later. In this type of possession we might find the person possessed—say, a writer of today—exhibiting the aforementioned "power," "wisdom," "therapies," "disciplines or skills" of the long dead but well esteemed writer who has possessed him. This "mounted" writer's work (e.g. a novel) might manifest aspects of the writer loa who has mounted him; these aspects could range from the loa's (dead writer's) core ideas or beliefs to specific literary techniques.

This houngan's nature deserves some emphasis as well. As already noted, houngans can become loas if a community reveres them enough to perform the *retirer* (preservation ceremony) after their deaths. But the *living* houngan can also call forth and manipulate loas. To do this the houngan needs the assistance of the loa "Legba," who acts as "God of the Crossroads," or the crucial "link between the visible, mortal world and the invisible, immortal realms" (Deren 97). Without Legba, no communication with "*les Invisibles*" ("invisible spirits," of loas and the souls of all dead people) is possible (Deren 97–98; 331). Therefore, the houngan must make offerings to Legba (often food) in order to call him to open the gate between our "visible, mortal world" and the "invisible, immortal realms" of loas and the dead (Deren 97). After the houngan successfully calls Legba, the former may communicate with loas and the souls of the dead. He may, in a sense, manipulate and control them.

We can now link these elements together to construct a broad picture of Reed's conception of authorship and identity, after which we can examine this conception in depth through an analysis of his writing tropes. Reed's vision of authorship and identity relies on a commingling of the three primary elements just addressed, namely, loa possession, houngan (priest), and the figure of loa Legba ("God of the Cross-roads"). The first of these, loa possession, presents Reed with a myriad of authorial possibilities. If loas range from individual spirits of the once living (e.g. past writers) to the sedimentary spiritual history of a "tribe," or ways of thinking, believing, and valuing, then numerous forms of possession exist.

However, this could present some problems for unitary authorship. For example, if a contemporary writer can be possessed by the loa of a long dead writer, then who actually *authors* the written text? If one is possessed by numerous personal loas (e.g. numerous past writers), then the problems merely compound. Similar questions result in the case of a writer possessed by numerous loas of thinking, believing, or valuing. An equally problematic case would arise with the writer possessed by numerous and historically disparate accumulations of tribal history or knowledge. All would devolve into the fundamental question of "who writes?"

Reed suggests a partial answer to this question of "loas" in the mediating figures of Legba ("God of the Cross-roads") and the houngan (priest). In fact, in *Mumbo Jumbo* Reed combines the two in the character PaPa LaBas to produce a pluralistic model of authorship and African-American identity. Specifically, LaBas becomes both Legba—"the God of the Cross-roads" who marks an intersecting point between divinities (loas) and materiality—and houngan -the mortal priest who calls forth the loas and manipulates them for "reassurance" and "the instruction of community," though according to his own creative play. Put more simply, the author is a kind of literary houngan who acts as an interested intermediary negotiating between the material realm and the spiritual realm of loas. He offers sacrifice to loas of both the distant and more recent past; this brings them all before him for his manipulation and according to his creative energy. Thus, in Reed's vision the author can call up the loa of W.E.B. Du Bois, Louis Armstrong, Bessie Smith, Malcolm X, or the loa of Black Nationalism, or some other aspect of accumulated spiritual history. The writer then allows these loa voices to speak in whatever configuration s/he deems.

But as I just stated, Reed offers this as only a partial solution to the question of "who writes?" We are still left with the possibility of an author's own head being possessed by one or many loas, not to mention the difficulties arising from an unruly *maît-tête* ("master of the head") of which one is or is not aware. In short, there is simply no telling where—precisely—the authorial voices comes from, or where -precisely- the writing will go. While it proves helpful to remember that Voodoo tradition demands houngans (or writers) utilize loa (e.g. spirits or techniques of other writers, or ways of thinking or believing) for "the reassurance" and "instruction of the community," this is by no means assured. The additional Voodoo belief in "bocor," nasty houngans who purchase loas for their own selfish goals, makes the authorial issue more of a predicament. To further problematize matters for individual authorship we should also recall my remarks earlier regarding the powers of loas; that is, loas have the power to "modify" but not "create" (Deren 55). A houngan (writer) can thus put loas (e.g. other writer's techniques or their content) together in myriad ways—i.e. "modify"—but s/he cannot "create" an *original* work. In this sense, we may see the houngan (author/writer) as one who plays with given loas (e.g. a previous author's writing technique), attempting to combine them in different, though not absolutely unique, ways.

The loas' ability to "modify" but not "create" has obvious affinities to postmodern conceptions of authorship. We could think here of Foucault's notions of "discourse" and "discursive formations." If we read in these terms, writers become something quite different. They are not unique creators—authors—of original works; instead, they only write already existing discourses—if in various combinations—which they inherit from their culture. Or, we might think of Derrida's notions of "dissemination" and "trace." Here, an author (or houngan) who writes texts with loas—regardless of whether he possesses them or they possess him—produces "[t]exts [which] are 'stratified' in the sense that they bear along with them a whole network of articulated themes and assumptions whose meaning everywhere links up with other texts, or other genres or topics of discourse" (Norris 25–26). This is to say that the author (houngan) writes texts which bare disseminating "traces" of other previous texts and meanings. More simply the writer's (houngan's) text always has loas (spirits) within it from past texts.

Interestingly, this Voodoo notion of authorship as loa possession dissolves the unitary writing subject in much the same way as postmodern poststructuralism. This is so because the subject writing (individual houngan) must necessarily possess loas to write, or alternatively, must be possessed by loas to write. In either case, the writing subject (houngan) disappears. In the former instance the disappearance occurs because the writing product (the text) has no trace of the writing individual, but only traces of the loas she used to write the text. In the latter case, the disappearance of the writing subject occurs precisely because of possession; that is, the writing voice is not that of the writer (houngan), but that of the loa(s). While the postmodern disappearance of the author occurs because of an obsession with linguistic concerns—the belief that language constructs and predates the self—the Voodoo disappearance of the writer (houngan) has to do with a religious belief in the accumulation and preservation of communal history and values. Certainly, poststructuralists such as Foucault and Derrida would insist on a "history" within texts, a sedimentation of meanings and values from previous texts, but their emphasis falls on linguistics and its attempts to deal with particular historical problems in western philosophy. As such, the two appear somewhat different. One could say that Reed arrives at postmodern conclusions, but he does so by following a different path than those laid out by poststructural theorists.

A concrete instance from Reed's work illustrates both his uses of satire and his vision of authorship as houngan (writer) possession. As well as offering an introduction to these topics, this selection from Reed's poem "Neo-HooDoo Manifesto" gives a general outline of his Neo-HooDoo aesthetic. As is typical of Reed's work, it critiques even as it constructs:

Politicizing Authority, Authorship, and Identity

Neo-HooDoo is not a church for egotripping—it takes its "organization" from Haitian VooDoo of which Milo Rigaud wrote:

> *Unlike other established religions, there is no heirarchy of bishops, archbishops, cardinals, or a pope in VooDoo. Each oum'phor* [each temple] *is a law unto itself, following the traditions of VooDoo but modifying and changing the ceremonies and rituals in various ways.* (*Conjure* 21)

Within this poem we get both clues about Reed's satirical targets—the "church for egotripping," which obviously refers to the (Catholic) Christian church's "heirarchy of bishops, archbishops, cardinals" and "*pope*,"—and clues about Reed's multi-voiced vision of authorship, identity and divinity, through reference to each "*oum'phor*" (temple, place of worship for houngans) "following . . . *traditions of VooDoo but modifying and changing ceremonies in various ways.*" The "egotripping" must certainly refer to two things. First, it refers to the notion of a single authoritative voice or God who issues and authorizes the one and only authoritative narrative. Second, Reed's sarcastic use of quotations around "organization" must surely refer to the mortals ("bishops, archbishops, cardinals" and "popes") who canonize this singular narrative and reproduce it and its power "heirarchy." Furthermore, the blatant reference to Catholicism (e.g. "*pope*") in conjunction with Reed's mention of "*VooDoo*" necessarily calls to mind visions of Haiti—Voodoo's birthplace—and the western Christian imperialism associated with its occupation. In *Mumbo Jumbo,* published the same year as "Neo-HooDoo Manifesto," this spirit of western Christian imperialism is personified in "Atonism," and Reed transports it to nineteen twenties New York to do battle with the American spirit of Voodoo called "HooDoo." Indeed, for Reed Haiti and America are two instances of the same historical repression. In each case the (white) Christian or Atonist spirit has sought to impose a hierarchy and a singular narrative voice. Thus, later in "Neo-HooDoo Manifesto" Reed calls Christianity "a CopGod from the git-go" (24) and remarks in *Mumbo Jumbo* that Atonism's method of dealing with dissenters is to "'beat the living shit out of them'" (172).

If we look elsewhere in the poem, we find other radical tendencies. For example, the poem's capricious capitalization ("*VooDoo*") and aberrant spelling (e.g. "*heirarchy,*" "*oum'phor*") indicate Reed's poetic attempt to speak at the limits of an inherited language and to articulate African-American difference. Putting "*e*" before "*i*" in "heirarchy"—correctly spelled "hierarchy"—helps accomplish this because it violates spelling "rules" (i.e. the "hierarchy" of "'i' before 'e' except after 'c'"). *Mumbo Jumbo* is peppered with such instances (e.g. LaBas says Atonists—those "devoted to Aton" (174)—are named after the Pharaoh "Akhnaton," though the correct spelling is "Akhenaten" or "Akhenaton"). This metaphorically reverses the priority of white over black to black over white in much the same fashion as Reed's symbols (●○) within individual chapters of *Mumbo Jumbo* reverse the priority of races; that is, the black circle coming immediately before the white circle signifies black as prior. The gesture ruptures the sacred white colonialist narrative of presence—the story of whiteness as the only and all encompassing narrative—that has been handed down to African-Americans in diaspora. Reed has commented on this unfortunate linguistic inheritance, observing that "our destinies are still being decided by the slave master. We use the language that he invented, and we have certain attitudes that he left with us" (Martin interview 1981, 182). Reed's strategic move with regard to both his spelling and his use of symbols is meant to counter this, to signify both the difference of the African-American position—the part of the "African" which is "American"—and the reversal of priorities, so that another story can be told, namely, African-American (his/hers)tory.

Reed's misspelling works also to locate the writer (houngan). For example, his misspelling "*oum'phor*"—he plays here on the Voodoo term "hounfor," which is "[t]he 'temple' of a Voudoun priest [houngan], including the paraphernalia of the service and understood to include the persons who serve there" (Deren 330)—serves to mark the place of difference for the African-American writer or houngan, that aspect of the author which is specifically American but serving the loas (spirits) inherited from Africa. Similarly, the capricious capitalization in "VooDoo" signals the difference of that author's African-American aesthetic, what Reed call "HooDoo." It will be characterized by the syncretism already noted and function along tropic lines.

Because Reed performs his reversals and these plays on words by writing understandable stories and poems, we have evidence that he still uses the given language. He therefore seems to recognize—like many poststructuralists—that it is impossible to step outside inherited systems of representation. Here we might revisit Reed's earlier remark which seems to signal his recognition of the fact ("our destinies are still being decided by the slave master. We use the language that he invented . . .") The best he can do is implement a variety of disruptions, misspelling being one, to draw attention to representation as a form of power and play with it so as to offer other ways of seeing, like the multi-voiced Voodoo tradition which has no "*heirarchy*" of authority. Reed's intertextual use of Milo Rigaud's own words in "Neo-HooDoo Manifesto" signifies this willingness to give up absolute authority (hierarchy) over language. In this instance he gives "proper credit" to Rigaud, but in *Mumbo*

Jumbo the precise origin of sources—the unitary authorial voices—is very often unclear, despite Reed's bibliography. Thus *Mumbo Jumbo* appears more like an amalgam of voices, none of which can be given ultimate credit.

What appears especially interesting in Reed's "Neo-HooDoo Manifesto" is the way it utilizes almost all aspects of satire but at the same time remains connected to the African-Haitian heritage. On the one hand it illustrates one aspect of satire in its scathing ("derogating") attack on western Christian beliefs and their destructiveness. By including Rigaud's text in the poem, Reed evinces intertextuality illustrative of satire as "mixed dish" or collage. Yet in its use of Voodoo elements combined with this "mixed dish" or collage it continues the Voodoo tradition of syncretism. While Reed's "Neo-HooDoo Manifesto" is helpful for understanding his revision of authorship, turning to a number of his primary writing tropes helps show how he implement his syncretic authorial vision to locate the place and activities of the writer. However, before we turn to these tropes, I have one final observation. The tropes analyzed—namely, jazz, dance, and cooking or food preparation—all illustrate the same basic vision of authorship, be it authorship of texts, cultural identity, or other narratives. Each simply represents a different way of envisioning a similar attitude, specifically, an attitude toward authorship.

Reed's HooDoo Satire and the Jazz Player as Trope

To begin, let us look at the first few pages of *Mumbo Jumbo*. In these first pages Reed announces the birth of jazz saxophonist Charlie Parker and appoints him to the status of "houngan," meaning "Voudoun [voodoo] priest. literally chief, *gan,* of the spirits, *houn* . . ." (Deren 330) Here is Reed's anointment of Parker as a "houngan": "1920. Charlie Parker, the houngan . . . for whom there is no master adept enough to award him the Asson, is born." (*Mumbo Jumbo* 16). That Reed anoints Parker a Voodoo "houngan" (priest) seems clear enough, though we still need to spell out this moniker's specific implications with regard to jazz, writing, and the saxophonist. But what does Reed mean by stating there "is no master adept enough to award him [Parker] the Asson"?

The answer to this question resides in Voodoo religion. In particular Reed draws explicitly on the Voodoo notion of *"serviteur."* A *"serviteur"* is, as the French suggests, a "servant." But this servant is also a houngan, one who calls forth loas to both possess him and for his possession. We see this double sense of being possessed and possessing throughout *Mumbo Jumbo*. For example, PaPa LaBas' fixation with "feeding" loas is exactly a calling forth of loas so that he may perform his "techniques and therapy" (28). He thus *possesses* loas for "the reassurance and the instruction of the community" (Deren 30). We can see an example of the *desire to be possessed* later in *Mumbo Jumbo* when an inquisitive Nathan Brown begs Benoit Battraville to "teach" him (Nathan) "how to catch Jes Grew," which is to say the African-American spirit of HooDoo (151–152).

We can now bring together several of Reed's ideas. The phrasing in the quotation about Parker clearly equates the saxophonist Charlie Parker to a serviteur-houngan, one who both possesses loas and is possessed by loas. But we must now address the question of the "Asson." According to Deren, the "Asson" is the "ceremony of priestly investiture" bestowed—usually by an existing houngan—upon those deemed worthy of the title "houngan" (Deren 80). Yet it is also a sort of instrument used to accompany Voodoo ceremonies (Deren 325). If we compare Reed's phrasing of Parker's anointment to Deren's description of the mythical Haitian Voodoo *serviteur*-houngan Titon and his anointment, some interesting parallels result. Deren, speaking of Titon, says, "he would . . . proclaim that there was no houngan great enough to give him the asson" (Deren 80). Here, again, is Reed's anointment of Parker: "Charlie Parker, the houngan . . . for whom there is no master adept enough to award him the Asson, . . ." (*Mumbo Jumbo* 16) Here, Reed, who took pains to include Deren's book in *Mumbo Jumbo*'s bibliography, clearly draws a direct comparison between Titon and Charlie Parker.

Titon, as Deren indicates, represents the sole inheritor of Voodoo and African tradition. While everyone else, including his brothers and sisters, had been converted to Christianity and had abandoned the faith, Titon alone remained loyal to the loas of his homeland. Though he excelled at the sacred ceremonies devoted to the loas and was better than most confirmed houngans (those who already had the Asson), he was poor and could not afford the cost of the Asson ritual. Therefore, "he would proclaim that there was no houngan great enough to give him the asson. It would be the loa themselves who would confer upon him this sacred instrument of divine power . . ." (Deren 80–81)

For Reed, Charlie Parker, and all the great jazz players and singers from the Harlem Renaissance to the present, are like Titon and must award the Asson to themselves. They appear like LaBas—who admits, "I awarded the Asson to myself" (*Mumbo Jumbo* 212)—as modern day HooDoo priests. They continue devotion to the loas, the spirits who moved from Africa to Haiti to America in the great forced diaspora. Charlie Parker—as a black man in racist America—is like the poor Titon, an outsider without resources, but one who carries the traces of the past within him and continues to worship these traces through his playing. As "Asson" also signifies a musical instrument used for

Voodoo ceremonies, one can view Parker's playing saxophone—and any playing by jazz musicians on instruments—as a form of priestly musical worship conducted for loas past. As a jazz musician, or author of a jazz text, he is at once a houngan-artist and Legba (the mediating loa figure between divinities and this world). As both a mediator of loas and an artist himself, he plays the past—past texts by earlier authors or jazz musicians—and brings it (historical past) and them (past texts) into the present.

While I have spoken about Charlie Parker's devotion to African-American tradition—the spiritual loas of his black inheritance—I have not exactly specified the nature and practice of this devotion, what it means to call these loa forth to possess one and to possess for one's manipulation. Here, again, Deren's comments on the *serviteur*-houngan prove helpful and move us some way toward a more complete explication. When a *serviteur*-houngan worships the loa—in Charlie Parker's case through playing the sax—his intention is to, in Deren's words,

> call upon everything of which he [*the serviteur*] was, himself, the final issue—to call not only upon the generality, the principles of his patrimony, but, beginning with the Marassa, the first men, upon the roll of that ancestral progression which had successively borne that complex forward: the African tribes, the Indian allies, the thousands of individuals whose blood had nourished it and whose diverse personal genius had swelled and elaborated its manifold and various aspects. His invocation was the genealogy of his own divinity, and condensed into the shorthand nomenclature, contained the record of the race, of all that which, flowing like a river forward in time, was to be funneled now into this single individual so that, in his own person, the accumulated force of moral history would be pitted against contemporary circumstance. (Deren 81)

This means that the serviteur-houngan—in this case the jazz musician as representative of the writing author—has within him or her the capacity to call up the entirety of tradition. In a very real sense, then, this *serviteur*-houngan jazz musician is a historian and allows history to speak through her or him. Reed states elsewhere, specifically in *Shrovetide in New Orleans* (1979), that this is part of his conception of composition: "This is what my kind of writing is all about. It leads me to places where I can see old cultures resurrected, and made contemporary. Time past is present" (3).

But what exactly is this cultural past and how does the jazz player or writer bring it to life? Earline gives an answer which helps us locate both jazz musician and writer in America in a conversation with PaPa LaBas:

> That's our genius here in America. We were dumped here on our own without the Book [The Text or The Book of Toth] to tell us who the loas are, what we call spirits were. We made up our own. The theories of Julia Jackson. I think we've done all right. The Blues, Ragtime, The Work that we do is just as good. I'll bet later on in the 50s and 60s and 70s we will have some artists and creators who will teach Africa and South America some new twists. It's already happening. What it boils down to, LaBas, is intent. If your heart's there, man, that's 1/2 the thing about The Work. . . . .Doing The Work is not like taking inventory. Improvise some. Open up, PaPa. Stretch on out with it. (*Mumbo Jumbo* 130)

Here, Earline clearly refers to the forced diaspora from Africa to America in her first line of dialogue ("We were dumped here on our own without the Book"). Because Africans were "dumped" in America without a complete and coherent statement of cultural identity ("without the Book to tell us who the loas are"), the Africans—now African-Americans—"made up" their own identities and cultural practices ("loas") from what they had at hand and could recover from memory ("theories of Juila Jackson"). "The Blues" and "Ragtime" are instances of that constructive and recuperative practice, instances which are inherited but are also "made up." References to "the 50s," "60s," and "70s" represent Reed's homage to "free jazz" musicians like Sun Ra, Ornette Coleman, and others who worked to construct African-American cultural identity through continuing avant-garde practices ("new twists") first seen in blues and ragtime.[22] Reed comments on this historical progression: "The Blues is Jes Grew, as James Weldon Johnson surmised. Jazz was a Jes Grew which followed the Jes Grew of Ragtime" (*Mumbo Jumbo* 214). Finally, there is Earline's plea to LaBas to "Improvise some. Open up. Stretch on out with it."

This plea for LaBas to "Improvise some" and "Open up" represents both the Voodoo syncretic tradition and satire as construction (the "mixed dish" or "collage"). The inclusion of references to jazz avant-garde ("free jazz")—if cryptic—clearly indicates the creative parallels between jazz and Reed's vision of writing. "Jazz," like Reed's vision of composition "is always understood as dependent on improvisation. It is music that drifts on a read. It starts with what is given and spins off new melodies, rhythms, and harmonies" (Jarrett 3). But to start "with what is given" and make "new melodies, rhythms, and harmonies" is to destroy the uniqueness of the unitary author's place and creation (the text). In particular, that which is "given" is itself indebted to that which came before it. To mix the poststructural (postmodern) and Voodoo conception we might think of the author/jazz musician (as *serviteur*-houngan) composing texts/jazz music (The Work/The Text/The Book of Toth as expressions of African-American spirit), which themselves always evince "traces" or "disseminations" of earlier writers'/musicians' compositions (loas). For this reason, LaBas marks the end of the singular author: "We serve the loas, . . . Charismatic leaders will become as outdated as the solo because people will realize that when the Headman dies the movement dies instead of becoming a permanent entity, perspirit, a protective covering for its essence" (*Mumbo Jumbo* 40). In another place where Reed discusses HooDoo aesthetics, he negates this singular godlike author by proposing a pantheon of composers. As LaBas puts it, "Voudun [Voodoo] aesthetic," envisions a "pantheistic, becoming, 1 which bountifully permits 1000 of spirits, as many as the imagination can hold. Infinite Spirits and Gods. So many that it would take a book larger than the Koran and the Bible, the Tibetan Book of the Dead and all of the holy books in the world to list, and still room would have to be made for more" (*Mumbo Jumbo* 35).

"Neo HooDoo Manifesto" and *Mumbo Jumbo* both reflect this singular author's undoing through syncretism and constructive satire. In the first work Reed asserts the following: "Charlie 'Yardbird (Toth)' Parker is an example of the Neo-HooDoo artist as an innovator and improvisor" (*Conjure*, "Neo-HooDoo Manifesto" 21). This reference to Charlie Parker as "Toth" occurs again in *Mumbo Jumbo,* where Reed draws a line of heritage between artists like Parker and Toth, the ancient Osirian recorder of sacred dances: "Osiris the Bull, the Seedman, . . . his faithful Birdman Toth at his side, taking it all down" (*Mumbo Jumbo* 165). The line drawn first refers to the saxophonist's famous nickname ("Birdman"), and then the reference in both the poem and novel to "Toth" serves to equate Charlie Parker jazz musician with the ancient transcriber of sacred dances. Parker is thus a sort of serviteur-houngan writer who, while improvising, pays tribute to the loas (spirits) and The Text (texts) of the past through the very act of playing on "what is given." Parker's act of playing-which represents improvisational authorship—is thus the "sounds—song, drum beat, asson and langage— which are like lines thrown out,[23] to become the cables of the bridge upon which man would cross that chasm; it is present, as physical fact, in the amnesia which makes even the sense of the loa inaccessible to the very 'horse' which bore him" (Deren 249). In short, Parker's playing is a "bridge" to "cross" the "chasm" of history and bring the past into the present through improvisation upon older texts. The metaphorical "amnesia" present when the jazz musician plays is caused by "the loa"—previous jazz musicians and their texts, as well as those musician's predecessors and their texts—which possess the musician in the present, in his act of textual/musical composition.

In this sense, the "loa" ride the musician like a "horse," even as the musician remains unaware of all the previous texts/musical compositions which inhabit his or her performance in the form of "traces." Similar, and in a self-conscious way, Reed's *Mumbo Jumbo* is composed of "what is given" from the past (traces). As we have already seen, he includes many texts and borrowed words within his work, and this illustrate the syncretic tradition of inclusion, but also the satirical constructive tradition of "collage." In this syncretic or collaged sense jazz is a "hound mongrel" (*Mumbo Jumbo* 20). The term "mongrel" signals this mixture.

But how, exactly, does one develop the artist's sense, the "Jes Grew"—or African-American spirit—of authorship. Reed offers one hint through the Haitian character Benoit Battraville. In this instance Nathan Brown asks Battraville how to "catch" "Jes Grew"; Battraville, after telling him to ask an American HooDoo expert like PaPa LaBas, says this:

> You see the Americans do not know the names of the long and tedious lists of deities and rites as we know them. Shorthand is what they know so well. They know this process for they have *synthesized* the HooDoo of VooDoo. Its blee blop essence; they've isolated the unknown factor which gives the loas their rise. Ragtime. Jazz. Blues. The new thang. That talk you drum from your lips. Your style. What you have here is an experimental art form that all of us believe bears watching. So don't ask me how to catch Jes Grew. Ask Louis Armstrong, Bessie Smith, your poets, your painters, your musicians, ask them how to catch it. Ask those people who be shaking their tambourines impervious of the ridicule they receive from Black and White Atonists, Europe the ghost rattling its chains down the deserted halls of their brains. Ask those little colored urchins who 'make up' those new dance steps and the loa of the black cook who wrote the last lines of the 'Ballad of Jesse James.' Ask the man who, deprived of an electronic guitar, picked up a washboard and started to play it. The Rhyming Fool who sits in Rē'-mōte Mississippi and talks 'crazy' for hours. The dazzling parodying punning mischievous pre-Joycean style-play of your Cakewalking your Calinda your Minstrelsy give-and-take of the ultra-absurd. Ask the people who put wax paper over combs and breathe through them. In other words, . . . Open-Up-To-Right-Here and then you will have something coming from your experience that the whole world will admire and need. (*Mumbo Jumbo* 152; italics mine)

This quotation speaks to the syncretic tradition as well as postmodern collage. Battraville says explicitly that HooDoo is "synthesized" Voodoo, but it is also the "new thang," that which jazz artists construct from the synthesis of both the American and African tradition. "The Jes Grew" or HooDoo within jazz comes from a mix of Voodoo—as an expression of African cultural inheritance—and from the historical inheritance of African-American artists (e.g. "Bessie Smith" or "Louis Armstrong"). In addition, it's the individuality added to the syncretic "mixed dish" by each artist ("your style," "The Rhyming Fool who sits in Rē´-mōte Mississippi and talks 'crazy' for hours"), a figure who almost sounds like anyone with the right mind, not just the famous artist ("the man who, deprived of an electronic guitar, picked up a washboard and started to play it," "the people who put wax paper over combs and breathe through them"). All of this is what LaBas intends when he says he "wanted them [African-Americans] to have the heads their people had left for them or create new ones of their own" (*Mumbo Jumbo* 217). In this scheme it would appear that anyone can create, but no single person may claim to be the sole creator of a work(s).

In a related sense Reed's ubiquitous employment of disparate texts also problematizes singular authorship. Here, Reed uses numerous texts—often without reference to their origin—and works them into his own prose. As a typical example, he often mixes newspaper articles and bits from history texts, as well as the "Situation Reports" and excerpts from literature,[24] to produce confusion not only about what belongs to which author, but also which source is fact and which is fiction. A text like Reed's *Mumbo Jumbo* thus seems to work very much along the lines of Derridean writing.

Having looked at Reed's similarities to some poststructural attitudes toward interpretation, improvisation, and the "riddling" of signatures, we can turn back again to some of Reed's distinguishing features. In particular we can look again at the notion of devotion. In terms of Reed's use of Voodoo, we cannot forget that for anyone to compose or author—professional artist or otherwise—requires devotion. These devotions take the form of "feeding," specifically, feeding loas (spirits). The importance of this practice is illustrated by the sign in PaPa LaBas' Mumbo Jumbo Kathedral stating, "REMEMBER TO FEED THE LOAS" (*Mumbo Jumbo* 28). Certainly, jazz artists "feed the loas" by playing music which bears traces of the past (i.e. texts/music of past artists). But there are other feedings required. Earline, LaBas' secretary and daughter, once forgets this practice and receives the wrath of loa Erzulie—the Voodoo goddess of love (Deren 62)—via possession.[25] As a result of this possession Earline seduces a trolley driver.

But what does "feeding" mean exactly? If we look to moments in *Mumbo Jumbo*, Reed offers some hints. In one section Reed shows feeding done by non-artists, those who are not themselves *serviteur*-houngan-musicians or writers, but who love the loas those artists worship. Haitian Benoit Battraville comments on this "feeding" saying,

> we know that when 1 [loa] comes about it must be fed, similar to the way you feed your Ragtime and Jazz by supporting the artists and making it easier for those who are possessed by those forms. Buying records and patronizing those places which are not in the hands of the Atonists. You know that if you do not don't do this, Ragtime and Jazz will turn upon you or unfed they will perish. (*Mumbo Jumbo* 151)

Battraville adds to this list as well, noting a new loa: "Similarly, we have a Radio Loa who just came about during this war" (*Mumbo Jumbo* 151). The two quotations serve to indicate that as time goes on and circumstances change (e.g. with the invention of the radio and recordings by African-American jazz artists) the nature of devotion to tradition changes as well (e.g. the necessity to "feed" "Jazz by supporting the artists" by buying their recordings).

As one last item, we should observe how Reed's jazz model of the artist and her work stands in stark contrast to those African American's who have entirely abandoned their past and pursue white western models of authorship and identity. It cannot be forgotten here that The New Negro model while embracing jazz as entertainment, never considered it authentic art, which was to be found traditional white models. In *Mumbo Jumbo* PaPa LaBas critiques "Black Marxists" for forgetting their cultural inheritance and embracing white models (e.g. Marx). Speaking of them LeBas says they "merely mimic . . . somebody else's thought, and somebody else's song" (51). Of course, this could also apply to the real Amiri Baraka during his Marxist phase, one where he demanded art conform to certain rules. Reed renders another critical jab at this abandonment of the African-American past when he intertextually inserts a rejection letter from a publishing house to Abdul Hamid. In it, the editors suggest the market in "The 'Negro Awakening'" literature has reached its peak, and he should try "returning to *serious* writing" like that of "Mark Twain" and "Stephen Crane," or take a look at "Claude McKay's If We Must Die and perhaps pick up some pointers" (*Mumbo Jumbo* 98; italics mine). The reference to Twain and Crane clearly pokes fun at those African-Americans who aspire to write "serious" literature by writing according to white western models. The reference to Claude McKay—while somewhat cryptic—drives home the point, since his poem "If We Must Die" falls into McKay's "post-Jamaican" period of poetry writing; in this period McKay concentrated almost entirely on the "sonnet form, eschewed dialect, and showed no strong inclination to experiment with rhyme, rhythm, and the other components of the sonnet. Further, he displayed the influence of his early reading of the English Romantics" (Mcleod 429). By his sarcastic inclusion of McKay, a writer clearly following white western composition techniques, Reed critiques the those African-American writers who deny their own tradition by constantly mimicking western models. Furthermore, Reed's inclusion of McKay draws attention to shortcomings heretofore ignored within "Harlem Renaissance" poets, a group too often uncritically embraced as representing the African-American spirit.

Having examined jazz as a trope and template for authorship, we may turn to another of Reed's tropes for the author and her activity. Next, we will examine dance and how it similarly refigures the authors place and activity.

Dance as an Authoring Trope

While Reed uses jazz as a trope and template for authorship, he also employs the bodily trope of dance to refigure the author's place and activity. Reed's intertextual insertion of prose from Joost Meerloo's *The Dance* takes us some way toward understanding this point:

> Dance is the universal art, the common joy of expression. Those who cannot dance are imprisoned in their own ego and cannot live well with other people and the world. They have all lost the tune of life. They only live in cold thinking. Their feelings are deeply repressed while they attach themselves to the earth.(Meerloo qtd. in Reed 60)

This statement corresponds to Reed's attitude toward white Christian Atonists who deny the carnal while also holding on to a singular—ego bound—vision of Authorship. It is no accident that near the beginning of *Mumbo Jumbo* Reed associates the fear and hatred of dance with these attitudes. For instance, at the moment of the "Jes-Grew" outbreak, "No Dancing posters are ordered by the 100s" (*Mumbo Jumbo* 17). Later, Reed intertextually inserts the book *Modern Dancing,* which cautions against performing "the Turkey Trot, the Grizzly Bear, the Bunny Hug, etc. These dances are ugly, ungraceful, and out of fashion" (*Mumbo Jumbo* 93). In another section of the book the body hating Muslim zealot Abdul Hamid warns all African-Americans to "[c]ut out this dancing . . ." (*Mumbo Jumbo* 34). Similarly, Moses, thief of The Text/The Book of Toth—itself a book of dances—and inheritor of Set's hatred of the carnal, declare that "there would be no savage dancing" at his "dignified concert" (*Mumbo Jumbo* 182) In the case of the *Modern Dancing* quotation we have both a declaration against jazz oriented—and thus black influenced—forms of dance, as well as a command to dance according to some other model (implied by "out of fashion"). This, of course, is reminiscent of the fears people like Henry Ford had during the jazz age. His solution was to require his auto executives to take courses in the minuet. The other instances merely mimic this white Atonist attitude.

But Reed offers an alternative. We see this in his ancient figure Osiris who authors dances: "Osiris . . . became known as 'the man who did dances that caught on'" (*Mumbo Jumbo* 162). Later, we see Osiris as having his dances choreographed: "Osiris did his basic dances for many days until Toth had them all down. A Book of Litanies to which people in places like Abydos in Upper Egypt could add their own variations" (*Mumbo Jumbo* 164). As the words indicate, the book constituted not just Osiris' authorship, but the ability of others to author from it. That is, they could syncretically borrow or collage together their own dance steps ("add their own variations"). Reed states this again on the next page and makes it multi-cultural: "Just as fast as Osiris would teach these dances the people would mimic him and add their variations to fit their country and their clime" (*Mumbo Jumbo* 165). This fitting the dance "to their country or clime" implies improvising upon one culture's dance—or text—and adapting it to your own cultural needs. Yet the fact that people would "add their variations" also introduces the individual into the mix. Reed has commented on this individual creative aspect in dance as well as its multi-cultural element: "If you look at the way dances arise, you know, they just come about. And that's part of the Voodoo tradition. And it's also multi-racial, multi-ethnic, and that's the sleeper that most people overlook" (Gover interview 16).

Reed's introduction of intertexts through pictures, concert announcements, news clippings, bits from history books, hand written letters, and radio announcements not only renders traditional narrative mimesis—which is to say "realism"—problematic, but also forces readers to *participate* in the jazz dance of writing, or authorship. If one were to think of a simple instance of this call to participate, Abdul Hamid's hand written note to LaBas offers one micro-example of this. If one inspects the note carefully, one sees that it remains impossible to determine the case of particular letters (e.g. "n" or "N" in "N/niggars, change!") (*Mumbo Jumbo* 201).[26] This call for reader/audience participation marks a critical, though not necessarily absolute, difference between African performance and classical European performance. Amon Saba Saakana writes on this difference (1995). Saakana sets European ballet and classical music performance against African musical performance and dance. In the case of ballet, observes Saakana, European tradition dictates audiences refrain from participating in actual performances; instead, they "applaud politely at certain high points, or preferably at the end of the performance" (332). Not surprisingly, European musical performance illustrate similar tendencies. The classical European mode of musical performance enthrones a singular "conductor," one who "selects the range of the repertoire and controls the playing of the performer and the flow of the music with a baton. This somewhat different from both African dance and African musical performance. For his part Saakana possibly overstates the case, remarking that "to an African such an unnatural performance of music would be *inconceivable*" (Saakana 332; italics mine). Citing J. H. Kwabena Nketia, Saakana observes that in regions of Africa, the Americas, and the Caribbean audiences remain central to the very act of performance, in a sense, helping author it. In Nketia's words, "The presence and participation of an audience influence the animation of a performance, the spontaneous selection of music, the range and textual improvisation, and other details; and this stimulus to creative activity is welcomed, and even sought, by the performers" (Nketia qtd. in Saakana 332). By way of comparison, Reed's Neo-HooDoo aesthetic—an aesthetic drawing on African mythology and musical tradition but also their distinctly African-*American* manifestations—similarly transforms readers into authors/artists. Reed would seem to imply as much in his poem "Neo-HooDoo Manifesto," where he comments on this more egalitarian and participatory vision of the exchange between author and reader. Reed uses the copulative to make this point explicit: "Neo-HooDoo believes . . . every man is an artist and every artist a priest" (*Conjure* 21). In his later work *Mumbo Jumbo,* he reiterates the point: "[A]t the time of Osiris every man was an artist and every artist was a priest" (164).

Of course, given *Mumbo Jumbo*'s persistent irony a caveat seems in order here; while Reed apparently grants the audience participation in authorship, the idea that separation between performer and audience is "inconceivable"—as Nketia claims—probably exaggerates Reed's position, mostly because his pervasive irony makes such absolute statements highly questionable. Nevertheless, the points above do seem to illustrate that dance is important for Reed as a way of conceiving of authorship. It is, like jazz, syncretic and collage oriented. It thus appears both traditional and postmodern. Now, in the next section I would like to look at another of Reed's authorial tropes, namely, cooking.

Cooking as an Authoring Trope

One piece of writing explicitly discussing the author's/artist's essentially improvisational nature is Reed's own poem "The Neo-HooDoo Aesthetic." The poem ostensibly represents two recipes, one for "Gombo Févi" and another for "Gombo Filé" (*Conjure* 26). Most of the poem consists of a list of ingredients for each of the two dishes. The recipe poem concludes with the following two statements:

> Why do I call it "The Neo-HooDoo Aesthetic"?
> *The proportions of ingredients used depend upon the cook!* (*Conjure* 26)

For Reed the cook is the artist or writer; she may utilize "ingredients"—which I read as inherited literary or narrative techniques or an historically bequeathed language—to create a dish (i.e. a work) conforming to her uniquely *individual* tastes. Therefore, we may discern that both cook and writer have creative freedom to express their individualities in their works (i.e. in their culinary dishes or their literary texts). However, there necessarily exists an inherent limit to any cook or writer's creative abilities. Both cook and writer can only cook or write with what is available, namely "ingredients" and combinations thereof in various "proportions." Any given cook finds the outer limits of her individual creativity in the food stuffs available to her and how those various food stuffs—in certain "proportions"—have been combined traditionally in the form of "recipes." She may, for instance, play with "proportions" of particular ingredients in a given recipe. Thus, she might alter the proportions of "crab" in the recipe for "Gombo Févi," adding or subtracting according to her *individual* tastes. Or she may improvise further on the recipe by adding a new "ingredient"—one taken from all of the historically available food stuffs—to an inherited recipe. For example, she might add a new ingredient cayenne to "Gombo Féve" in her own particular "proportions." In terms of composition, this might look like a syncretic or collage sort of borrowing from available narratives, something along the lines of Reed's intertextual insertions of other author's works, which themselves carry loas (spirits) with attitudes (e.g. ideologies). But again, this is not creating ex-nihilo because like the cook who can only pick from the historically available food stuffs, the writer can only pick from narrative strategies, plots, etc. that are historically available. The writer can, if you will, use the loas of other previous writers in the form of narrative techniques or whatever; but since loas—according to Voodoo—cannot "create" but only "modify," the writer's position is one of rearranging these techniques in a new way.

This represents the syncretic and collaging moment of composition, namely, improvisation. Reed alludes to this in his "Neo-HooDoo Manifesto," and *Mumbo Jumbo,* where he brings together cooking of food and improvisation. In "Neo-HooDoo Manifesto" Reed states that "Neo-HooDoo is BAR-B-CUE of Amerika" (*Conjure* 22). In *Mumbo Jumbo* he offers a "soul food" item from a restaurant frequented by jazz types: "BAR-BE-CUED FISH" (100). In one we see the African-American spirit of artistic creation as difference (the misspelling "Amerika"). Moreover, taken together, "CUE"/ "CUED" invite a syncretic or collaging participation. As *Webster's New World Dictionary* notes, the definition of "cue" is "hint, intimation, suggestion," "frame of mind, mood, temperament," "the few notes or bars of music directly preceding an instrumentalist's or vocalist's part and serving as a signal for him to begin" (357). Reed's words operate in all these senses, at once indicating a creative frame of mind and a call for a response. The connection to music cannot be missed, neither can Reed's deliberate association with food.

Beyond this, Reed's vision of the author as cook includes more. Interestingly, the middle of the poem also urges cooks to prepare the dish "according to the taste of the consumer" (*Conjure* 26). This remark proves important for several reasons. First, writing, like cooking, is not an exact science. The experienced cook must sample a dish during preparation so that proportions of ingredients attain the desired gastronomic results (i.e. satiated consumers or consumers who simply enjoy eating), despite vagaries of individual kitchens and cooking appliances. Writers must do the same by testing and implementing narrative techniques and language for successful communicative expression within their particular historical circumstances. In metaphorical terms, cook and writer must "adjust the seasoning" of a "dish" or "work" according to contextual demands of a particular time and place. Demanding a chef always cook in one way would ignore the exigencies of individual historical situations. Similarly, demanding a writer compose according to one set of rules disregards that writer's particular time, place, and history at the moment of composition.

Yet a tension also arises here with Reed's language use. Reed says that "Gombo" should be prepared "according to the taste of the consumer" (*Conjure* 26). Certainly, the cook and writer represent the first consumers. The dish prepared and text written reflect their individual tastes at a particular place and time. And again, the cook and writer prepare/compose according to the exigencies of particular historical circumstances (e.g. availability of ingredients or availability of specific language and narrative techniques). However, the term "consumer" does not seem to apply only to individuals composing meals or texts (i.e. cooks and writers). It also appears to apply to other consumers as well (i.e. the people for whom the cook cooks and the writer writes). That is, the cook and writer must always attend to those eating and those reading as "consumers."

This fact about cooking also relates to Voodoo and the cook or writer's use of loas. As Deren observes, loas are brought into this world by houngans for "the reassurance and the instruction of the community" (Deren 30). Here

I would read the houngan as houngan-cook or houngan-author. Both act as intermediaries (like the loa Legba) between the divine and the worldly. But they—cook and writer—have a responsibility; they must provide "reassurance," and "instruction" to their "community." Thus the cook and writer must always consider their place in the community. They—cook and writer—are not solitary creators producing independent artefacts of no value to the community. Rather, they remain in the public space creating, through syncretic and collaging practice, in order to promote that community.

At the same time, it seems unwise to suppose that the irony inhabiting Reed's writing in *Mumbo Jumbo* should not also show itself here. Certainly, preparing the dish/text according to the "taste of the consumer" could apply in the numerous ways noted above. But if read ironically, the phrasing "taste of the consumer" might just as easily refer to feeding the appetite of mass market culture, which is propelled not by a motivation to better community, but by a market driven ideology whose sole motive is profit. Taken this way, the author's position seems ironic in that she must produce not just for herself or communal betterment, but also for the machine of capital, which would seem bent on exploiting both author and community.

The many examples of irony demonstrated in this chapter would seem to indicate Reed's ambivalence about granting singular authorships of any kind, though he especially problematizes autonomous authorship and the authoring of African-American cultural history and identity. In terms of African-American cultural history and identity, this point is clearly most evident in LaBas' counter-narrative of HooDoo, which is itself ironized. At the same time, we have also seen how aspects associated with postmodernism (e.g. poststructuralism) bear close similarity to Reed's reinterpretation of these issues via Voodoo and its American counterpart, HooDoo. This results, it seems, in an authorial practice which combines postmodernism and traditional inherited forms. But there are certain problems with this characterization, especially as it is sometimes conflated with claims suggesting poststructuralism's power to explain African-American tradition. I will address some of these problems in Chapter Four.

Chapter Two
Combative Textualities: Kathy Acker's *The Adult Life of Toulouse Lautrec by Henri Toulouse Lautrec*

In the present chapter I want to move from the writer of texts to the text itself. Here, we will examine how one postmodern writer, Kathy Acker, attacks traditional narrative construction within two literary genres. The text under analysis is Acker's *The Adult Life of Toulouse Lautrec by Henri Toulouse Lautrec* (1975, hereafter referred to as *ALTL*),[1] which parodies genres in order to unmask—at levels of *form* and *content*—what she feels these constructions attempt to conceal or repress, namely, destructive social relations under patriarchy and capitalism.[2] Both capitalism and patriarchy Acker traces—at least in large part—to what Kaja Silverman calls the "Oedipalization of the subject . . . and the phallocentricity of that symbolic order" (131).[3] For Acker this state of affairs has much to do with reason, notions of static and autonomous subjectivity, as well as reified social relations.

It must be said, moreover, that Acker's parodic attacks are informed to a large degree by her own idiosyncratic absorption of poststructural theorizing, including especially the ideas of Derrida, Foucault, and Lacan, as well as feminist readings of these figures. Acker has herself admitted these influences on her work in numerous interviews and within her own writing.[4] Because Acker is a writer of fiction, and not—strictly speaking—a philosopher, use of Derrida, Foucault, and Lacan within her fiction does not conform perfectly or consistently with their theories.

While I believe Acker's opus worthy of a book length treatment regarding these issues, for purposes of time and space I will focus primarily on Acker's disruption of the traditional realistic narrative generally, and how that disruption can be seen through shifts in genre, as well as moments of interdiscursivity and intertextuality within those genres. Though Acker's text does in fact address many genres, I will focus on how this disruption operates within only two, namely, the genres of historical narrative and detective fiction.[5] I have chosen to examine Acker's undermining of historical narrative and detective fiction because both genres represent quintessential instances of supposedly realistic narrative, namely, narrative possessing certain primary realist conventions of supposed referentiality with equally conventional tight emplotment. As seems obvious, few narratives are more absolute in their referentiality than historical narratives; similarly, few narratives are as tightly emplotted as the traditional detective novel. Here, however, I should indicate that Acker's methodical undermining of realist narrative demonstrates a certain tension—especially as concerns the genre of historical narrative. Acker's writing does disrupt real historical reference, but it simultaneously seems to embody an opposing desire to alert readers to the very history subverted.

While I will address this tension in the last chapter, for purposes here it is more important to appreciate Acker's attitude toward these genres. Specifically, Acker believes the aforementioned literary genres help reproduce dominant power relations within capitalism and patriarchy. For Acker these innocuous innocent literary practices *interpellate*—and in so doing construct—reading subjects, which is a necessary part of reproducing social relations under capitalism and patriarchy.

In this regard we should remember that genres act as "literary *institutions,* which like other institutions of social life are based on tacit agreements or contracts. The thinking behind such a view of genres is based on the presupposition that all speech needs to be marked with certain indications and signals as to how it is properly to be used" (Fredric Jameson qtd. in Porter 84). The points here are two. First, genres as "literary institutions" are subject to social forces and help in the process of "acculturation" (Porter 84). Second, and as a consequence, they are ideological and part of what Louis Althusser calls the "Ideological State Apparatuses" (Althusser 1971). Hence, we have my earlier mention of the term "interpellation," which in this case means the way a genre "'recruits' subjects among individuals . . ." (Althusser 174) That is, a genre offers reading subjects a subject position, an identity to take up, but as it is ideological, it does not necessarily correspond to reality.

In terms of genre I need to emphasize a further important and related point. Acker's unmasking effects are to some degree implemented through her deliberate mixing of popular genres, each of which represents an instance of traditional narrative. Acker's jumbling of genres, her refusal to let genres settle within her text, destabilizes the idea of a unified text belonging to a single genre. Instead she shows texts and genres as penetrated or inhabited by numerous discourses we rarely notice. At this level is a further implied critique of various realist narratives as instances of all encompassing and singular accountings of fact. An easy example of such narratives would be simple linear fictions which offer closure and pretend to offer up transparent visions of reality and history. Acker believes such accounts are lies, myths which ideologically reproduce capitalism and patriarchy by reifying social life into some frozen eternal state of affairs.

But Acker does not simply critique and destabilize unified texts. She also critiques and destabilizes the *unified subject within the text.* By this I mean that Acker attempts to destabilize subjectivity's model in the literary work, namely, that subject modeled in the work which "is constructed in language and in discourse," but as such is necessarily "ideological" and a misrecognition (Belsey 660). She does this in two different ways. First, she interrogates the notion of singular narration as she moves within and between genres. Here, Acker constantly shifts the speaking "I," or narrator, which results in a receding or distancing of that narrator. But Acker also shifts speaking "I"s more generally, which causes another series of displacements. This incessant shifting—a textual characteristic virtually impossible for readers to ignore—is a form of unmasking the reified "I." It marks the break between the speaker who speaks and the speaker who is spoken of. The effect within the text is to fragment that speaking and spoken of "I."

For Acker this view of wholeness of self and world, of fixed unities and relations, represents not a true state of affairs but an *ideological* position. Writing and reading in this mode—and here, again, I mean "realistic" writing following traditional narrative progression—must perform a trick to pass itself off as whole, complete, and unified. Catherine Belsey, using the work of both Pierre Macherey and Jacques Lacan, explains this bit of ideological magic:

> In its attempt to create a coherent and internally consistent fictive world the text, in spite of itself, exposes incoherences, omissions, absences and transgressions which in turn reveal the inability of the language of ideology to create coherence. This becomes apparent because the contradiction between the diverse elements drawn from different discourses, the ideological project and the literary form, creates absence at the center of the work. The text is divided, split as the Lacanian subject is split, and Macherey compares the 'lack' in the

consciousness of the work, its silence, what it cannot say, with the unconscious which Freud explored. (667)

Moreover, as Belsey further remarks, "The unconscious of the work (*not*, it must be insisted, of the author) is constructed in the moment of its entry into literary form, in the gap between the ideological project and the specifically literary form. Thus the text is no more a transcendent unity than the human subject" (667). Acker wants to pull the curtain on this ideological magic show to reveal what is in the gap.

Her reluctance to reify the subject (in the form of a stable "I") and her equal unwillingness to give texts—and genres—a similar fixed nature suggest Acker follows Lacan's reading of the subject, which is somewhat Marxist in nature. For those who are unaware of Lacan's position, he "condemns as grossly inaccurate the common *hypostasization* of the 'I,'" which "contributes to," in Lacan's words, '*chosifiant l'être humain*' (reifying the human being)" (Hogan 10; Lacan qtd. in Hogan, *Criticism and Lacan* 10; italics mine). To "hypostatize" the "I" is to consider it a "distinct substance," or to hold it as "actual," a "reality." For Lacan, as for Acker, this remains an impossibility because the "I" cannot "be" a thing, but is always *in process*, never whole, unified, or complete. It is only, as Lacan remarks, "certain schools of psychoanalysis, of . . . 'psychologism'" which hypostatize the "I," or reify it (Hogan, *Criticism and Lacan* 10).

While both men and women are equally subject to hypostatization through "interpellation," that "freely" accepted call into a position of subjectivity within the social system, there nevertheless exist marked differences in what happens to the two. Women, according to Catherine Belsey, remain especially inhabited by contradictory discourses as a result of being split as subjects. On this point Belsey remarks that "[w]omen as a group in our society are both produced and inhibited by contradictory discourses" (Belsey 661). Specifically, women "participate both in the liberal–humanist discourse of freedom, self-determination and rationality and at the same time in the specifically feminine discourse offered by society of submission, relative inadequacy and irrational intuition" (Belsey 661–662). Of course, in the Lacanian system, inadequacy of women relates directly to entrance into the "symbolic" (an entrance into structured language), which is marked by the phallus, a situation making for a binary adequacy and inadequacy between males and females. Yet, the unfinishedness of the subject, that the subject is in process and not whole, is promising in terms of women's liberation since it means that change is possible (Belsey 662). Or, so one version of this feminist theory goes.

Now, a more general point needs to be made about all this. For Acker mixing of genres, which is to say the mixing of supposedly distinct categories, undermines the previously mentioned phallic base of meaning and unifications.[6] This has, in part, to do with the already noted affiliation between Acker's thought and Lacan's, but it also relates to Derrida's attitudes regarding logocentrism. In this respect we may say that Acker adopts the two thinkers in the following way. Firstly, she agrees with Lacan that "The Law of the Phallus" marks "the principle of psychic division and sexual difference" (Benstock 6). Since the Phallus marks entrance into the symbolic (entrance into language) and women do not possess it, they are forced outside it, namely, outside the realm of meaning.[7] Or, as Jacqueline Rose puts it, "there is no feminine outside language . . . because the 'feminine' is constituted as a division in language which produces the feminine as its negative term" (Rose qtd. in Benstock 14). So the category of Woman is not simply a function of social construction generally, but "is constructed as a (non)-category in language that signifies the fantasy of wholeness and guarantees (but also resists) the Phallic order" (Benstock 14).

Acker's Derridian aspect relates to the issue of fantasized "wholeness" or completeness. In Derrida's many writings his metaphysical *bete noir* and frequent whipping boy is any notion of unity or wholeness, the idea that entities exist purely in themselves. Rather, Derrida finds all such entities inhabited by elements outside them; in fact, according to Derrida, these entities depend on this outsideness—this "otherness"—for their very identity. Now, for Derrida—and for Acker who follows his lead—"genre" is susceptible to just this sort of contamination by "otherness" because it slots literary works into fixed categories, namely, fixed genres. That slotting into categories gives the work, like the genre itself, a stable identity with boundaries. Like many such indivisible identities, it is very much about boundaries, about legally marking off territories of identity. In the case of genre the law is clear; "The Law of Genre" indicates that "genres are not to be mixed" (Derrida, "The Law of Genre" 202). That is, the law of genre commands genres be specific, whole, complete, and pure. It is here that gender and genre come togther: Gender is similar to genre (or "The Law of Genre") in that it represents a *command*. Like "The Law of Genre," the phallus demands purity, wholeness, and absolute distinction in that it calls an individual to take up an identity (male or female, but not both). But for Derrida and Acker "The Law of Genre," like the law of gender, ultimately fails because in order to have them one has to posit what is not them, namely the other genres and the *other* gender. Within the very definition of a specific genre or gender is the "absent presence"—excuse the PoMo catch phrase—of its opposite. With regard to gender, as I have already hinted, "Woman" remains the necessarily absent term, or the "other." In all these senses, Acker believes, much like Derrida, that the present culture is phallically hierarchized ("phallocentric") but also partakes of a more general "metaphysics of presence," otherwise known as identity, unity or wholeness, which is popularly referred to within deconstruction as "logocentrism"; Hence, if we put the terms together, we get "phallogocentrism," what Acker and Derrida take as a fundamental way of thinking in our culture.

As an important aside, however, we should note that Acker posits an additional "other" (beyond woman) which remains invisible but also repressed. This invisible other are the poor who constitute victims of globalized capital. For Acker, they share a similar victimization as woman in that they are the impoverished invisible term necessary for capitalism to exist and expand. In *ALTL* Acker unites the idea woman and the poor through characters who are, quite literally, poor whores in a Montmartre brothel. These characters and their experiences drive home Acker's disgust with present material conditions for women and the poor in this country as well as those inhabiting so called "third world" countries.

Subverting Readable Narrative and Identity: Text, Self, and Gender:

This section is designed to show how detective fiction serves as a model for the traditional narrative text, what I will later designate the *lisible* (readable) text. But it will also engage the issues of gender and capitalist exploitation which Acker feels are reproduced by the *lisible* text. In addition it will show how Acker's *ALTL* undermines traditional *lisible* narrative along with the unified subjectivity and world that model of fiction portrays. Some elements making for this include tight logical-temporal connection between narrated events, addition of certain linguistic details beyond those strictly necessary to tell the tale, and presentation of so called "character." As I will attempt to show in this section, Acker seems particularly interested in undermining these elements as they appear in realistic detective fiction,[8] which for her presents a particularly unified vision of world and subject, but also one which is phallic in its rational pursuit of truth. I must say, however, that we should not lose the forest for the trees and continually remember that Acker's attack on unified world and subject within the rational detective's universe does not exist for itself, for the sake of undermining. Again, to her mind Acker attacks these targets for the way they reify social relations and reproduce—or attempt to reproduce—present material relations.

We can begin to examine Acker's *ALTL* by seeing how, exactly, the detective genre mirrors traditional narrative structure. First, as Dennis Porter observes, every "detective story always proceeds from a fixed point of departure to a fixed destination. It moves both from mystery to solution and from crime to punishment or, if not to punishment, at least to arrest"(85).[9] Following Barthes' work on codes in *S/Z* (1974), Porter further remarks that this pattern makes detective fiction "a genre dominated by a combination of the two sequential, non-reversible codes"; one is "a highly visible hermeneutic code," the other "a strongly determined proairetic code" (Porter 85–86). The *hermeneutic code* is, as Porter recounts, "the sum of units whose function in a given text is to formulate a question and its answer, as well as the various events which prepare the question or delay the answer"; the second code accompanying the first, the *proairetic code,* "refers to any succession of acts, evoked in a novel and modeled on empirical actions, that constitute themselves into a nameable sequence, such as a murder, a journey, the eating of a meal, or the taking of a bath" (Porter 87). In a very simple case, we might say that the hermeneutic code has to do with questions and answers accompanying actions which the author has written in the text. So, we might have a novel beginning *in media res* with nothing more than a description of an actor walking down a street. The actor or character's progress walking down the street would be an element of the "strongly determined proairetic code," while the "highly visible hermeneutic code" would be the many planted questions which would arise upon reading this. Some of these questions would be things like: "Who is this character?" "What is this character doing on the street walking?" "Where is she or he walking to?" I used the word "planted" in reference to the hermeneutic code to stress, as does Porter, the degree to which "a reader's desire to know is stimulated by the author in such a way that it functions as a 'structuring force'"; in the case of detective fiction, the dead body or murder at the beginning of the novel immediately structures the tale into a search for answers (Porter 86). Of course, the "structuring force" of traditional detective is such that this search for answers will come to an end in a final revelation (e.g. who committed the murder).

It is here that we see detective fiction mirrors the classic realistic text, one form of traditional narrative story telling. This is because detective fiction, like the classic realist text, has the structuring codes just mentioned. Reading these sorts of texts is easy because they flow logically; primary questions are answered; the world represented appears understandable. They are, in a sense, unified wholes, or at least they pretend to be. Roland Barthes designated such texts as "*le lisible,*" which means "readable."[10] Though they did not elaborate the codes like Barthes did, it is this tight structuring, this *lisible* aspect, which led writers ranging from Pierre Macherey (1978) to Catherine Belsey (1997) to note the connections between realism and detective fiction.

In Belsey's words, "The project of the [detective] stories themselves, enigma followed by disclosure, echoes precisely the *structure of the classic realist text*" (670; italics mine).

In terms of individuals reading, or those being interpellated, we may say that for Acker "[d]etective fiction is a metaphor of the reader's search for meaning in the fictional work. The cognitive activity of the investigator engaged in solving the mystery parallels the cognitive activity of the reader as he attempts to make sense of the text" (Cannon 46–47). In this sense readers will, in the process of reading, attempt to close what Wolfgang Iser calls "gaps of inconsistency" so that the text will make sense as a whole (Iser qtd. in Cannon 47). But for Acker, unlike reception theorists like Iser, the reading encounter does *not* produce radical revision of belief in the reader, nor a new way of seeing the world, but rather, in the words of Terry Eagleton, the reader is "simply returned to him or herself as a more throughly liberal subject" (Eagleton, *Literary Theory* 69). More simply, each reading of a traditionally constructed work interpellates individuals—makes them into subjects within the social system—and reconfirms again and again the unitary subjectivity they supposedly possess. From this perspective, how to read is very much a matter of the previously mentioned acculturation, which is assisted by texts constructed in particular ways. For her part Acker wants to attack the acculturation process by destroying—or at least disrupting—the *lisible* text's role within the acculturating institution of literature.

Hints that Acker will target the *lisible* text and the detective fiction genre as its perfect illustration, appear very early in *ALTL*, in fact, at the very beginning. Two important elements make this evident. The first element, the one primarily addressed in this section, is a reference Acker uses to indicate the tradition of the *lisible* (readable) text. The second element is an early citing of the detective genre, which will receive primary attention in the next section. This *lisible* reference appears on the first page of the book, even before the first chapter's title. It consists of a short dialogue between a character named "Fielding" and some as yet unknown "I": "'Make sense,' Fielding said. 'Tell the real story of your life. You alone can tell the truth!' 'I don't want to make any sense,' I replied" (Acker 188). The I's response, "I don't want to make sense," represents Acker's first announcement that her work will not be *lisible*. That is, it will not conform to the readerly model of sensible action, recognizable world, and solution of all enigmas. Though I have not yet mentioned this sort of anti-lisible text, it too has been named by Barthes and is called, quite appropriately, *le scriptible,* or "the writable." Dennis Porter, summarizing Barthes, calls the "writable" narrative one that cannot be read in traditional ways; instead, remarks Porter, "It has . . . the character of a pre-text, of a work in which the reader is required to acknowledge and participate in the writing process . . . (Porter 83). Though this should become apparent through the rest of the essay, suffice it to say that for Acker the reader's participation should be critical in nature, criticizing the naturalness or truth presented in the individual genres.

In order to initiate this critical participation Acker makes an explicit reference to "Fielding," which is intended to fill several functions. First, she clearly intends to indicate English writer Henry Fielding (1707–1754). Acker wishes the proper name ("Fielding") and words that proper name "speaks" to stand in for an entire view of unified textual construction and truth. "Fielding" substitutes for this discourse, acting like a sort of advocate for the *lisible* text and demanding our anonymous "I" tell its "real story," one containing "the truth." The command is metaphysical; "Fielding" wants the truth about the "I" and about the world it inhabits. Use of the name "Fielding" is Acker's initial act of "interdiscursivity," a strategy she applies throughout *ALTL* along with her occasional use of "intertextuality." Very generally, "interdiscursivity" is when "a single narrative voice speaks a mix of different discourses . . ." (Bal 65).[11] By placing the Fielding reference and quotation at the beginning of her novel, Acker wants to call up elements of that discourse—one demanding unified stories of the truth and self—in order to interrogate them throughout the rest of the book.

As part of this interdiscursivity we may associate Fielding's name and period of literary production with the rise of the novel as a literary form, one Acker wishes to subvert. Acker, taking her cue from the structuralists, believes that the novel constitutes a "primary semiotic agent of intelligibility" (Culler, *Structuralist Poetics* 189). Put more simply, and as I have been trying to suggest, she considers the novel—in its classical narrative form—as offering a unified world with unified subjects and static social relations. The novel is a semiotic device which calls in reading subjects and constructs for them both a world and an identity; in so doing it represents at least one method by which the world and subjects become whole or complete.

Directly illustrative of the above is the fact that mention of Fielding brings to mind *Tom Jones* (1749), perhaps Fielding's best known work and an example of the novel form. To understand the implications we should remember that *Tom Jones* retains much of its canonical reputation based on Fielding's ability to *construct varied characters* involved in *complex actions* (Hornstein, et al. 449–452). As Hornstein notes, part of Fielding's success is due to his production of "dramatic tension" between "extraordinarily *individualized* and realized characters" (Hornstein, et al. 450; italics mine). In *Tom Jones* the reader gets a protagonist ("Tom") who has an "identity"; Fielding offers him as a so called "round character" which, for those who need reminding, means he "is complex in temperament and motivation and is represented with subtle particularity; such a character therefore is as difficult to describe with any adequacy as a *person in real life,* and *like all real persons* is capable of surprising us" (Abrams 24; italics mine).

For Acker the reading subject does not escape reification in this process because it has individual "character" as a prototype within the novel form. Fielding's novel gives it to us. *Tom Jones* is one work in long line of novels offering such identity prototypes. Readers are invited to identify with his characters' wholeness, which performs for the former—Fielding's readers— just what is suggested above, namely, it offers them unitary subjectivity. In this sense Acker, somewhat like Philippe Sollers, sees the traditionally constructed novel as enticing individuals into an act of misrecognition whereby they imagine themselves as unified subjects. Or, as Sollers put it so eloquently, "Our identity . . . depends on the novel, what others think of us, what we think of ourselves, the way in which our life is imperceptibly moulded into a whole. How do others see us if not as a character from a novel?" (Sollers qtd. in Culler, *Structuralist Poetics* 189)

In terms of the aforementioned complex actions within a coherent world *Tom Jones,* like the detective novel which mirrors its traditional structure, is *lisible* and maintains a "unity of action" wherein all activities are finally subordinated to a singular goal, namely squaring Tom with Sophia and Squire Allworthy. In this regard, as one critical source puts it, the "interrelated actions are managed so skillfully that suspense and a sense of movement are always present; at the same time all the major developments of the plot are so well prepared for in advance that, despite Fielding's addiction to coincidence, we have always a sense of logical unfolding of what the author often calls a '*history*'" (Hornstein et al. 450; italics mine).[12]

Acker calls up these elements within Fielding in order to remind readers of the implicit "narrative contract"—again, a Barthesian term—in Fielding's *lisible* text. Loosely defined, "narrative contracts" in the novel (e.g. realistic detective fiction) are basic agreements—placed formally within the text—between writer and reader as concerns the text read. We might, for example, say that part of a narrative contract—at least for a realistic text like Fielding's—would be that readers, "through their contact with the text" will "be able to recognize a world which it [the text] produces or to which it refers," and that there will exist "at least some elements of the text whose function it is to confirm this expectation and to assert the representational or mimetic orientation of fiction" (Culler, *Structuralist Poetics* 192–193). Thinking of traditional detective fiction in these terms, a reader would expect the contract would prevent, for example, a murder victim returning from the dead to kill himself, since that would fly in the face of mimetic expectation.

Moreover, for Acker this aspect of confirming "reality"—remember, again, that Fielding's narrator says it tells a "history"—gives readers another means of identification. That is, in a general sense Acker would submit that within Fielding's *lisible* text the reader identifies not only with characters per se—as with the instance noted earlier—but also with a more distant narrative voice, one offering a position of absolute knowingness. For Acker Fielding's *lisible* text, one which is predominately realistic,

> offers the reader a position of knowingness which is also *a position of identification with the narrative voice*. To the extent that the story first constructs, and then depends for its intelligiblity, on a set of assumptions shared between narrator and reader, it confirms both the transcendent knowingness of the reader-as-subject and the 'obviousness' of the shared truths in question. (Belsey 664; italics mine)

From Acker's perspective this narrative voice—whose maximum veneer of objectivity can sometimes come in the so called "third person"—helps interpellate readers, and in so doing makes them subjects who view the world and themselves with a similar "obviousness," namely, they take these ideological views as prima facie true. [13]

Acker's interdiscursive use of Fielding shows she clearly understands, and at least partially buys, the structuralists' belief that identifying narrators and securing their vision is pivotal to constructing the realistic narrative. Jonathan Culler, speaking on this structuralist belief, observes the following:

> Identifying narrators is one of the primary ways of *naturalizing* fiction. The convention that in a text the narrator speaks to his readers acts as one support to interpretive operations which deal with the odd or apparently insignificant. In so far as the novel is, as George Eliot says, 'a faithful account of men and things as they have mirrored themselves in my mind,' the reader may treat anything anomoulous as the effect of the narrator's vision or cast of mind. (Culler, *Structuralist Poetics* 200; italics mine)

Thus, according to structuralists the narrator is made into a subject. This subject tells "'a faithful account of men and things as they have mirrored themselves'" in its mind. But the truthfulness of the account is based on convention, namely, the reader's trust in the narrator, that that narrator delivers a "faithful account." Parts of the account appearing strange or "anomoulous" are normalized or naturalized by blaming it on the narrator's "cast of mind," an aspect of its subjectivity.

Since Acker appears conscious of this realist necessity to identify narrators, she also seems to know how to prevent, or at least frustrate, such identification. This is seen especially in her use of first person narration wherein Acker refuses to give readers a singular and unified speaker. That Acker intends to trouble the unified speaker is hinted at by her book's title (*The Adult Life of Toulouse Lautrec by Henri Toulouse Lautrec*), but is also accomplished through her dialogue between "Fielding" and the "I," as well as text placed above the first chapter's title on the opposite page ("I'm too ugly to go out into the world. I'm a hideous monster" (189)), which is repeated later by a narrating Toulouse (194). For Acker the intended effect of all this is to disallow any identification of the narrating "I" by splitting it so many times that its unity disappears and becomes an impossibility. Again, to emphasize the point, Acker frustrates the reader's identification with individual character, but that is often accomplished through frustrating the singular character of first person narration.

As I just indicated, an initial identification problem occurs in Acker's book title (*The Adult Life of Toulouse Lautrec by Henri Toulouse Lautrec*). The first displacement of the narrating "I" comes from the title of Acker's work itself and the supposed writer of that work. Now this gets complicated, but it can be sorted out. Acker's novel is entitled "The Adult Life of Toulouse Lautrec by Henri Toulouse Lautrec." The beginning of the title ("The Adult Life of Toulouse Lautrec") would seem to announce a *narrative* about a subject called "Toulouse Lautrec." But at the same time, a later part of this beginning announcement also *names* (i.e. the pronouncement "Toulouse Lautrec"). Furthermore, the naming is doubled within the title of the work itself. What do I mean? Well, we initially have an announcement of a narrative that names ("The Adult life of *Toulouse Lautrec*"), but the title of the work continues on: "by Henri Toulouse Lautrec." In so doing the supposed author of the work names himself twice, once as the subject of the narrative "The Adult Life of Toulouse Lautrec," but also as its author and guarantor ("by Henri Toulouse Lautrec"), all of which is in the book's title itself ("The Adult Life of *Toulouse Lautrec* by *Henri Toulouse Lautrec*"). Moreover, the addition of "Henri" to the second name ("*Henri* Toulouse Lautrec"), a name whose referent (i.e. the person named) is supposed to be identical to the first naming ("The Adult Life of *Toulouse Lautrec*"), marks the sameness/difference of the subject from one enunciation to the next (i.e. from the enunciation "Toulouse Lautrec" to the enunciation "Henri Toulouse Lautrec"). But the movement does not stop here since this naming is done by the supposed author himself, one "real" Toulouse Lautrec. Thus, Henri Toulouse Lautrec names "Toulouse Lautrec"—namely, the subject of the narrative of "The Adult Life"—but also the author of that narrative, which is "by Henri Toulouse Lautrec."

What does this mean? Again, if we look to Lacan, we see that Acker wishes to follow his train of thought by distancing the "I" which speaks (i.e. the subject in process, Toulouse Lautrec) from the "I" which is spoken of (i.e. all those instances of naming "Toulouse Lautrec"). Following Lacan, Acker here wishes to indicate what she believes is a mistake, namely, the act of reifying the subject, of making the subject into a thing whose gender, class, social status, and subjectivity remain fixed and natural. For Acker the subject is in process and any attempts to enunciate it—attempts which amount to so many acts of misrecognition—will always fail precisely for that reason; in short, the subject is always more and separate from what can be enunciated.

Taking this as a general pattern in Acker, we can look at three other examples related to this. In the first, we have the earlier mentioned claim by an anonymous "I": "'I don't want to make sense,' I replied." (Acker, *ALTL* 188). Here, the narrating "I" distances itself several times. First, there is the speaker who speaks of itself in refusal ("*I* don't want to make sense"). But there is also another level of speech which refers to an "I" outside the quoted statement ("I don't want to make sense,' *I replied*). But this other "I" outside the quotations ("' . . . ,' *I* replied") is yet another instance of speech. The speaker, the supposed entity which utters the words, is nowhere present, at least not for Acker. Who, we might wonder, is the speaker who speaks these many levels? Where is the individual speaking? Leaving that question open for the moment, we should note yet a third instance of Acker's distancing which relates to this one. It is on the opposite page above the chapter's title; it reads, "I'm too ugly to go out into the world. I'm a hideous monster" (188–189). The speaker enunciates itself in these two sentences, and thus also distances or misrecognizes itself. This seems plain enough and does not appear to point beyond what I have already said, except for the fact that precisely the same statement is uttered by the character Toulouse a few pages later (194).

Here, a number of issues with respect to Lacan, misrecognition, and gender hierarchy begin to come together, but it requires some explication. The first thing we may note is the distancing I talked about in the aforementioned title of Acker's work (*The Adult Life of Toulouse Lautrec by Henri Toulouse Lautrec*). Here, we have "information that is 'always already' involved, that relates to an extra textual situation, in so far as the reader is acquainted with it" (Bal 119). What I mean here is that we have a reference to an actual historical figure, the artist Toulouse Lautrec, and whether or not most of us have studied his work, as members of western culture his name, as well as his artistic and cultural associations, remain part of our "frame of reference," by which I mean "information that may with some confidence be called communal" (Bal 119). Now, as Mieke Bal observes, historical figures have an *image* within our frame of reference, but when they appear in texts, "the image we receive of them is determined to a large extent by the confrontation between, on the one hand, our previous knowledge and the expectations it produces, and on the other, the realizations of the character in the narrative" (Bal 121). Moreover, that an author decides to use a "referential character"—one like Toulouse Lautrec—"implies . . . opting for such confrontation" (Bal 121). The author, in this case Kathy Acker, uses the "referential character" (Toulouse Lautrec) to force a confrontation between what the reader knows about him and what Acker's text will present. This confrontation is exactly what Acker wants, and it constitutes the sort of textual "trap," to use Bal's term, she sets to destroy or disrupt reader's expectations.

While I have not yet brought us back to Acker's use of Lacan and her beliefs about gender hierarchy, we can work toward understanding these issues by looking at readers' expectations of Toulouse Lautrec and what Acker's text actually offers. From there, we can begin to trace our way back to the aforementioned quotations concerning the "I" and how all this relates to Lacan and gender. To begin, in first pages of *ALTL* Acker gives some of what readers expect of the character "Toulouse Lautrec." We have a character "Vincent," who readers would probably suppose was Vincent Van Gogh, berating a character named "Toulouse." He says, "Toulouse . . . What are you going to do with your life? How're you ever going to make any money? You're a deformed crippled beast. Look at your hairy chest, your huge nodding head. Your legs are spindly" (*ALTL* 189). We also get information from Vincent that Lautrec is an artist: "How are you ever going to get famous and get fucked? Your such a lousy painter" (189). In the first instance the text offers an historically accurate picture of what Toulouse Lautrec might look like, namely, a man suffering from a severe bone growth problem that made him look like a dwarf with misshapen legs (Frey 71). In the second quotation we have evidence that Lautrec is an artist, a "painter." So far the picture seems roughly historical, even if Vincent's comments seem in bad taste, pornographic, and quite mean spirited.

However, on the next page this somewhat historically accurate portrayal undergoes radical changes, having Toulouse utter the following: "I

Combative Textualities

ache and I ache and I ache. I feel a big huge hole inside my body. I see a man I like about to stick his cock in my hot pussy" (190). The surprise for readers in this description goes without saying since the narrative contract—a promise of mimesis—is violated. The book's title, which calls to mind the western cultural image of a *male* artist (Toulouse Lautrec), but also asserts the tale told will be by the artist himself, is not at all what most readers would expect. Our male Toulouse has now become *female,* which is evident from the reference to "my hot pussy." Changing Toulouse's gender makes readers question the legitimacy of the text's description of an historical character (i.e. the real Toulouse Lautrec). That is, the real artist Lautrec was a male, not a female. Further troubling historical reference to the real artist is the character Lautrec's obscene language ("cock," "pussy"); would the real Lautrec have used such words?

We may also note, however, that spontaneous shifting of gender troubles not only the reader's sense of reality, but also identification more generally. As to the first question, reference to the real, in everyday experience males do not spontaneously become females. This spontaneous change disrupts the reality effect, and as a consequence disrupts reader identification since there no longer exists any firm basis upon which to make identification. How is a reader to identify with such a shifting character?

For Acker this problem of identification is intended. But we might wonder where she is going with all this. If we continue to examine the text closely, some clues emerge as to Acker's motivation. For example, we see four pages later that our problematically gendered Toulouse practically repeats—if in reverse—the words appearing above the first chapter's title. Here is the original passage followed by its later reversed form: "I'm too ugly to go out into the world. I'm a hideous monster" (189); "I'm a totally hideous monster. I'm too ugly to go out into the world" (194). While the two sentences from the first example are reversed in the second example, the sentences are nevertheless similar, though separated by four pages of text. The repetition of the sentences—though reversed and with the word "totally" added to the second instance—enables us to link the first declaration of the "I" (189) to the second (reversed) declaration of the "I" (194). We can therefore say the "I" announced at the beginning of the book—above the first chapter's title—represents a declaration of the character "Toulouse" since the second example is definitely spoken by her. Moreover, I would further suggest that Acker wants us to identify that "I" with the "I" on the first page of the book who argues with Fielding ("'*I* don't want to make any sense,' *I* replied").

At first glance, then, definitive identification of the self seems possible after all. But such an assertion would be wrong. While Acker does want readers to link the three instances of "I" ("'I don't want to make any sense,' I replied"(188); "I'm too ugly to go out into the world . . ." (189); "I'm a totally hideous monster . . ." (194)) for a very limited sense of identification having to do with gender inequality—something I will discuss momentarily—definitive or absolute identification of the subject is not at all what she intends. Instead, Acker wants the movement from the first "I" ("*I* replied") to the second ("I'm too ugly to go out into the world. I'm a hideous monster"), third ("I'm a totally hideous monster. I'm too ugly to go out into the world."), and finally the fourth utterance ("I ache. . . .") to stand for the subject in progress which cannot, as Lacan says, be conceptualized in language. The "I" which replies ("*I* replied") is the first instance of the individual putting her/himself in language; it is the first instance of misrecognition, but the content of its speech ("'I don't want to make sense") also represents a refusal—though a fruitless one—to enter the symbolic, the realm of language, and to take up an objectified or reified subject position. The addition of the term "totally" to the third utterance ("I'm a *totally* hideous monster"), as well as the reversal of sentences from the second to the third speech act, again signals difference of the subject from moment to moment, from speech act to speech act, but also the impossibility that any speech act could do justice to the speaker speaking. That is, there is always difference, the gap, between the subject who speaks, and the subject who is spoken of. For Lacan, of course, that gap is the unconscious.

Acker wants to make this unconscious visible, unmask it formally in the text. We might therefore also assert that Acker's reversal of the above sentence and her use of the term "hideous" are intended to signal the missing term which is the feminine, something which cannot be represented since it operates as the negative of the primary term, namely, the phallus. The sentence reversal would represent something like the reversal of the binary male/female. For Acker it would be that moment when the male artist "Toulouse Lautrec" becomes a female artist "Toulouse Lautrec." This new reversed Toulouse is necessarily "totally hideous" given her new gendered position. We might offer two examples as evidence for this. First, just after Toulouse formally announces her femaleness in the text, she says, "I don't know how to present my image properly" (194). Here, Toulouse cannot represent herself ("present my image properly") within a phallic based system where she remains only a negative term. In addition, directly after Toulouse's third utterance of "I" ("I'm a totally hideous monster. I'm too ugly to go out into the world") comes this line: "If I was living with a man, I would have someone who'd tell me if I'm hideous" (194). Here, again, the female Toulouse must have the male, and the accompanying phallus, to signify herself, even if that is impossible given the fact that woman remains outside signification (i.e. outside the phallus as the primary signifying moment). Her hideousness is a given since she is (already) castrated; nonetheless, she needs him ("If I was living with a man . . ."), or what he has, to signify her hideousness ("I would have someone who'd tell me if I'm hideous").

The issue of female hideousness and its relationship to the phallus brings us back to my earlier mention of the pornography genre. If we look at a passage from *ALTL*, one which occurs on the same page but after the revelation of Toulouse as female (or at the very least, of mixed gender), we start to get a feeling for why Acker uses pornography and its frequently obscene language. Here is the passage: "Here all the women know everything. They know if they don't spread their legs, no man'll notice them; when they spread their legs, they get fucked not loved. They're worn. They know they have to turn to the brothel" (194). Before continuing, I should say that a good deal of the novel's action occurs in this brothel. In fact, the first murder in *ALTL*, and much of the detective work, such as it is, take place in this brothel.

If we look at the language of the passage carefully, we can discover more about what Acker intends to communicate regarding both the brothel and women who turn to it. Now, *ALTL* is predominately narrated by a "character bound narrator" (hereafter, "CN"), Toulouse, a fe/male. A CN would be any "I" narrating and playing a role in a sequence of events recounted. At the same time, there are elements that also make the novel appear as though it were somehow also narrated by an "external narrator" (hereafter, "EN"), namely, an "I" narrating but not playing a role in the sequence of events recounted.[14] The use of both CN and EN within sentences or passages of writing is often referred to as "free indirect discourse." If the above passage is not exactly free indirect discourse, it certainly comes close to it. As for elements of the EN, we have the use of third person plural pronouns ("they") in Toulouse's (?) passage above (e.g. "They know if they don't spread their legs, no man'll notice them . . ."). The use of the third person is sometimes, though not always, associated with EN. Beyond this are elements of the "personal language situation" where "deixis," or "words that only have meaning in the context in which they are uttered, such as 'I' and 'you,' 'yesterday,' 'here,' 'there'" are used (Bal 30). As an important aside, it should be noted that the above passage, which continues on at some length, never mentions the CN, Toulouse, by using "I." Moreover, in terms of deixis we can note the use of the word "here," a clearly deictic reference. All this might suggest Acker intends the mixed CN and EN to be read as "we," thus further problematizing identification.

Equally important and intimately related to the "personal language situation," or "deixis" is the strong *coloring* of the passage, the way attitudes and values are plugged into the text. Narratologically speaking, these values and attitudes are communicated via "focalization." As Mieke Bal remarks, "focalization" is an "aspect of the story" told by the narrator, here, a fe/male Toulouse; it represents the "'colouring' of the fabula," or the coloring of all the events experienced by actors within the story (19). The narrator, as a point of view, colors the events seen in the tale. Moreover, as Bal further asserts, "The fact that 'narration' has always implied focalization is related to the notion that language shapes vision and world-view, rather than the other way around" (19). This point is important in reference to Acker and her Lacanian vision of self and world. The importance stems from the previously mentioned dominant role language plays for Acker in construction of "world view" and the reified subject. For her the world view is constructed by language as it is used and reproduced materially. Thus, it is not hard to see how, from Acker's perspective, realistic texts set up and reproduce within reading subjects a world view which is false, namely, one which reifies subjectivity and history.

A specific instance of this coloration can be seen in value terms and phrases from the above passage. In this strange passage our combination EN/CN utters "when they spread their legs they get *fucked* not *loved*"; "They're *worn*"). Regardless of how we take the previous deictic word "here" (mentioned above) the attitude of the narrator in these colored statements seems clear. The statement, "when they spread their legs they get fucked not loved" obviously indicates the narrator's disgust and anger at the relations between the genders. Similarly, the use of the word "worn" betrays the narrator's feeling that the women are used up, their human spirit and physical bodies depleted. In all this our narrator's allegiance also seems clear, even if the type of narration does not; its allegiance falls squarely on the side of women.

However, allegiance to the brothel's women does not mean readers can locate this narrator; nor does it mean that readers can identify with it. In fact, neither is possible, and that is by design. In using "free indirect discourse"—mixing of EN and CN—or what is very close to it, Acker continues her Lacanian refusal to reify the subject. The subject she refuses to reify is the narrator, and that is why locating it and identifying with it are nearly impossible. Instead, Acker makes narration hover between the personal language situation (CN) and the impersonal (EN). This hovering is Acker's attempt to keep the subject in process and prevent—or at least disrupt—misrecognition.

While this formal intervention at the level of EN and CN troubles (mis)recognition, thematic elements also appear illustrating Acker's attitude regarding gender relations and capitalism. One of the ways Acker communicates gender relations and their connection to capitalism appears when Toulouse—Acker's now female narrator—speaks about her subordinated relationship to men and their privileged place society: "They're masculine which means they know about a certain society, this polite-death society which is their society, with which they know how to deal. So I don't have to deal with it. I don't want to. They provide a base for me in a society to which I feel alien. Otherwise I've got no reason to be in this world" (200). But how, exactly, is the male a base for the female? The answer comes in the next sentence: "I can't get a man unless money's involved. I found this out in the brothel" (200). That is, Toulouse—a woman—finds that the relation between the sexes is that of exploitation; women are whores, and men are johns. This, according to Acker, is the "everything" "women know" (194). While it is not exactly clear here how Acker interprets Lacan's phallus—as "master" signifier—it seems more than evident that she envisions a society dominated materially by patriarchal masculinity.

The powerful force of this patriarchal relationship between men and women—one which Acker reads as systemic in capitalism—can also be seen by looking at the exclusion of women from the economic realm, which is overwhelming controlled by men. Thus, Acker would say, we have the traditional—often enforced—economic dependency women have had on men. There exists no relationship between women and men which is outside that dependency. Here, Acker's representation of woman as whore deliberately and crudely unveils gender based divisions of labor ("economic" verses "domestic"), but also gender relations more broadly, for what she thinks they really are within patriarchal-capitalist society. Thus, during a discussion of recent news, including the "Paris Commune" and a related disruption at "the Stock Exchange," Giannina (a whore) says, "That stuff doesn't concern us. We're women. We know about ourselves, our cunts, not that stuff you read in the newspaper" (201). The description of woman as "whore," or alternatively as "cunt," merely serves for Acker to highlight in the starkest and most disturbing vocabulary what she takes to be woman's position within patriarchal-capitalism. Women are whores economically dependent on men, or they are simple body parts used for copulation ("cunts"). Giannina's comment with regard to politics (the "Paris Commune") and economics (the "Stock Exchange"), that "that stuff doesn't concern us" illustrates the women's lower position in the binary hierarchy of male/female. Women are outside politics and economics, and thus outside control of their own material destinies.

The Case of The Copper Hearted Critique; Or, Deconstructing The Detective Narrative

In the preceding section we noted how detective fiction has a *lisible* (readable) structure which mirrors the realistic narrative's readable structure. In addition, we have discussed the hermeneutic code of question and answer, as well as the tendency of that question and answer process to close in a final all-encompassing answer, so that the text attains a kind of wholeness. Moreover, in our earlier discussion I tried to show how Acker is intent on disrupting such readable texts by substituting what Barthes calls the *scriptible* (writable) text. Let us now see how Acker tries to disrupt the traditionally *lisible* (readable) detective genre by introducing a *scriptible* (writable) detective tale.

To begin, we should remember that earlier in this essay I mentioned the link between Pierre Macherey's project and Jacques Lacan's. Specifically, we discerned how a writer, in attempting to shape a text into "a coherent and internally consistent fictive world," would pay a price for that shaping; that price is a series of "incoherences, omissions, absences and transgressions which in turn reveal the inability of the language of ideology to create coherence" (Belsey 667). The gap inevitably occurs because the writer uses various and contradictory components from different discourses. More specifically, what we have are discourses from different realms, one representing "the ideological project," the other its shaping into "literary form"; this, it must be said, makes for a black hole at the heart of the text, so that it "is divided, split as the Lacanian subject is split, and Macherey compares the 'lack' in the consciousness of the work, its silence, what it cannot say, with the unconscious which Freud explored" (667). Again, to be clear, the act of making ideology into literature (its form) creates a gap, which is the unconscious.

Acker wants to make the gap visible. Through interdiscursive use of the detective fiction genre she will point to the "gap between the ideological project and the specifically literary form" (Belsey 667). That is, she will use the detective fiction genre—in its predominately realistic form—in order to pull out and expose hidden ideologies necessarily buried in the production of such literary texts. In the slang of hard boiled detection we might say that Acker's detective text is "copper hearted," which means to be an "informer by nature" (Chandler, *The Notebooks* 57). That is, Acker's detective story, like a snitch in the hard boiled tale, will "inform" on the detective genre itself, exposing from within its hidden ideology. It should be noted that this process of informing is accomplished in a double movement. At once, she wants to point to the naturalized ideology behind detective fiction, and in so doing show how its view of reality is not a natural or eternal state of affairs, but rather an historical construction which benefits some to the disadvantage of others. But at a more formal level she will also deconstruct its pretensions to wholeness by refusing to let her detective story be *lisible* (readable).

The sign Acker will do this first appears on the opposite page of the earlier Fielding reference as the first chapter's title: "The Case of the Murdered

Twerp" (*ALTL* 189) Obviously, this title (interdiscursively) invokes the detective genre. In specific, its employment of the phrase "The Case of the Murdered . . ." immediately calls to mind the many classic as well as pulp detective tales which employ some variation of this in their titles.

On the second page of the book Acker gives us what the genre promises, namely, a murder and a witness; in this case the witness is a "young girl," also referred to as the "twerp," who runs into a brothel screaming "I saw a murder. MURDER!"(190). Immediately, then, the text calls up detective fiction's typical hermeneutics of question and answer. As called for by the genre, Acker introduces the most rational of rational detectives, Agatha Christie's "Poirot," to answer the question of who murdered who and why (197).

Using the character of "Poirot" within the detective genre is pivotal for understanding many of the points I indicated earlier. First, detective fiction is very much about the upholding of law. This may seem an obvious point, but for Acker it directly effects how gender hierarchy is maintained. Understanding this point requires some explanation. As Dennis Porter indicates, detective fiction concerns "the discourse of the law" (120). This discourse is communal or community based, since it would be impossible, barring certain religious tenets, for a person to commit an illegal act outside of a community context. That is, we may say that "a crime implies the violation of a community code of conduct and demands a response in terms of the code" (Porter 120). A crime, we may say,

> always depends on a legal definition, and the law, as both Gramsci and Althusser make clear, is a key element of the superstructure in ensuring the reproduction of the existing power relations in a society. As a result, in representing crime and its punishment, whether evoked or merely anticipated, detective novels invariably project the image of a given social order and the implied value system that helps maintain it. (Porter 120–121)

But equally important on this point is that detective novels of the classic type rarely call into question their own social orders or value systems (Porter 121). The genre, that is, never questions the legitimacy of the law; it merely supports it without questioning. So, echoing points made earlier by Althusser and Jameson, the genre of detective fiction as a "literary institution" and part of the ideological state apparatus, merely reproduces a given social order and its values.

But what, we might ask, does an unquestioning support and reproduction of "the discourse of the law" have to do with gender hierarchy? For an answer we can turn again to Lacan. "The Name-of-the-Father," or what I will broadly call "The *Law* of the Father"—because it emphasizes "law"—is central to entrance into the "symbolic." This entrance—which is also entrance into language and society—is directly related to the phallus as the aforementioned primary signifier. It also has for Acker, as it does for Lacan, a *legal* and *legislative* aspect. As Malcom Bowie explains of Lacan,

> The Name-of-the-Father was the symbol of an authority at once legislative and punitive. It represented, within the Symbolic, that which made the Symbolic possible—all those agencies that placed enduring restrictions on the infant's desire and threatened to punish, by castration, infringements of their law. It was the inaugurating agent of law, but also gave birth to the mobility and the supple interconnectedness of the signifying chain. (108)

In fact, as Bowie further indicates, for Lacan "The-Name-of-the Father" is the central "'paternal metaphor'" that proves "an essential anchorage for the subject" (109). The power of "The Law of the Father" or "The-Name-of-the Father" is legislative, law-like, and part of its law is the "paternal metaphor" enabling identity, or, if you will, that entity called the "subject." But as should be clear, woman does not stand under the threat of this law (i.e. under threat of castration), even as she is subject to it as an all pervading cultural phenomenon. That is, even though she can't be castrated, the force of the law nevertheless gives her a place as a "subject," and that place is outside, be it outside reason or outside representation. And it goes without saying that since she possesses no phallus, she necessarily takes up a lower place in the law of gender hierarchy. The effects of this will become clearer when we discuss the role of reason within detection and how that aspect, for Acker, necessarily precludes woman.

But law comes in another way as well, one having to do with class and the detective's place within a specific class. Certainly, he is the consummate upholder of law, but he performs his role in a particular way and holds particular values. The detective, from the moment of his birth in Poe's "The Murders in the Rue Morgue"(1841), a time which coincides roughly with the rise of organized police forces as enforcers of law (Porter 150),[15] up to Agatha Christie's incarnation of him as "Poirot" in the nineteen twenties, is increasingly cerebral and a man of leisure. Sir Arthur Conan Doyle's Sherlock Holmes, for instance, has an "urbane lifestyle" and lives an "upper-middle-class bachelor life" as does Poe's Dupin, the latter offering the model for the former (Porter 156; Chandler, *The Notebooks* 33). This is especially the case with British detectives; the investigator is not the common person, but a brilliant, stylish, and well to do individual, one who solves murders for leisure. In typical form, of course, Christie's Poirot—and Acker's use of that character—foregrounds issues of class, though Acker's use is an interdiscursive attempt to call it directly to the reader's attention.

The ideological import of the two topics just discussed, namely class and law, cannot be stressed enough. Christie's detective stories—stories containing the character Hercule Poirot, which are immediately called to mind when Acker uses "Poirot"—were geared to a certain readership with certain values. As Carl Lovitt has observed, Christie's fictions were intended for the Bourgeoisie, a bourgeois readership (Lovitt 69). As such, they were expected to "speak" in a certain way and uphold certain values. Essentially, what we are talking about here is *écriture,* which is to say a kind of writing that represents a "national style" but is also "a class style" (Porter 133). It—*écriture*—is, in the words of Stephen Heath summarizing Barthes, "the choice of a set of values, a way of seeing, an act of socio-historical solidarity" (Heath qtd. in Porter 134). In the case of Christie's very rarified detective tales we have an insistence on "good taste," which means the language of the lower classes is entirely missing, as is overt class conflict.[16] Her detective fiction's *écriture* therefore does exactly what marxist V.N. Voloshinov says it does. Namely, as a linguistic product of "the ruling class," it "strives to impart a supraclass, eternal character to the ideological sign, to extinguish or drive inward the struggle between social value judgements which occurs in it, to make the sign uniaccentual" (Voloshinov qtd. in Porter 136). In short, her fiction's language makes class difference and class war disappear, or at least it tries.

But the language and setting of Acker's detective fiction—her Hercule Poirot story—unearths this repression refusing to let it be pushed under the rug. The aforementioned use of profanity (e.g. "fuck," "cunt," "cock") which peppers the detective tale, as well as innumerable graphic sexual descriptions (e.g. "More and more of his cock hits the back of my throat" (*ALTL* 196)) bring up a vocabulary and language style outside that ruling class realm.[17] Also, much of Acker's detective tale takes place in a Montmartre brothel, surely not the stuff of ruling class tales like those told by Christie. Moreover, the brothel's location, Montmartre, is itself described as "filthy," as a place where "[g]arbage cans and dogshit lie strewn over the sidewalks" and "[b]ums lie under the garbage for warmth" (*ALTL* 217). Through the course of his investigation the polite detective must not only enter this area of Paris, but must go to its poorest section, where he is forced to deal with the malnourished mother of the murdered twerp; there, he must see real suffering: "The woman [the mother] blinks at us. She understands nothing. Obviously poverty's destroyed her mind. 'Mrrlrrp,' her mouth gurgles" (*ALTL* 217) Again, this is not the setting or action we would expect of Christie's detective; her fiction's action and language always remain within "respectable" society. This is seconded by Porter, who observes that Poirot's "triumph is the triumph of subtlety and the sedentary life. Poirot does not indulge in Holmes's elaborate disguises, nor does he expose himself to the risks of penetrating the underworld of London's East End dives, its riverside, and opium dens, let alone hotfoot after his criminal adversaries or even on occasion tangle with them" (159).

Moreover, and at least as important, beginning with Poe's work, we have detective tales highlighting the powers of pure reason (Porter 163). For example, we can recollect that in "The Purloined Letter" Dupin says to the policeman Monsieur G——, who has come to ask for help in his investigation, that if the matter "is any point requiring reflection, . . . we shall examine it to better purpose in the dark" (Poe 468). Dupin considers the art of detection as an exercise requiring nothing but the reasonable meditative mind. Empirical evidence gathered in the light of day is useful in a court of law, but its discovery is secondary to the reasoning act itself. Hence, after Monsieur G—— leaves his home, Dupin in the comfort of his dimly lit study is able to deduce through pure reasoning the whereabouts of the purloined letter. Though as Porter points out, this "pure ratiocination" required more demonstrative action to become part of popular literature, something that Christie surely accomplished with her fiction, the detective is nonetheless a premiere exemplar of reasoning (163). It is significant that Christie's addition of more action does not eliminate the importance of reason. As Porter indicates, Agatha Christie's Hercule Poirot remains "wholly cerebral" (159).

Poirot's wholly cerebral character makes him the consummate puzzle solver; the reader can depend on him to use his logician's mind to discover all the clues and solve the murder. This, taken together with the fact that he is always associated with polite society (i.e. the ruling class) and commands greater pop culture allegiance than Poe's detective, Dupin, make him appealing for Acker. While Acker uses all these associations in her attack on detective fiction, it is perhaps most important here to register the cerebral or logical element within Poirot as detective. This is because Acker's parodic attack targets both the *lisible* (readable) detective genre and the all powerful phallic logic that drives it.

Understanding this helps us gain further insight into the kind of detective fiction she constructs. It seems obvious from what has already been said that Acker's version of the detective genre hardly resembles the one to which we are accustomed. Nonetheless, she gives us all of the traditional trappings.

As we saw earlier, Acker does offer us a murder, as announced by the first chapter's title ("The Case of the Murdered Twerp"). The first murder and dead body—what can be said to start Acker's detective tale—is not within the text. Rather, it is only testified to by a witness, the so called "twerp," who runs into "Restaurant Norvins," for all intents and purposes a whorehouse, and screams, "Norvins, . . . you've got to help me. I just saw a murder. MURDER! I myself . . ." (*ALTL* 190). Unfortunately for the twerp, no one in the brothel believes her; so, she runs into "the bar's back room" (190). The brothel's owner, Norvins, is afraid the girl's ranting will ruin the party she is staging, so she tells Theo—Acker's incarnation of a referential historical character, namely, Vincent Van Gogh's brother—to take the twerp and "hide her in the library that's opposite the dining room" (*ALTL* 195).

In a classical detective story the twerp's public announcement and action, as well as Norvins' command and Theo's subsequent act of escorting our twerp to the dining room, would constitute clues. Using razor sharp reasoning the classical detective would take these clues and others gathered through the course of the story to determine—and announce—the guilty party, namely, the murderer, blackmailer, or whatever. In this revelation the hermeneutic process comes to and end, and the text gives readers a feeling of wholeness and coherence. But Acker's detective tale will not do this; instead, as we shall see, it offers an abundance of clues like the ones above, as well as numerous suspects, but Acker's text ultimately refuses to provide any answers.

Indeed, things just get curiouser and curiouser in Acker's novel. The original murder supposedly witnessed by the twerp is never mentioned again. But, as we see a few pages later after Norvins' party, there has been another murder; this time our victim is the witness to the first murder, the twerp. Ostensibly, then, we have another clue (the twerp's murder) and can guess that the killer who murdered the first unseen victim must also have murdered the witness to that crime (i.e. the twerp). This relatively reasonable series of events would seem to indicate that the hermeneutic process is functioning normally, and we could eventually arrive at the identity of the killer or killers. Indeed, after the twerp's murder the detective Poirot acts as if that is the case, saying "Maybe she [the twerp] had seen a murder" (*ALTL* 198).

Acker's use of the Poirot adds to this sense of a well functioning hermeneutic process as it interdiscursively brings to mind Agatha Christie's Hercule Poirot, the aforementioned "wholly cerebral" detective. That Acker clearly intends us to read her detective as Christie's Poirot seems clear by references like "Poirot's stroking his moustaches like a big fat cat" (*ALTL* 198). Anyone familiar with Christie's detective is surely acquainted with the man's moustache. The scene of Poirot's introduction appears after Norvins' party when Toulouse tells him of the twerp's murder. As Toulouse puts it to Poirot, "At the end of the party . . . she was dead" (*ALTL* 197). Poirot then begins his detective hermeneutic of question and answer: "'Where'd she die Toulouse?'" (*ALTL* 197). In response Toulouse tells him that Paul—another of Acker's referential characters, this time noted painter Paul Gauguin—found the twerp's body in a barrel of water they were using to bob for apples at the brothel party. Poirot then asks Toulouse, "Do you always bob for apples? Whose Idea was that?" (*ALTL* 198). Toulouse responds by saying s/he does not know. This series of inquiries and answers goes on for much of the page, with Poirot asking questions and Toulouse responding with answers. Here are several typical examples wherein Poirot inquires and Toulouse answers: "'Tell me, this Norvins, who runs the bar, what's she like?' 'A good person. Efficient. Hard on her girls and her whores, but she has to be. Looks like a society dame'"; "'Were any of these people holding any sort of grudge against the young dead girl?' 'How could they? She was so, so full of shit. She did keep saying she had seen a murder'"; "'Who exactly was at this party and what was the layout of the place?'" (*ALTL* 198). After this last exchange, Toulouse helps Poirot construct a laundry list of possible suspects and then hands him a sketch of the brothel's layout.

By offering this series of events, as well as the dialogue and sketch, Acker means to call up conventional elements of detective fiction, if in parody. First, she uses the above questions and answers to get the hermeneutics of detection going. By planting these questions and answers in an apparently conventional way (i.e. they are presented as common elements in a detective fiction plot), Acker makes the reader ask certain questions, ones which mirror the detective's own consciousness (e.g. "Did Norvin's kill the twerp?"; "Was the twerp killed because of a grudge?"; "Who are the suspects?"; "Of these suspects, which one is the murderer?"). The sketch itself (see above) is interesting in this respect because it brings up questions all on its own (e.g. "There is only one entrance, so could the murderer escape without being seen?"; "Peter and Rhys' rooms are near the dining room where the twerp was found. Did either of them, or both, do it?"). Moreover, the sketch acts as another of Acker's parodic moments because it calls to mind the sort of logical diagraming done—if not always so literally, at least figuratively—in so many "who done its."

Now, in classical detective fashion these questions and answers are meted out over the course of the tale. Though the text offers some answers quickly (e.g. the body's location; the list of suspects), full revelation (i.e. who is the killer) is not. The reader must go through numerous periods of question and answer in order to arrive at that end point. This "hermeneutic delay," or postponement of revelation, is part of the enjoyment of traditional detective fiction. The reader is happy to forgo the orgasmic pleasure of full disclosure by reading through a series of smaller questions and answers. In fact, as Dennis Porter indicates (54–55), some of these hermeneutic delays can be quite enjoyable (e.g. Raymond Chandler's descriptions of Los Angeles and the Sternwood mansion in *The Big Sleep* 1992).[18]

But for Acker such enjoyable delays in traditional detective fiction are nevertheless secondary pleasures to the final orgasmic pleasure of full revelation. Thus, Acker would seem to roughly agree with Roland Barthes, who condemned traditional detective fictions as *"textes de désir"* (Barthes 1973; Porter 53).[19] Detective fictions exemplify *"textes de désir* to the degree that they exploit the linear nature of narrative in order to stimulate end-oriented desire in a reader" (Porter 53). The connection to traditional detective fiction is easy enough to see since its whole modus operandi is about ends (i.e. the identity of the wrongdoer).

It is not difficult to see the link between such *textes de désir* and the earlier mentioned *lisible* (readable) texts; after all, in both cases the categories come from Barthes himself. In addition, the goal oriented *textes de désir* and *lisible* (readable) text have a wholeness or coherence element in common. That is, *textes de désir* in the fact and process of achieving their goal are *lisible* (readable). The detective pursues clues to discover the murder and reveal him or her as such; this is the goal. But in so doing the text is entirely *lisible* (readable) because instructions for reading (e.g. planting of clues within the text) demand the text take a certain shape, namely, one which constructs a naturalized world of coherence and wholeness. Moreover, as part of that naturalizing process the text includes elements designed to give the fictional world believability.

Now Acker springs a textual trap on the reader by giving all of the aforementioned clues which should lead to the goal of revelation (i.e. who murdered the twerp as well as all the other victims). But that goal will never be achieved because the clues lead nowhere; moreover, in the process the coherent world expected within the *lisible* conventions of detective fiction (e.g. clues lead to answers; the world presented makes sense, is logical) will be destroyed—or at least disrupted—by a number of other narrative techniques. As we earlier discussed some qualities of lisible texts, we can take those observations and look first at how Acker disrupts readability in her vision of detection. Then, we can investigate more generally why Acker attacks the goal oriented nature of detective fictions as *textes de désir.*

To begin, we can recall earlier remarks in this essay indicating that *lisible* texts like traditional detective stories carry with them "narrative contracts." We will remember that these contracts are formalized within the *lisible* text itself. In so doing, readers, "through their contact with the text" will "be able to recognize a world which it [the text] produces or to which it refers," and that there will exist "at least some elements of the text whose function it is to confirm this expectation and to assert the representational or mimetic orientation of fiction" (Culler, *Structuralist Poetics* 192–193).

While I earlier discussed character in this respect and gave a general idea of how a coherent and whole "real" world is communicated, if falsely in Acker's view, I have not done so for the detective genre, one of her targets. To understand Acker on this point we can again refer to Barthes. In Barthes' view of literature there is no "pure context"; instead, as Robert Scholes observes, "all contexts come to man already coded, shaped, and organized by language, and often shaped in patently silly ways" (Scholes 150). That is to say, the writer composes in historically inherited codes and the reader reads those codes to discover meaning; however, according to Barthes it is a mistake for the writer to believe she or he has access to "reality"—to some pure "context"—and for the reader to believe that she or he has equal access to that same reality through reading. With this as a given, the problems for realism seem clear. Again, Scholes explains Barthes on the issue: "The great error of the 'realist' in literature or in criticism is to assume that he is in touch with some ultimate context, while in reality he is simply transcribing a code" (Scholes 150). Therefore, for Barthes what a realist writer—in this case a realist writer of detection—writes as "reality" is nothing but a series of codes. For Barthes, and I would say Acker follows him in this, it is a particular use of these codes which makes a text "realist" in nature and gives readers the "reality effect," a sense that the text reports truth.

Having said this, what does it have to do with Acker's detective fiction? The easiest answer is to say that Acker will prevent or disrupt the "reality effect" in her detective tale, thereby pointing to the conventionality of all traditional detective tales reporting "reality" as unified and whole. To do this, Acker will attack a fundamental technique of realism, and thus of traditional (realistic) detective fiction. In specific, she will disrupt the narrative contract—as it appears formally within the text—"by blocking the process of recognition" that is required to shuttle from a "text to a world" (Culler, *Structuralist Poetics* 193). That is, Acker will exclude what Jonathan Culler calls "descriptive residue," or "items whose only apparent role in the text is that of denoting a concrete reality (trivial gestures, insignificant objects, superfluous dialogue)" (Culler, *Structuralist Poetics* 193). In particular, Acker deletes long descriptions of rooms and other locales, "insignificant objects," as well as what we would usually consider normal conversational dialogue. In its place she substitutes the already remarked upon interdiscursive historical narratives, but also moments of *iteration* which destroy senses of time, place and identity.

Combative Textualities 95

To demonstrate how Acker's writing technique disrupts this "reality effect" we can compare two more traditional versions of detection with brief passages of Acker's *ALTL*. The first is from Arthur Conan Doyle's famous detective novel *A Study in Scarlet* (1981), an earlier instance of the genre; the second instance comes from Raymond Chandler's *The Big Sleep* (1992), a later hard-boiled version of detection. The last two examples come from Acker's *ALTL*:

> Far away on the extreme verge of the alkali plain there rose up a little spray of dust, very slight at first, and hardly to be distinguished from the mists of the distance, but gradually growing higher and broader until it formed a solid, well defined cloud. (Doyle, *A Study in Scarlet* 80)

> The air was thick, wet, steamy and larded with the cloying smell of tropical orchids in bloom. The glass walls and roof were heavily misted and big drops of moisture splashed down on the plants. (Chandler, *The Big Sleep* 7)

> They [men] take hold of me; they shove me around. (Acker, *ALTL* 200)

> We're the meat. That's how we get loved. We get cooked. (Acker, *ALTL* 201).

If we look at the first two examples, Doyle and Chandler, we see clear instances of "descriptive residue," namely, "items whose only apparent role in the text is that of denoting a concrete reality" (Culler, *Structuralist Poetics* 193). For example, Doyle writes of the "little spray of dust" that rises from "the alkali plain" and becomes "a solid, well defined cloud." Chandler, through his narrator Marlow, describes Sternwood's greenhouse as a place with heavy air that is "wet, steamy and larded with the cloying smell of tropical orchids in bloom." Marlow narration even takes us down to the level of descriptive minutia, when he notes how "big drops of moisture splashed down on the plants" from the walls and ceiling of the greenhouse.

The points to see are two. First, we can clearly observe how both authors, Chandler and Doyle, use descriptive language in a fashion that does not move the story forward. That is, these descriptive elements play no role whatsoever in the story per se. It would be fair, then, to call both cases instances of hermeneutic delay. At the same time, these delays serve a clearly realist function, in that the level of details—exemplified through language like "the alkali plain," "well defined cloud," "tropical orchids in bloom," and "big drops of moisture"—serves to give readers a recognizable and coherent picture of the world, one which is finished and whole.

This, however, is not the case with Acker's language in the above passages. While she sometimes offers what can be called realistic descriptive language (e.g. her instances of historical narrative, bare bones descriptions like the one already noted of the slums of Montmartre), Acker includes little "descriptive residue." Instead, she offers moments of *iteration* which disrupt *narrative rhythm* and, as a consequence, interfere with realistic presentation of the world. This disruption or interference has the further effect of pointing to power relations between the genders.

To understand this point we should note that in narratology "iteration" has to do with the frequency of events within a story (Bal 110–112). Now, there are, of course, a number of ways to represent the frequency of an event or events within a story. An event could occur regularly (e.g. going to the grocery store every week) in a story, or it could occur only once. Moreover, as Mieke Bal observes, there also exist several other options in regards to frequency. I will not discuss them here because it is not necessary to make my point. Instead, I need only indicate that in some postmodern texts—and Acker's *ALTL* is one example—iteration troubles our efforts to envision a coherent world. Troubling iteration, and thus coherence, is not particularly desirable in traditional detective fiction precisely because it is concerned with reason and coherence. If frequency of events is disrupted, then world takes on a very unreal character.

If we look at the above examples, we can see how Acker accomplishes this disruption. Let us take, for example the passage from *ALTL* where Acker writes, "They [men] take hold of me; they shove me around." Toulouse, the character who makes this statement, never divulges *how often* "they take hold" of her/him. Furthermore, s/he never reveals how frequently men "shove" her/him "around." Much the same is true of the other statement presented above: "We're the meat. That's how we get loved. We get cooked." Again, the frequency of the event is left open, forcing readers to ask, "How often are they [the whores] loved? How often are they cooked?" Besides the obvious textual fact that such instances point directly to gender oppression (e.g. "they [men] shove me around," "We [women] get cooked"), we should note that issues of iterative frequency occur directly within the detective tale and serve to interfere with coherence. In failing to stipulate frequency, such iteration creates not a logical or coherent world, but a world called into question.

As I have already mentioned, besides disrupting coherence, such iterative passages pointedly criticize current gender relations. In passages like the above Acker wants indicate how men literally and figuratively "shove me [a woman] around." In the phallically based world, there are only oppressors (males) and the oppressed (females). As the lesser of the two terms (i.e. male/female), women are reduced to the level of animal flesh to be "cooked" and consumed by men.

Moreover, we should note that the effect of these iterative disruptions is to ruin, if that is the correct term, our detective tale's *rhythm*. To do so is also to disrupt the reality or coherence of the tale as well. Rhythm, as Bal indicates, is something like the relationship between "the amount of time covered by the various events or series of events, episodes" and "the *amount of space in the text* each event requires: the number of pages, lines, or words" (Bal 100–101; italics mine). In this respect, what we are really talking about here is how "attention is patterned" (Bal 101). This issue is critical in understanding the difference between the detection Acker creates and traditional detective narratives. If one grants that traditional detection, like that of Doyle and Chandler above, is piled high with "descriptive residue" (i.e. it takes up a lot of space in the text), such description helps give traditional detection a certain rhythm. Now, that rhythm may slow down the telling of the story because text space is taken up with "descriptive residue." Nevertheless, that slowing effect, namely slowing of rhythm, does nothing to interfere with the ideological project of realistic detection. In fact, it aids that project, as I have already noted in my discussion of "descriptive residue."

On the other hand, in her use of iterative moments Acker attempts to disrupt or destroy that realist detective project. She peppers her detective tale with bits of iterativity; these iterative moments—moments like those noted above—take up a lot of text space, jumping in frequently to disrupt the detective story. In this respect, it is not "that the story has no narrative rhythm. On the contrary, it seems hasty and fragmented, frantic and verging on the incoherent" (Bal 110). As Bal observes, it is precisely "by disrupting the correlation between fabula and story in this respect that the [postmodern] novel achieves its postmodern 'feel'" (110). In this sense, the world represented is thus not whole and complete, but fragmented and unfinished.[20]

We should note that this iterative attack on coherence within detective fiction is closely related to Acker's assault on reason and logic within detection. To get a sense of her intent, we can return to the clues Poirot finds in the course of Acker's story. Through the early portions of *ALTL* he adds to the clues I mentioned earlier in a fashion expected of a *lisible* (readable) detective story. He cites a "coroner's report" that shows the murdered twerp was indeed killed at the brothel party; from this and the earlier clues he surmises that the murderer must have been in attendance at the party since there is only one entrance to the brothel, and no one reported seeing anyone enter beyond those already there (*ALTL* 209). Poirot also learns that the murdered twerp's real name is "Marie," and so he drags Toulouse along to interview the victim's mother in the "poorest section of Montmartre" (*ALTL* 199; 216). There, he is forced to hear of yet another murder, that of Marie's brother, Melvyn (*ALTL* 218).

Unfortunately for the rational Poirot things only get worse from there, as murders and clues pile up (e.g. a "Haitian voodoo killing" that supposedly occurred "three days before the murdered twerp got bumped off" and two other killings related to it; killings during a gang shootout (*ALTL* 222; 223)). But Poirot, for all his investigative power, cannot solve these murders, nor can he make sense of the clues. To borrow a phrase from Toulouse, who predicts Poirot's ultimate failure, "Poirot's stumped" (*ALTL* 200). In fact, the degree of his failure is measured by the fact that he and his narrative of detection disappear forever near the end of Chapter Three, as he wanders back to the brothel to requestion suspects and gather more evidence.

What does Acker mean by this? Well, if we combine a bit of autobiographical information with our previous analysis and elements from *ALTL,* we can get a good idea of her intent. First, we should recall my earlier comments about Acker's affiliation with Derridian and Lacanian ideas, as well as her feminist bent. Remember, Acker believes, much like Derrida, that the present culture is phallically hierarchized ("phallocentric") but also partakes of a more general "metaphysics of presence," otherwise known as the belief in identity, unity and wholeness. For Acker the two ideas—phallocentrism and logocentrism—go together, but the element that starts it all, at least for her, is "The Law of the Phallus," which marks "the principle of psychic division and sexual difference" (Benstock 6). All other hierarchized differences stem from this fundamental moment of difference. Therefore, notions like subject, object, male, female, etc., as well as all other *identities,* can be traced to this moment.

The idea of *identity* is pivotal here, because for Acker it is directly associated with the masculine scientific and rational mind, and this is exactly the logical mind of Hercule Poirot, the "wholly cerebral" detective. While Acker does not believe that science "invented" identity, she does believe that in its pursuit of knowledge it has become wholly masculinized in its infatuation with it. Some writers, such as Susan Bordo, have traced this masculinization back at least to Descartes, who believed that "the scientific mind must be cleansed of all its 'sympathies' toward the objects it tries to understand. It must cultivate absolute detachment" (Bordo 104). In this respect Bordo, quoting from Evelyn Fox Keller's *Reflections on Gender and Science* (1985) observes the following:

> [T]he scientific mind is set apart from what is to be known, i.e., from nature, and its autonomy is guaranteed . . . by setting apart its modes of knowing from those in which the dichotomy is threatened. In this process, the characterization of both the scientific mind and its modes of access to knowledge as masculine is indeed significant. Masculine here connotes, as it so often does, autonomy, separation, and distance . . . a radical rejection of any commingling of subject and object. (Keller qtd. in Bordo 104)

Here, it seems important to remark that in affirming identity—a trait evinced by separation—there is also discarding or purging. This process is precisely the purging of nature and the feminine. As Bordo indicates, in order to have a mechanistic view of the world—a noted shift in science of the seventeenth century—it was necessary to rid the world of an "organic cosmology" which envisioned "the natural world as mothered" (Bordo 101). We can, of course, trace this in Western culture to Plato and Aristotle (Bordo 101–102). There is no need to go into detail on Plato and Aristotle; rather, the important idea for understanding Acker's view is to note, as does Bordo, that in Descartes' creation of a mechanized view of nature, "nature became *defined* by its lack of affiliation with divinity, with spirit. All that which is God-like or spiritual—freedom, will, and sentience—belong entirely and exclusively to *res cogitans*. All else—the earth, the heavens, animals, the human body—is merely mechanistic" (Bordo 102).

It is not hard to see this, at least from Acker's mixed Lacanian and Derridian point of view, as a further logical expression in the cultural sphere of the Phallus' all encompassing signifying power. That is, from Acker's viewpoint pushing nature outside the *res cogitans* is merely a further logical expression of a culture based on the Phallus. The Phallus as the root of meaning and language—that place where *res cogitans* can operate—pushes the feminine into unreason; nature and the feminine may operate, but they cannot have reasoning "sentience" or "will." It is in this spirit that Acker's cerebral detective, Poirot, tells Toulouse, "You lack the analytical mind. You're too emotional to have planned this murder" (*ALTL* 200). The feminine—or at least partially feminine—Toulouse is incapable of male reasoning "sentience" or "will."

Moreover, to understand Acker we need to see another important sense of exclusion or loss with regard to the feminine. It is, as Bordo puts it, a rejection of "that cluster of epistemological values, often associated with feminine consciousness . . ." (102). In particular, I am talking about a rejection of "sympathetic thinking," which is a mode of thought explicated by, among others, Herbert Marcuse (Bordo 103).[21] Interestingly, Acker in fact studied under Marcuse and later followed him to U.C.S.D. For Marcuse, and I think Acker as well, "sympathetic" thinking means "being receptive" or "passive" in one's attitude toward the object studied (Marcuse, *Counterrevolution and Revolt* 74). Bordo, describing Marcuse's position, observes that for him "sympathetic thinking" represents "the only mode which truly respects the object, that is, which allows the variety of its meanings to unfold without coercion or too-focused interrogation" (103). Sympathetic thinking—which Descartes rejects and in so doing changes the very definition of "logical" scientific thinking—envisions a merging of the "objective and subjective"; together they "participate in the creation of meaning" (Bordo 103).

It is important to see the conflict here between the two scientific conceptions and that each is associated with one pole of the binary opposition male/female. In Descartes' masculine vision "scientific mind is set apart from what is to be known"; therefore there exists an absolute "autonomy, separation, and distance . . . a radical rejection of any commingling of subject and object" (Keller qtd. in Bordo 104). In Lacanian terms Acker sees this conception rooted in the phallus as first signifier of (absolute) difference. It is that moment of misrecognition when identities (e.g. subject vs object) are formed. But this vision can only be achieved by throwing out, rejecting, "commingling of subject and object" or the destruction of absolute difference, which is associated with the female side of the pole.

Acker's failed detective tale can then be seen as a deeper attack on a particular kind of phallogocentric thinking, namely, that associated with the masculine and the formation of absolute identities. As we have seen, Acker blends Toulouse the historically male figure with her own vision of Toulouse as female. She crosses the inviolable "logical" boundary of male/female. But Acker also refuses to let Poirot, our "wholly cerebral" detective, succeed in his incisive masculine logic; as a practitioner of Descartes' logical method, he is thwarted at every turn. He never solves the murders. This renders ironic Toulouse's statement that "Poirot'll figure everything out. He's my father" (199). At the same time, I think Acker means Toulouse's words to have a number of meanings. Poirot may, for instance, stand in for the father as castration threat, but he also represents the logic behind the phallus as first signifier, as well as the consequences of that logic, namely, reification and oppression.

Acker's Use and Abuse of Historical Narratives:

To understand Acker's undermining of historical narrative, it is useful to consider Linda Hutcheon's conjectures about postmodern writing's treatment of literature and history. According to Hutcheon, "What the postmodern writing of both history and literature has taught us is that both history and fiction are discourses, that both constitute systems of signification by which we make sense of the past ('exertions of the shaping, ordering imagination')" (Hutcheon, *A Poetics of Postmodernism* 89). In this sense, "the meaning and shape are not in the events, but in the systems which make those past 'events' into present historical 'facts'"; in terms of strategic intervention, this means that "[t]he postmodern . . . effects two simultaneous moves. It reinstalls historical contexts as significant and even determining, but in so doing, it problematizes the entire notion of historical knowledge" (Hutcheon, *A Poetics of Postmodernism* 89).

In terms of Acker's work, reinstallment of historical context and the simultaneous problematizing of historical knowledge are intimately bound with formal elements (e.g. the personal language situation, deixis), as well as profanity, tawdry setting, and equally tawdry actions. The use of these, combined with specific historical contexts, as well as intertextual and interdiscursive references to those contexts, "challenge narrative singularity and unity in the name of multiplicity and disparity"; such a technique, according to Hutcheon, "offer[s] fictive corporality instead of abstractions," but also destabilizes unitary "subjectivity of character" and the unity of historical narrative (Hutcheon, *A Poetics of Postmodernism* 90). In this sense we may say that Acker's writing reflects a critical vision of history somewhat similar to Michel Foucault's, in that both see history as "dispersion, disparity," and "difference" (Smart 55), rather than unified and linear.[22]

We may say here that Acker's disruption of traditional historiography generally resembles her disruption of subjectivity and realist detective narrative. That is, disruption occurs via a number of formal and thematic methods. On a formal level, Acker's detective tale and her ruptured historiography, refer to themselves as constructions. But such self-reference is forbidden in traditional realism and its cousin, historical narrative, which wish to hide the place and moment of enunciation. As Hutcheon puts it, "Historical statements, be they in historiography or realist fiction, tend to *suppress grammatical reference to the discursive situation of the utterance* (producer, receiver, context, intent) in their attempt to narrate past events in such a way that the events seem to narrate themselves" (*A Poetics of Postmodernism* 92; italics mine).

Acker begins this self reference by shifting *ALTL*'s genre into that of a school text book, wherein she deploys a supposedly objective economic-historical narrative to make specific points about capitalism. Here, formal concerns mesh with thematic ones, as the "other" remarked upon earlier extends beyond just women to the poor, namely, the trace supporting globalized capitalism's existence and growth. Acker's shift into the genre of economic-historical narrative points directly to the third world "other" and the capitalist imperialism that made it possible:

> Capitalism as a world system had its origins in the late fifteenth and early sixteenth centuries when Europeans, mastering the art of long-distance navigation, broke out of their little corner of the globe and roamed the seven seas, conquering, plundering, and trading. Ever since then capitalism has consisted of two sharply contrasting parts: on the one hand a handful of dominant exploiting countries and on the other hand a much larger number dominated and exploited countries.
>
> In the beginning the relations between the developed and underdeveloped parts of the world capitalist system were based on force. The stronger conquered the weaker, plundered their resources, subjected them to unequal trading relations, and reorganized their economic structures (e.g., by introducing slavery) to serve the needs of Europeans. (*ALTL* 275)

While this was "gradually replace by 'normal' economic relations of trade and investment," there was nevertheless no softening of "the basic development pattern, or stopping the transfer of wealth from the periphery to the center" (*ALTL* 276). In fact, this section of the novel goes on for a good number of pages outlining the history of capitalist exploitation up to its more recent globalized postmodern incarnation in so called "flexible accumulation," as seen in these passages: "Keynesian economics . . . has had its day (if it ever had a day)"; "Keynesian economics has failed because of its politics and not its techniques—in broadest terms, because it attempted to paper over the class conflicts present in a capitalist society" (*ALTL* 286). That is, the liberal economist John Maynard Keynes never saw the problem at the core of capitalism, namely, its logic of class conflict and its valorization of individual self interest. Instead, says David Harvey, Keynes sought merely "a set of scientific managerial strategies and state powers that would stabilize capitalism, while avoiding the evident repressions and irrationalities, all the warmongering and narrow nationalism that national socialist solutions implied" (129). Keynes believed the capitalist system could be maintained by small regulatory tweaks in the system, and therein lies his problem according to Acker. The system is based in part on a thoroughgoing selfishness, as well as a set of laws and contradictions that inevitably produce suffering. Mere tinkering with an essentially flawed system will ultimately fail. As Harvey indicates, such thinking never foresaw capital's ability to infiltrate the very state agent assigned to corral it. Through a series of changes—e.g. "flexible production systems," "formation of a global stock market," "accelerated geographical mobility of funds," as well as corporate investment in the infrastructure of the nation state itself (Harvey 161, 165)—the lines between nation and capital blur, such that there is "a shift toward the empowerment of financial capital *vis à vis* the nation state" (Harvey, *The Condition of Postmodernity* 165). More simply, financial capital controls the state if not in whole, at least to a high degree. Therefore, reform through regulatory tweaks becomes almost impossible.

We should note here that Acker's shift in genre to an overtly didactic social-historical-economic narrative indicts capitalism's exploitation of so called "third world" nations, but also that such concerns are brought together with the poor more generally (e.g. the brothel in *ALTL* is in Montmartre, a poor working class area of Paris) and gender (woman as whore) to draw a parallel between denigration of women in the male dominated system and the denigration of the poor, third world within the capitalist system. Such a reading is difficult to avoid because of the sheer weight of the previous portions of the book which speak about and from those exploited positions of female and worker.

In a directly related sense, we should also understand that for Acker no relationship exists between men and women that is not commodified or outside the cash nexus. When the narrator, Toulouse, says, "They [women] know they have to turn to the brothel" and later utters, "I can't get a man unless money's involved," finally finishing with "I found this out in the brothel," she is indicating exactly this: the capitalist world is a whorehouse where everything and everyone have been commodified. Hence, by implication, the relationship between people is that of the atomized commodity. Everyone is for sale. It is fitting, then, that Toulouse and many of the other women in the book are whores, women for sale as sexual objects. Hence the prostitute Berthe says, "We're part of the meat market. We're the meat" (200).

But seeing the capitalist world as a whore house would seem to make Acker's picture somewhat contradictory. It seems, for instance, that the whores in the brothel are also men. But Acker's females, many of whom are often termed "waitresses," appear to participate in equally whore-like activity of giving themselves over to the power of men for money. While this seems a bit confusing, I think we can postulate that for Acker we are all whores within the capitalist system. But men, though they are commodified, at least have the signifier—the chance to represent—while woman does not, and is therefore outside, "other."

From a more traditional psychoanalytic perspective, Acker's image of the whore in the world's brothel may communicate a solution for the male fear of women, but one that *critiques* Freud's system by revealing in stark pornographic terms the plight of female sex workers in this system. The whore, as many of us know, represents for Freud a "splitting in two of the maternal figure" which allows the male to avoid the incest taboo and the castration which it represents. The avoidance is achieved because in its splitting the maternal aspect is separated from the "love of the whore" (Kofman 86). Sarah Kofman explains this splitting, observing that "prostitutes" represent "women of humble birth sufficiently debased to exalt man's sex and to banish any association with incest . . ." (84–85). But despite defensive male attempts to efface incest with the mother, the maternal image in the prostitute remains. Again, we can look to Kofman on this issue, who remarks that "this choice of an object [a prostitute] apparently so different from the maternal object in fact unquestionably betrays a maternal prototype: the whore is a simple substitute for the mother and she retains all the mother's characteristics . . ." (86).[23] Thus, the "waitress" Veronique, who is also obviously a whore, makes the following comment about her male artist clientele: "What these artists really want are pillows. Nice soft sweet female pillows. We can't be that way. We've got our work" (*ALTL* 197). The male clientele want mothers with comforting bosoms, women as "sweet female pillows." But as Veronique says, "We can't be that way. We've got our work." Specifically, she and the other "waitresses" have their work as prostitutes, whores, and you cannot be both a whore and a mother.

While the critique of gender relations presented above remains almost exclusively subjective, and our earlier example of historical-economic analysis presents itself in the guise of objectivity, Acker combines the two below, moving abruptly from objective to subjective in an effort to bring actual suffering subjects into the historical-economic narrative:

> The managers are becoming owners, deriving an ever-larger portion of their income not from their managerial skills but from the stock they own in their corporations.
>
> You don't give a damn if he never comes around. You never want to see him again. Fuck his round face and his blond hair and his five feet ten inches lean body. Fuck him in shit. Fuck his screwed-up mouth and skinny legs. Fuck him in piss. (*ALTL* 280)

Here, in moving from one paragraph to the next, Acker injects subjectivity into the objective historical narrative. While at first we had the rhetoric of the "objective" historical narrative (e.g. "The managers are becoming owners . . ."), we now have a text inhabited by those who suffer the costs of the system about which the narrative speaks, namely, exploited workers like the whores of Montmartre, who suffer at the hands of a male dominated capitalist system ("Fuck him in piss.").

We should note, however, that the shift does not simply draw attention to the writing of historical-economic narrative; if we interpret such excerpts in conjunction with the novel's widespread profanity, its tawdry setting, and formal use of deixis, we may understand how *ALTL* avoids history as *nostalgia,* an accusation leveled at mixed textual works like Acker's by Fredric Jameson (1983, 1997).[24] Who, after all, could be nostalgic for a "filthy" Montmartre covered in "dogshit" and populated by whores who are "fucked not loved." It is, in short, quite the opposite of the mystified nostalgic glaze of Parisian life presented in Baz Luhrmann's recent film *Moulin Rouge,* wherein whore's dance, sing, and generally revel, with real life figures like Lautrec.

In other parts of *ALTL* history is troubled somewhat differently even as it is called up for the reader's attention. While we have already noted deixis—the personal language situation—as a problematizing component in delivering of truth, in terms of ruptured historiography we may add to it Acker's employment of various *interdiscursive* and *intertextual* historical references. These also trouble objective history even as they point to the actual history of class war and women's oppression. Here, we can examine both interdiscursive and intertextual moments which not only call up historical discourses (i.e. interdiscursivity), but also verifiable statements spoken by real historical figures (i.e. intertextualiy).

For the sake of time and space I will address only three instances here, all occurring within two pages of one another. While one of the instances is culturally distant from the other two, all three refer to action occurring within a span of fifteen years. Moreover, all refer to revolutionary attempts to change material relations, and all are intertwined with the experiences of the Montmartre whores. The effect unites the whores' class and gender position with that of revolutionaries struggling for social change. At the same time, the breadth of interdiscursive and intertextual reference, as well as the whores' uniting of them in their own speech, would seem to disrupt the continuity one usually demands of traditional historiography.

The first reference is both interdiscursive and intertextual and concerns the French anarchist Charles Gallo. In it Berthe, a whore, tells another prostitute, Giannina, about Gallo's activities as reported in the newspaper:

> The other day the cops arrested Charles Gallo. . . . The anarchist who threw a bottle of vitriol into the middle of the Stock Exchange; fired three revolver shots into the crowd, and didn't kill anyone. When the cops got

him, he said, 'long live revolution! Long live anarchism! Death to the bourgeois judiciary! Long live dynamite! Bunch of idiots!' (*ALTL* 201)

Before addressing Gallo's actions and words, we should note that the passage is interdiscursive because it refers to a particular political movement and its discourse, French anarchism, as well as to that movement's role and development. Acker brings up this discourse to point to revolutionary history generally, but also to specify it with the case of the French anarchist movement's attempts to gain power for workers and the poor. Acker obviously means for us to equate Giannina and Berthe with the poor, as they are both prostitutes working in a brothel in Montmartre, a poor working class section of Paris. Moreover, it seems clear from Acker's text that the whores support anarchism as an alternative to the hierarchical political and economic system of so called "democratic" capitalism. As evidence, shortly after Acker's Gallo reference Berthe remarks, "If we lived in a society without bosses . . . we'd be fucking all the time" (*ALTL* 201). Obviously, Berthe's "society without bosses" refers to the anarchist society's lack of hierarchical authority.

More generally, we can say that the interdiscursive moment evoked through Gallo brings up the history of anarchism, but it also calls up the social conditions in France that made for the anarchist movement. Juxtaposing the whores Giannina and Berthe with the anarchist revolutionary Gallo in the above passage recalls the historical struggle of workers in France to achieve social and economic justice. In this respect it should be remembered that the capitalist development of France in the nineteenth century was very gradual, and industrialization and an organized industrial working class were slow to develop as a result; in fact, industrialization cannot really be said to occur in France until the later part of the century, though even then industrial activity took place primarily in a small number of places (Ridley 15). Gallo, who committed his actual feat of "terrorism" in eighteen eighty-six, thus falls into this sparsely industrial period. Before this period, say, in mid nineteen hundreds, seventy percent of the population remained living in the country occupied in agricultural activities (Ridley 15). Industry, such that it was, remained confined primarily to small workshops, in what might be called the craft trades; as a result, (industrialized) labor's ability to organize was feeble because of its small numbers. Moreover, despite the French state's talk of liberation, from the time of the revolution in seventeen eighty-nine to around eighteen eighty-four the French government adamantly opposed labor's attempts to organize trade unions; its opposition was in fact so strong that it actively legislated against organizing for higher wages or striking (e.g. *droit de coalition*) or organizing period (e.g. the *Le Chapelier* law) (Ridley 20).

Such laws effectively made workers organizing into law breakers. It is amongst all this that the anarchist movement arose from theoretical writings of Pierre-Joseph Proudhon (1809–1865). As Peter Sterns observes, Proudhon represents "France's greatest contribution to socialist thought and was one of the few non-Marxist socialists of any importance after 1848"; moreover, his thinking can be said to have commanded "French labor movements in the third quarter of the nineteenth century . . ." (11). Thus, his influence can be said to extend into the thought of radical French workers during the Paris Commune (1871) we see represented in Acker's *ALTL*.

Proudhon's anarchist theory, based in part on Hegel's logic and published in his work *Qu'est-ce que la propriété?* (1840), sought to reconcile property with communistic collectivization; on the one hand, "property and the state were closely linked, the one was the *raison d'êntre* of the other. Its unequal distribution led to the exploitation of the weak by the strong, the tyranny of the rich over the poor" (Ridley 26). On the other hand, collectivization destroyed liberty because "it merely increased the power of the state, making it absolute tyrant" (Ridley 26). Using Hegel's notions of "thesis," "antithesis," and "synthesis," Proudhon reconciled property and collectivity by performing a "synthesis":

> This was the abolition of property (i.e. the unequally distributed forms that gave rise to unearned income) and its replacement by possession (i.e. the peasant's possession of the land he cultivated, the worker's possession of the tools he employed). Widespread ownership, individual and communal, would create a system of checks and balances in which none could dominate. (Ridley 26)

Yet for Proudhon justice demanded a further step because "authority is itself evil" and would produce injustice; regardless of its form, authority would always produce similar unjust consequences (Ridley 27). Democracy was equally flawed for Proudhon in that it simply spread authority out among the many, and despite its claims always exhibited itself in singular tyrannical institutions like the judicial system (Ridley 27). Acker's anarchist Charles Gallo follows Proudhon proclaiming, "Long live anarchism! Death to the bourgeois judiciary!" (*ALTL* 200). To such a repressive system Proudhon offers the solutions of "reciprocity" and "mutuality." Reciprocity was Proudhon's alternative to authority; instead of acting on authority, under reciprocity people acted reciprocally, by "co-operation between individual and individual, group and group; it meant society based not on the rights of capital but on the free and fair exchange of services" (Ridley 27). This would produce what Proudhon called "mutualism," which meant independent groups negotiating and acting with other groups to form things like "mutual aid" and "reciprocal guarantees of markets"; the combination of the two—"reciprocity" and "mutualism"—would dissolve the state and its authority as we customarily know it (Ridley 27). The appeal of such a system to Acker's Montmartre whores is thus easy to understand for reasons of both gender and class, since the stress on autonomy within anarchism would dissolve the power of men over women as well as the power of the capitalist over the worker (or working whore). In terms of gender and class in anarchist society Berthe remarks, "We [women] wouldn't have to be images. Cunt special" (*ALTL* 201). Her use of the term "images" points to the power of male representation of women, while the reference to "Cunt special" evokes the idea of women as commodities on a diner menu. For Berthe, neither of these would take place under anarchism.

I have discussed Proudhon here to give us sense of the interdiscursive political discourse and history Acker invokes by bringing up the real historical actor Charles Gallo. While time and space do not permit much further investigation of this, it would be remiss, of course, not to add to this discourse and history of anarchism the influence of Karl Marx, Auguste Blanqui, Mikhail Bakunin, and Peter Kropotkin. In fact, Proudhon was well acquainted with both Marx and Bakunin, though the second figure, Marx, eventually dismissed Proudhon's ideas and later became embattled with followers of the anarchist Bakunin (Ridley 25–30).

Though all remain essential for understanding the French worker's resistance to state and capitalist repression, in terms of Acker's *ALTL,* Blanqui seems, in addition to Proudhon, of special importance here. This is because Charles Gallo's call really embodies a mixture of historical influences; while Gallo was surely influenced by Proudhon's position, the latter's views were primarily theoretical and needed concrete suggestions for their implementation (Stearns 11). Here is where the influence of thinkers such as Auguste Blanqui (1805–1881) is especially evident. Blanqui was a lifetime French revolutionary who advocated violence to overthrow the repressive state; he was also once proclaimed the "honorary president of the first session of the [Paris] commune" in eighteen-seventy-one (Ridley 34–35). Thus, under this Blanquist influence we have Acker's Gallo throw a bottle of "vitriol" in an act of violence, and in a moment of intertextuality declare, "'Long live the revolution. . . . Long live dynamite!'" (Acker 201). The precise words Gallo speaks have been variously reported, but the incident itself is true, and Acker's language roughly approximates Gallo's. In fact, according to my research the declaration "Long live dynamite" is an exact quotation ("Ephéméride Anarchiste" 5).

Combative Textualities

Acker's intertextual and interdiscursive references to Blanquist influence in Gallo's speech takes us to another of her interdiscursive moments, but earlier in time. Here, one page after her reference to Charles Gallo in *ALTL* is the declaration of the failed Paris Commune of eighteen seventy-one, of which Blanqui was president, if only briefly:

> On Sunday May 21 the first detachment of Versailles troops entered the capital. This entrance caught the Commune unawares. Thiers' army made up of prisoners of war and provincial recruits shot everyone in sight. They killed 25,000 people. The Communards, retreating from Paris, burned as much as they could. Marshal MacMahon of the Versailles army declared order was restored. The death of the Paris Commune was the death of the workers' revolutionary power. Now we have to give up our lives to cause any destruction of this society. (*ALTL* 202)

Time and space prohibit an exhaustive exploration of the Paris Commune, but we may say that it was composed of many of the sort of workers I have already mentioned. specifically, the Commune consisted of eighty-one members, elected not as parliamentary representatives, but as directly beholden to the people for every decision made, so they could be excused at any time (O'Carroll 3–4). Roughly thirty five of the eighty-one members were "manual laborers"—again, primarily craftsmen as I indicated earlier—and roughly fourty members "had been involved in the French Labour movement and most of them had joined the international" (O'Carroll 3–4). As so many had been involved in frustrating attempts to put unions together under state scrutiny, they had a lot of suspicions regarding power and politics; this, as I have already tried to convey, gave them a strong anarchist Proudhonist bent.

On the whole, Acker's interdiscursive presentation is roughly correct as regards actors (e.g. Theirs, General MacMahon), as well as chronology and death toll. Indeed, as Acker correctly states, Theirs and the army entered Paris on the twenty-first of May, though the last barricade did not fall until the twenty-eighth of May; her death toll is roughly correct as well, if something of an underestimate; the impressive carnage actually totaled more like 30,000 dead (O'Carroll 6–7).

The slaughter, of course, was horrific in scale, and Acker's conveys her attitude about it in the above passage through another instance of deixis—the personal language situation of the CN—mixed with the so called third person form of narration, namely, EN. We can note that the last sentence of this historical narrative reads as follows: "Now we have to give up our lives to cause any destruction of this society" (*ALTL* 202). This passage uses "now," an adverb of time which is clearly part of the personal language situation, as is the first person plural use of "we" and "us." Both, in fact, are instances of deixis, of CN. Moreover, the focalized coloring of the narration, namely, its desperate cry that only death can destroy the system ("we have to give up our lives to cause any destruction of this society"), seems clearly to indicate an attitude toward the Commune's destruction and equally reveals CN.

But the rest of the passage is told in an almost cold and analytical voice, namely, that of the supposedly "objective" third person voice of history (EN). The problem is this narrator never "steps down," to borrow a phase from Mieke Bal, so that we get, again, a mixed narrative (free indirect discourse) which denies the comfort of history as a finished and objective narrative. This occurs because a character bound narrator (CN)—through deixis and coloration—undermines a third person narrator (EN), which claims to speak the objective narrative of history. For Acker this formal experiment is meant to show that "history" is always a process of interpretation and involves the conscious shaping of events into a whole. But that wholeness is a false reification enacted through a third person narrative (EN) which veils the interpretive or shaping act. Acker's mixing of CN and EN (free indirect discourse) might possibly be read as falling roughly in line Foucault's rereading of history, as noted earlier. That is, those who write the supposedly objective historical account—namely, history as EN, with its "narrative rhetoric of truth" (Bal 22)—remain unaware of the fact that their writing is itself conditioned upon their own particular historical-social context—namely the pollution of the writer himself (CN)—which is signaled by free indirect discourse (mixing of EN/CN). The mix then, perhaps, suggests one fundamental insight of narratology, namely, that "'I' and 'he' are both 'I'" (Bal 21; see also endnote 13). In any case, the effect makes coherent history appear plagued by the aforementioned "dispersion, disparity," and "difference" noted in Foucault (Smart 55). While there are problems with aligning Foucault's reading of history with Acker's, I will save discussion of them until Chapter Four. Setting these aside, however, we might also note that Acker's view of history can, in a sense, be considered Lacanin. It conveys the falseness of reified history, history as done, over with, finished, complete. Instead, Acker wants to see history as alive, in process, and in the present.[25]

In terms of Acker's historical interdiscursivity, we can also look at a final passage that invokes class war but also gives her Montmartre whores a recovered image of female power. The passage, appearing a few lines down from the Gallo reference, is spoken by the prostitute Berthe: "My heroine is Sophie Perovskaya. . . . Five yeas ago March First The People's Will, a group she was part of, murdered Tsar Alexander II. As she died, she rejoiced, for she realized her death would deal a fatal blow to autocracy. . . . I'd like to have the guts to follow that woman" (*ALTL* 201). In this passage Acker again uses interdiscursivity. Her character Berthe is speaking about a real historical figure, Sophia Perovskaya (1853–1881), who was a leading member of one splinter group ("Narodnaya Volya," "People's Will") which formed in eighteen seventy-nine from the break of the first political party in Russia to call for active revolution ("Zemlya i Volya," "Land and Liberty") (Moss, *Alexander II and His Times* 34).[26] Narodnaya advocated terrorism as a means of forcing the Russian government to pay attention to the needs of the rural and urban poor. Sophia Perovskya, and Acker is correct here, did indeed carry a bomb to kill Tsar Alexander II on March first, but instead of throwing it she was forced by logistical circumstances to command others members to throw their bombs. The planned assassination succeeded; Alexander II was killed (Moss 37). Subsequently, Perovskya was apprehended, tried, and eventually executed.

Acker's interdiscursive reference to Perovskaya is interesting not only because it calls up a third historical instance of class conflict and of workers attempting to change the system, but also because it provides for the whores Berthe and Giannina a powerful female role model in class struggle. Hence, we have Berthe's statement: "My heroine is Sophie Perovskaya. . . . I'd like to have the guts to follow that woman." The shaping of history is, for Acker, too often portrayed as an arena of action for men only. Woman's presence is obliterated, if not always in fact—through forbidding women's participation—then by erasing or concealing their roles in history. Acker, by referring to the female Russian revolutionary Perovskaya, puts women back into history and gives our poor Montmartre prostitutes an active and powerful model, even in her failure.[27]

While I will save extended discussion of this until Chapter Four, I would like to conclude this chapter with two final points. First, it is interesting to note that Acker is not alone in her use of history as text; in the last chapter we saw how Ishmael Reed's *Mumbo Jumbo* invokes an expansive and parodic series of historical references so as to critique history, even while he shapes a counter-image of it. Much the same thing occurs in Don DeLillo's *White Noise,* wherein he invokes a number of historical references, the most striking of which is Adolph Hitler.

My second point is really a question. It concerns the ethical grounding of Acker's textual critique. We have seen that Acker desires to undermine subjectivity, and that she adopts a sort of idiosyncratic Lacanian view of the subject. At the same time, this view is supplemented with a critique of history not unlike Foucault's in that it sees history and historical narrative as constructed from disparate and different phenomena, none of which can be unified into a true history. While I will talk about this problem in strictly poststructural terms later in the book, it is worth noting here that Acker's use of history is ethically driven; she desires to overturn patriarchy and capitalism as they have been historically inherited. At the same time, she seems to hold a vision of history as itself made historical by the narratives in which it is recounted. But such a vision must succumb to its own logic, in the sense that the very claims one is making about history are themselves defined by one's own social-historical moment and do not correspond to a distinct, ascertainable reality. How, then, is it possible to make factual claims about the history of capitalist and patriarchal domination—or make ethical claims that such things should be overthrown—when one's own vision of these phenomena is itself historically conditioned and when generalizations and causal explanations are the residue of our own reifying narratives?

Chapter Three
Don DeLillo's *White Noise:* Reading Consumers and the Politics of Commodified Education

In the last chapter we investigated how Acker's *ALTL*, at the level of *text,* undermines traditional narrative form. It is appropriate, then, that we should now turn to investigate the consumer of texts, namely, the *reader.* I have chosen Don DeLillo's *White Noise* (1985) for this purpose. Many writers have said DeLillo's book discusses the plight of postmodern subjects in so called "postmodernity" (e.g. a fairly recent anthology edited by Frank Lentricchia 1996). Though these investigations are enormously important and do comment extensively on subjectivity, most have little to say about subjects *reading* DeLillo's text and what makes that text appealing.[12] The present chapter is a contribution toward understanding this aspect of postmodernism in general and DeLillo's novel in particular.

One thing we can safely say of DeLillo's *White Noise* is that as a piece of writing it remains very accessible. This is especially true if we compare it to the other two postmodern novels already discussed. In the first novel we examined, Ishmael Reed's *Mumbo Jumbo,* we saw Reed invoke myriad references to history and culture (e.g. history of America, Haitian Voodoo culture). But in many cases his references are to historical minutia (e.g. Julian the Apostate), which, though central to the work's meaning, require in depth research to understand their deeper significance. Moreover, Reed's work contains pictures and drawings without explicit reference to their origin or significance. If we add to this Reed's fanciful dropping of an android into nineteen twenties Harlem, we have a book that is certainly not for everyone.

Much the same can be said of Acker's *The Adult Life of Toulouse Lautrec by Henri Toulouse Lautrec.* It refuses the narrative closure promised

113

when it invokes the realist detective narrative. Moreover, it mixes the gender identity of a central character. Then there is Acker's constant use of profanity. These elements come together to make a book we can assume would not be terribly popular with readers of traditional narratives, be they readers of detection, members of The Book of the Month Club, consumers of Danielle Steel, or even afficionados of *Penthouse Forum* which, despite its possibly "objectionable" content, nevertheless offers traditional narrative structure and closure.[3]

We should say that an obvious element dividing DeLillo's postmodern work from Reed's and Acker's is its fairly straightforward narrative. It contains almost none of the experimental elements seen in Acker and Reed (e.g. drawings, cryptic references to history, refusal of narrative closure). But we can still consider DeLillo's novels postmodernist. Or, to introduce some precision, we might say his novels speak about individuals living within *postmodern culture,* which is to say that disconcerting economic and cultural condition of late capitalism. His characters—like many of his contemporary western readers—experience living in a culture driven by mass produced images and products. More on this later. For now, I simply want to remark that my aforementioned description of his work enables us to can classify DeLillo's novels as postmodern if by that we mean, as does Patrick Hogan, works which "represent and reflect upon postmodern culture and the postmodern condition" (Hogan, *Philosophical Approaches* 204).

Here, it is interesting to note another related difference between DeLillo's work and that of Reed and Acker. Specifically, unlike Reed's and Acker's work, DeLillo's has found a wide audience. DeLillo's fairly recent book, *Underworld* (1997), spent more than a few weeks on the *New York Times'* "Best Seller" list.[4] Moreover, as Janice Radway has remarked, *White Noise* was also offered as a book selection for members of the popular Book of the Month Club (Radway, "The Book of the Month Club" 1989). At the same time, DeLillo has received as much attention as Reed and Acker from a much smaller circle of readers in academia, as testified by numerous book length treatments of his work (LeClair1987; Kavadlo 2004;), collected essays edited by Frank Lentricchia (1996), not to mention essays published in scholarly journals (e.g. Maltby 1996).

Discovering DeLillo's Readership: Discursive Communities and the Use of Genre

Though reading narrowly circulated (academic) writing may prove helpful in codifying and articulating the qualities of postmodernity, its inescapable presence in our own lives (e.g. through ownership of a television, exposure to mass media) and the consequent overlapping of what we may loosely call "discursive communities," means that "getting" *White Noise*—appreciating its rendering of contemporary experience—is something open to a good many readers, even if they have never heard of Baudrillard's "simularcrum," or even the term "postmodernism." Granted, understanding of DeLillo's work may be different for academic and lay reader. But since both live in the same world of globalized media effects under late capitalism and share—at least to some extent—a similar inherited literary tradition, we may say that their "discursive communities" overlap; thus, it may be that they both appreciate, if differently and in somewhat different contexts, DeLillo's work.

Following Linda Hutcheon, we may say that a "discursive community" is not "'a sociorhetorical construct'" which remains "'neutral in terms of medium and unconstrained by space and time'"; rather, it is a concept which "acknowledges those strangely enabling constraints of discursive contexts and foregrounds the particularities not only of space and time but of class, race, gender, ethnicity, [and] sexual choice," as well as "nationality, religion, age, profession, and all the other micropolitical groupings in which we place ourselves or are placed by society" (Hutcheon, *Irony's Edge* 92; Swales qtd. in Hutcheon, *Irony's Edge* 92). However, this concept is similar to the "socio-rhetorical 'discourse community' in that it recognizes how "we all belong to many overlapping (and sometimes even conflicting) communities or collectives" (Hutcheon, *Irony's Edge* 92).[5] With expansive overlapping "discursive communities" it is possible, I think, to broadly categorize DeLillo's readers, especially if we also take American literary tradition and genre into account.[6]

The college novel and its sub-genre, the college mystery, offer particularly fruitful insights in this respect. As already noted, genres act as "literary *institutions,* which like other institutions of social life are based on tacit agreements or contracts. The thinking behind such a view of genres is based on the presupposition that all speech needs to be marked with certain indications and signals as to how it is properly to be used" (Fredric Jameson qtd. in Porter 84). Not surprisingly, then, genres as "literary institutions" are subject to social forces and help in the process of "acculturation" (Porter 84). Consequently, they are ideological and part of "Ideological State Apparatuses" (Althusser 1971). In this respect any given genre "'recruits' [or "interpellates"] subjects among individuals. . . ." (Althusser 174). In short, it offers readers a subject position, an identity, but as it is ideological, it does not necessarily correspond to reality. *White Noise* gives readers the reassuring subject position offered by the college novel genre, but its stretching of the genre's boundaries and constraints disturbs such identification in order to conduct a larger ideological critique of the university and society.

White Noise *as College Novel and Mystery: Crafting Genre for Molar and Molecular Readers*

That *White Noise* is, in part, a novel of college life seems evident from the fact that much of its action takes place in the university setting, "College-on-the-Hill." In this respect it follows the pattern of college novels published after World War II, which primarily focus on academic characters and their activities (Martin 1988; Lyons 1962). DeLillo's narrator in *White Noise* is himself an academic, a certain professor Jack Gladney; what is more, narrative focus rests primarily on his life around school and at home. For these reasons DeLillo's novel often seems to fall within the category of "college novel." As an important aside in this regard, we should also observe that a good many of these college novels, including those of the mystery variety, satirize academics; here, English novels like Malcolm Bradbury's *Stepping Westward* (1966), or David Lodge's *Changing Places* (1978) and *Small World* (1986) serve as notable examples, with Mary McCarthy's *The Groves of Academe* (1952) and Robert Grudin's comical *Book: The Novel* (1992) representing but two American instances (Lyons 1962; Bevan 1990; Parini 2000). Indeed, this satirical aspect is present almost from the very beginning of *White Noise,* when Gladney discusses his invention of "Hitler studies" and shortly after in representations of the "popular culture department" (*White Noise* 4, 9), all of which play on what some readers believe is the university's odd, disconnected and esoteric pursuits.

The mystery aspect of DeLillo's novel seems easily supported by a peripheral examination. We may, for instance note that a central aspect of *White Noise*—one rooted very early in the novel—is professor Jack Gladney's sleuth-like endeavor to discover who, exactly, supplies his wife (Babette) with the mind altering drug called "Dylar," a substance said to rid the user of the fear of death. In fact, Jack discovers his wife is using the medication early on, but does not understand its purpose until he confronts her much later in the novel, after which he pursues her supplier (Willie Mink) and shoots him, though ultimately has a change of heart and saves the man's life (*White Noise* 37, 196, 189–193). Such plotting suggests we are talking about *more* than the basic hermeneutic model of question and answer, a principle driving virtually every kind of novel.

Instead, *White Noise* gives a "nameable sequence"—or a proairetic code—which plots events out according to the strongly determinative hermeneutic code of detective or mystery fiction (Porter 86). This seems evident enough in the brief but compelling instances above which, when taken together, contain elements of suspense and its (partial) relief through

Don DeLillo's White Noise

tight plotting. This plotting is important to traditional detective or mystery fiction, and further demonstration of it in DeLillo might be fruitful. However, what I would like to focus on is the other predominant code, namely, the hermeneutic code. From our previous discussion of the hermeneutic code's role in detection (see chapter three), we know that it works by offering tantalizing questions which the detective or mystery text will answer, all in the slow push to final revelation or disclosure. Certainly, *White Noise* as part college mystery exhibits this tendency, as seen in the above example wherein Jack finds the drug dealer, Willie Mink. However, there are occasional—and I would say crucial—moments when DeLillo short-circuits that traditional (mystery) reading process by offering questions without answers. These moments speak to readers even as they disappoint expectations of revelation.

While I believe *White Noise* possesses a good number of these reader-unfriendly moments, I will confine myself to two here. In the first example Jack tells us about his proposal to the university chancellor that College-on-the-Hill start a Hitler studies program: "When I suggested to the chancellor that we might build a whole department around Hitler's life and work, he was quick to see the possibilities. It was an immediate and electrifying success. The chancellor went on to serve as adviser to Nixon, Ford and Carter before his death on a ski lift in Austria" (*White Noise* 4).

In the second example Jack runs into Murray Siskind, a professor in "American environments" at the college who, earlier in the novel, announces his bitter power struggle with another professor, Dimitrios Cotsakis, over teaching rights to Elvis Presley and the late King's pop-culture legacy (*White Noise* 64–65). In a latter chance encounter at the supermarket Murray tells Jack of Cotsakis' demise:

> 'You know that matter you helped me with? The Elvis Presley power struggle?' 'Sure. I came in and lectured.' 'It turns out, tragically, that I would have won anyway.' 'What happened?' 'Cotsakis, my rival, is no longer among the living.' 'What does that mean?' 'It means he's dead.' 'Dead?' 'Lost in the surf off Malibu. During the term break. I found out an hour ago. Came right here.' (*White Noise* 168)

Now, let us return to the episode between Jack and the chancellor and analyze it. Since Jack is the narrator of *White Noise* and the story involves, at least in part, his activities in the university, it makes sense that our first example has him comment on how he became chairman of Hitler studies ("I suggested to the chancellor that we might build a whole department around

Hitler's life and work"); equally, it seems relevant to register the chancellor's excitement about the idea ("he was quick to see the possibilities"), and to observe that the department was indeed created and that it attained popularity ("It was an immediate and electrifying success"). However, Jack's genealogy of Hitler studies concludes with remarks that not only raise questions, but also seem out of place ("The chancellor went on to serve as adviser to Nixon, Ford and Carter before his death on a ski lift in Austria"). The information offered does not illuminate the tale told, at least not overtly; in fact, the chancellor is never mentioned again. Nor, would we say this sentence functions to achieve a "realistic" effect within the narrative; there is no list of extraneous material objects located around their meeting place to give the weight of real material existence. But the sentence does do something else. It imposes a hint of foul play relating to the precise nature of our chancellor's death on some far away Austrian "ski lift." But DeLillo drops this issue, never to return to the chancellor or his rather suspicious death.

The second example, involving Murray and Cotsakis, does something similar, while simultaneously illustrating an operative principle in college mystery. Conventions of college mystery are seen in its characterization, while its similarity to the sentence just examined stems from an equally frustrated hermeneutic code. To see how it does both these things, let us first segue through its use of college mystery convention and then go on to see how that plays into the question of hermeneutic frustration.

To begin, we can note that university mysteries, especially American, frequently portray learning institutions as places populated with "eccentrics" obsessed with their subject matter (Kramer, "The American College Mystery" 8). While there are numerous American examples, an early one is Vladimir Nabokov's *Pnin* (1957), about a Russian emigre academic with bad teeth who slaughters American vernacular speech (Bevan 1990); a good later instance is Robert Grudin's *Book: A Novel* (1992), which satirizes professors through the lens of their individual theoretical *idée fixe,* be it deconstruction, feminism, or Marxism. *White Noise* follows this tradition. Indeed, College-on-the-Hill's American environments department gives readers exactly this eccentric faculty; Jack, our narrator, calls them "a curious group" and notes that the department "is composed almost solely of New York émigrés, smart, thuggish, movie-mad, trivia-crazed" (*White Noise* 9). Now John Kramer observes that once a group of eccentric faculty have been assembled in a college mystery, it is left for the teaching institution to "systematically pit them against each other in a blizzard of conflicting situations"; these often involve "intense competition over small stakes" (Kramer, "The American College Mystery" 8). In the college mystery, of course, such competition frequently leads to foul play. Indeed the episode

Don DeLillo's White Noise

above would seem to promise that. Here, Murray—a character observant readers might reasonably see as the beneficiary of a faculty competitor's death—reveals that "Cotsakis," his "rival, is no longer among the living"; he is, as Murray succinctly puts it, "dead . . . Lost in the surf off Malibu." In this instance DeLillo *appears* to invoke the typical college mystery form. Our text has already informed readers of Murray's rivalry with Cotsakis; the "small stakes" of their rivalry are, of course, the meager salaries paid at most liberal arts schools; but they are also stakes for intellectual turf—in this case Elvis's legacy—the cultural capital over which eccentrics like Murray and Cotsakis battle. The disappearance of Cotsakis and Murray's clear rivalry with him invoke the reading contract of college mystery, namely, that a murder has surely occurred (Cotsakis') and that the murderer (Murray?) will eventually be exposed. But DeLillo's novel is as frustrating in this instance as in the chancellor example. *White Noise* offers no explanation here or elsewhere for the exact circumstances of our victim's death. The issue is simply dropped. DeLillo leaves it as a mystery never solved.

However, such puzzling features do not necessarily drive away readers. Indeed, if we divert our attention from DeLillo's use of information seeming to serve no immediate function in the events recounted, we can find a certain attraction in the two selections just examined. For example, rivalries such as those between Murray and Cotsakis, as well as Jack's clever scheming to start his own department, speak directly to readers teaching in universities. As Kramer remarks, "the college mystery," gives academics "a chance to read about the peccadilloes of people very much like themselves and their fellow denizens of academe. It allows them, as well, to witness hyperbolized versions of the dramas they regularly experience as part of their working lives" (Kramer, "The American College Mystery" 13).

On the other hand, for non-academic readers—especially if they were once undergraduates in universities themselves—the university based mystery can offer a kind of "belated insight"; as John Kramer remarks,

> many undergraduate find the higher education environment mysterious, and that portion occupied by faculty not only mysterious but threatening as well. By reading college mysteries former students learn, or at least think they learn, the ugly details about the dark undercurrents of academe which they always suspected were present. ("The American College Mystery" 13)

If we return momentarily to the small section DeLillo devotes to the chancellor, we can see a clear illustration of a common aspect in college mystery related to the aforementioned ugly and dark elements, but it also takes us beyond the confines of a single genre, and thus to different readers. In particular I refer to Jack's comment that "the chancellor went on to serve as adviser to Nixon, Ford and Carter before his death." Here, academia (i.e. via the chancellor) is linked to death (his) and the presidency (through service to Nixon, Ford, and Carter). Nixon, perhaps the most infamous of the three, certainly brings numerous ideas to readers' minds. Regardless of whether or not one reads alternative or marginalized press, most of us know about the secret criminal break-ins conducted at the behest of president Richard Nixon; the break-ins, of course, were subsequently revealed and make for the now famous "Watergate" scandal which destroyed Nixon's presidency. This connection between the sacrosanct value of a democratically elected presidency, the betrayal of that presidency via Nixon's secret crimes, and death occurs within the space of a mere two sentences. In close textual proximity to these remarks is Jack's proposal of Hitler studies to the chancellor, which occurs in "1968," a year when Nixon was in office. But in that connection it also elicits the specter of the Vietnam War. It thus brings to readers' minds various unsavory activities of the United States government, including one action which actually took place in sixty-eight (the My Lai massacre), but also America's earlier surreptitious undermining of democratic elections in Viet Nam and the wholesale invention of "facts" leading to the "Tonkin Resolution," not to mention the very character of the war itself, which—regardless of claims about the communist "domino effect"—was rooted in imperialism, colonialism, and a variety of capitalist interests (e.g. oil).[7]

While some of these connections require readers to appreciate Nixon's lesser known crimes (e.g. his COINTELPRO shenanigans),[8] almost all of us are aware of "Watergate." Moreover, we should note that regardless of readers' familiarity with Nixon's lesser known crimes, the social effects of his better known offences have been long lived; therefore, it does not seem outlandish to note a certain contemporary cynicism in many quarters of public consciousness regarding the viability of the democratic political process, and along with it an accompanying suspicion that secret or illegal political dealings persist.[9] More to the point, such social history leaves readers with a troubling sense there exist secrets or conspiracies as yet unrevealed.

At the same time, if we return to the deaths of Cotsakis and the chancellor, we find DeLillo connecting such secrecy to the ordinariness of supermarkets and their surroundings. In sentences I did not include above, but which directly follow the chancellor's death, DeLillo inserts various mundane quotidian sights on the way to the store: "At Fourth and Elm, cars turn . . . for the supermarket. A policewoman . . . patrols the area looking for cars parked illegally, for meter violations, lapsed inspection stickers. On telephone poles all over town there are homemade signs concerning lost dogs and cats . . ." (*White Noise* 4). These sights are at once comforting in their regularity—one would expect the policewoman tickets everyday—and reassuring in their implied small town communal spirit; surely kind neighbors will see the "homemade signs" posted "all over town" and return these lost pets to their owners.

In our second example Murray's revelation of Cotsakis' death takes place in "the generic food area" of a supermarket (*White Noise* 168). Here, the conjunction of death and supermarket causes Jack to see differently, to become "aware of the dense environmental texture" of the locale; in this case even the market's electric doors attain a quality of life all their own ("doors opened and closed, breathing abruptly"), and the store's environment attains a certain clarity, even if it is not entirely understandable ("Colors and odors seemed sharper") (*White Noise* 168).

In sum, then, we may say that our numerous connections above bring together horrific mass killing ("Hitler") with mysterious individual death (Cotsakis,' the chancellor's) and conspiracy or intrigue ("Nixon"). But DeLillo's text surrounds these with the quotidian banalities of supermarkets, though even these become endowed with phantasmagorical character ("doors . . . breathing"). As a result *White Noise* gives readers the comfort of the everyday, but tinges that everyday with menace and mystery, putting in layer upon layer of uncertainty. In fact, it would be easy to cite numerous other instances entailing mystery. For example, we have DeLillo's abiding concern with language that implies deeper unknown or undecipherable elements in contemporary reality: "Remarks existed in a state of permanent flotation. No one thing was either more or less plausible than any other thing" (129). Here, statements of supposed facts ("remarks") lose veracity and are reduced to "a state of permanent floatation" wherein truth is indiscernible, since "no one thing" seems "less plausible than any other thing." In another case, knowledge itself becomes problematic: "What good is knowledge if it just floats in the air? It goes from computer to computer. It changes and grows every second of every day. But nobody actually knows anything" (149). In this case knowledge attains at best an ephemeral quality, or at worst becomes simply gas-like ("it just floats in the air"); though it "grows every second of every day"—and thus at exponential rate—it does so only as information in memory transferred "from computer to computer"; hence, no one can access it or analyze it ("nobody actually knows anything"). In fact, nothing escapes this effect as even the private sphere of home life becomes tangled in mystery. Thus in one instance Jack gazes around his daughter's room and sees nothing but a locale "rich in codes and messages, an archaeology of childhood . . ." (*White Noise* 103)

But we may also locate another element indicative of mystery which expands audience beyond readers of college suspense to readers demanding just a little more from a literary work. This element reveals itself if we examine "The Book of the Month Club" (hereafter BOMC) and its offering of *White Noise* to readers as an alternate selection for the month. I take my cue here from Janice Radway, who explicates that club membership in her cogent essay, "The Book-of-the-Month Club and the General Reader" (1989). While I will also use Radway later in this essay to make other points about DeLillo's readership, here I employ her work primarily to show how *White Noise* uses a certain literary technique which at once evokes mystery, but also calls in readers looking for certain so called "high" literary modes. At the same time, we will see that the technique exists in tension with a more dominant element whose presence assures retention of a wider reading public.

We can begin by examining the BOMC's book selection criteria and setting it against Fredric Jameson's rather arcane construel of modernist literature's key characteristic. Jameson considers linguistic experimentation— pushing language to its limits—as "the *molecular* project of modernism" (Radway, "The Book of the Month Club" 271; italics mine). But the editors' "reader reports" for BOMC.—primary determinates of club offerings to its members—center "on a few of the abstract *molar unities* (constructions produced by the reader to create plot, personality, coherent character, and so on)" within works (Radway, "The Book of the Month Club," 271; italics mine). More plainly, Jameson finds the essence of modernism in the "individual sentence, the electrifying shock of the *individual word or the individual brush stroke*" (Jameson qtd. in Homer 87; italics mine). In short, it is a text's ability to push language at the smaller level of sentence, word, or phrase (i.e. the molecular level).

On the other hand, BOMC editors, "are not interested in those books that foreground their interest in language to such an extent that they are *about* language, its possibilities and constraints" (Radway, "The Book of the Month Club 273). Instead, they locate much—though not all—of their interest in the work's larger (molar) elements, namely, aspects which—when taken together—unify the work (e.g. plotting, character cohesion).[10] That is, BOMC editors favor—at least in large part—exactly the opposite set of characteristics as those exhibited in "high" modernist literature; or, if we were to employ Jameson's phrasing, the editors prefer "'the continuity of personal identity, the organizing unity of the . . . personality,'" and the part each takes "in the creation of a significant narrative" (Jameson qtd. in Radway, "The Book of the Month Club and the General Reader" 272).[11]

Don DeLillo's White Noise

DeLillo's *White Noise* is in fact very molar in character. DeLillo's narrator, professor Jack Gladney, is a well formed character. He is a professor of "Hitler studies," has a wife and children; he lives in a small town, shops, converses with colleagues (e.g. Murray Siskind) and confesses his fear of death to readers: "I don't want to die first. Given the choice between loneliness and death, it would take me a fraction of a second to decide" (*White Noise* 102). More to the point, he centers the narrative. His character is relatively static through the entirety of the work, as readers see him pursue Babette's drug dealer, learn German, and face shopping malls.

At the same time, certain elements in *White Noise* speak to readers of the "high" modernist sort. These elements appear very similar to those Jameson describes as molecular; in particular, they represent usages of language which do not correspond to common grammatical rules and also appear out of context within the primary narrative. There are times when the molecular elements seem somewhat contextual in that they appear within Jack's narration of his jaunt through a supermarket: "Kleenex Softique, Kleenex Softique" "Dristan Ultra, Dristan Ultra" (*White Noise* 39; 159). But in another case DeLillo inserts the molecular while Jack is discussing death with Babette, his wife, over a plate of eggs: "MasterCard, Visa, American Express" (*White Noise* 99). At another point, such elements interject as the Gladney family flees the "airborne toxic event": "Krylon, Rust-Oleum, Red Devil" (*White Noise* 153).

While these moments may have a message, and indeed I think they do, their presence disrupts traditional reading habits of those concerned primarily with story and plot. On the surface of things, their inclusion appears jarring and apparently out of context. This effect is due in part to language, namely, language presented outside the structuring force of the sentence. The individual reading DeLillo's text has, up until each of these moments, been reading a narrative composed of ostensibly meaningful sentences, one following from another logically. But here, we have no verb, no complete meaning, no sentence. In short, we have the molecular intrusion into the molar.

This, I think, has several effects. On the one hand, such molecular moments would appeal to readers seeking *more* than the commercial college novel—or commercial novels generally—namely, it would speak to those people looking for books containing something beyond the traditional solidifying and coherent elements (e.g. absolutely unifying college professor-narrator who precludes fragmentation of meaning at the molecular sentence level). On the other hand, DeLillo's novel also does the opposite; since the narrative is overwhelmingly controlled by the molar (e.g. plotting, character, narrator), it never repels readers accustomed to traditional molar works.

Though molecular elements intrude (e.g. "MasterCard, Visa, American Express"), DeLillo never lets them take over the book. Finally, what DeLillo also creates is a tension between the molar and molecular which produces mystery or enigma. The (molecular) language noted above is so jolting and incompatible with what has come before it—namely, stable and coherent narrative—that readers cannot help but shift into a very conscious hermeneutic hide and seek. Or, put by way of a question, "What possible meaning could fragmentary bits of language like 'MasterCard, Visa, American Express' have for this tale?"

In this respect such molecular moments may bear a striking resemblance to the frustration effect noted earlier in the deaths of Cotsakis and the chancellor. As such, they contribute to the pervasive sense of mystery within *White Noise*. In fact, language intimating mystery and enigma actually recurs so often that readers—mystery fans and otherwise—always feel uneasy anticipation while reading, a sense that full revelation awaits, if only on the next page. That is, despite his book's solution to its apparently central mystery—namely, the nature of Dylar and its distributor—the frequency and number of other puzzling linguistic moments (like ones above) leave readers at the novel's end in a state of unfulfilled expectation, but more importantly, mystified and disturbed about the nature of contemporary reality. Though DeLillo's book is only partly a college mystery, his questioning of the contemporary nevertheless illustrates how college "who-done-its" and college novels more generally have "matured from . . . narrow novel[s] of academic manners into . . . highly philosophical novel[s]" (Martin 52).[12]

Indeed, much of the discussion connecting Nixon's corruption to academics (e.g. the chancellor, but also Jack Gladney as professor of "Hitler studies") hints at this maturation. At the same time, we should still register the very traditional appeal of the corrupted academic to readers. For example, in a conventional sense what we observe above is a case of guilt by association. That is, for readerly pleasure DeLillo practices the old art of insulting academics by linking them—in this case through the chancellor—with the politically and morally corrupt Nixon administration. Much the same could, of course, be said of professor Jack Gladney whose specialization is the corrupt and evil Adolf Hitler. The two instances thus illustrate a common attitude not only about academics, but the learned more generally. This practice, as Richard Sheppard indicates, is evidence of a "primitive fear" found not only in college mysteries, but literary tradition back to the "middle ages" (22). As John Lyons puts it, "The traditional literary picture of the professor is not complimentary. He is either a pedant whose studies have ill-equipped him to deal with life, or he is a person who has used his knowledge to control others" (106). Easy examples extend from Chaucer's Jankyn and his professorial ranting about woman's natural sinfulness to the professor characters in numerous instances of the *Bildungsroman* (Lyons 106–107). For more recent cases, we might think of Ian Fleming's portrayal of nefarious scientists (e.g. *Dr. No* (1958)), as well as the "quasi-criminal and morally dubious academics" seen in both American (e.g. Marion Mainwaring's *Murder at Midyears* (1954); Robert Parker's *The Godwulf Manuscript* (1974); David Slavitt's *Cold Comfort* (1980); Robert Grudin's *Book: A Novel* (1992)) and British novels (Reginald Hill's *An Advancement of Learning* (1971) Colin Dexter's *Last Bus to Woodstock* (1975)) (Sheppard 24; Kramer and Kramer 1983)).[13]

Richard Sheppard speculates that the denigration of academic for reader pleasure is "an inverted compliment or . . . a sinister threat . . ." (Sheppard 22). That is, we may say that "the learned, especially if they are scientists, alchemists or psychologists, pose a very real threat—not least in a culture which prides itself on its empirical common sense. . . . The learned know things which, although apparently useless in the eyes of others, make them feel ignorant . . ." (22). The academic, one form of learned person, owns knowledge that can menace lay people, even if that knowledge is merely a refined vocabulary and a honed ability to reason over problems. Nobody likes to feel stupid, and the academic is just the sort of know-it-all who can make a person feel that way simply by displaying knowledge or reason publicly.

Yet both academic and university are positioned paradoxically, at once straddling the world of dominant culture while also interrogating that culture. The fear we observed above is rooted partly in the idea that intellectual endeavors are very much about "opposing or subverting conventional wisdom," which prides itself—as noted above—on "common sense"; as such, academics' insignificant research or explorations "may well turn out to be deeply disturbing if not (literally) world-shattering. And that, from the conventional point of view, can look very much like subversive folly, irresponsible knavery, social treachery, or dabbling in the black arts" (Sheppard 22). This, in part, accounts for DeLillo's association of the chancellor with Nixon, who had little patience for legality in his role as chief executive. The chancellor as law breaker is similar to the academic researcher who revises "our world views"; at the same time, the chancellor—as academic—is very much a part of the law itself, much like the presidency as an institution, despite Nixon's abuses. In this function the chancellor—as academic—is actively involved in "standardizing current knowledge and ideology," if often doing so through bureaucratic channels (Martin 55). In this sense we can see the teacher and her teaching institution as "at once progressive and conservative" (Martin 55); more plainly, academics and schools have pursued free and sometimes revolutionary thought, while at the same time attempting to reproduce the present status quo.

However, this reading seems only partly satisfying. Its close association of academics (the chancellor, Jack Gladney) with Nixon's corruption and the even more depraved figure Adolf Hitler would seem to demand more in the way of interpretation. Moreover, the ongoing decline of the humanities' importance—a decline evinced in sheer number of courses—would seem to problematize ideas about interrogating and liberatory instruction. We can, however, achieve a more satisfying interpretation of all this if we consider one recent development in both the college novel and its mystery sub-genre. I mentioned earlier that college mysteries have become "highly philosophical," but we may add to this an idea that seems implicit in some of what has already been said, namely, that such novels have started to exhibit "an interest in the university as a social, political, and cultural microcosm" (Martin 55). A good English example, as Gyde Christine Martin notes, is Malcolm Bradbury's *The History Man* (1975), with its scathing critique of anti-humanism in the university, something Bradbury himself blamed on social-political "sadomonetarism" or "economic functionalism" extant in society more generally (Martin 55; Bradbury qtd. in Wilson 1990 61).

White Noise *and the Move to a Corporatized University*

It should come as no surprise that the university should offer a "social, political, and cultural microcosm" of larger communal relations. In this respect university can mirror larger social realms in a number of ways, but DeLillo's chancellor—corrupted on only the fourth page of the novel by ties to Nixon and Hitler—marks an important instance of such mirroring. More to the point, it says something about the state of education, but also about conditions in contemporary American society, culture and economics. That DeLillo announces this connection in the first few pages of *White Noise* illustrates the importance of it to the book's wider project. Of course, as I have tried to suggest, to make such connections and observations is to speak about lived experience in contemporary America; thus, *White Noise* speaks to people more generally—that is, to a wider discursive community—than just the community interested in college novels or college mysteries.

If we return again to the chancellor, we can see but another of the ways DeLillo's college novel element reflects the smaller and larger realms of university and nation. We can note, for instance, that the chancellor represents a high academic-bureaucratic figure who reigns over the university. While he is probably qualified to teach, his responsibilities—like those of Nixon and

Hitler—are primarily on a higher administrative level that interacts with political and economic interests both inside and outside the immediate institution. In the case of Nixon and Hitler the immediate institutions are governmental (the U.S. presidency and German chancellorship), while the college chancellor's unique province is heading an educational institution. But the three are similar in that they all possess the air of corrupted bureaucratic or administrative power.

In a very general sense DeLillo's corrupted chancellor mirrors higher bureaucratic corruption at the party level. Here, the sequential service of the chancellor to both republican (Nixon, Ford) and democrat (Carter) illustrate the degree. His political pliability can only be accounted for in a few ways. It may be that he has no particular ideological commitment to either party, but if that is so, he is nothing but a mercenary. He may also compartmentalize his advisory service to different ideologies—under the guise of "it's my job"—but that would simply make him a victim of that ideological tendency under capitalism to divide labor and reify. Lastly, we may look at it somewhat differently. Perhaps DeLillo merely wishes to invalidate the distinction between democrat and republican, namely, by showing the two parties as essentially the same. In other words the chancellor's sequential service to presidents Nixon, Ford, and Carter signifies the increasingly delegitimized state of the two party system; the two are essentially the same and serving similar masters. It really does not matter whether DeLillo's chancellor serves for selfish mercenary reasons or from a compartmentalizing viewpoint. Either way, the chancellor's individual choices—themselves indicative of the capitalist ideology which valorizes autonomous subjectivity and achievement—illustrate *visible* examples of raw power (i.e. the way things change but remain the same). The visibility of the example—the chancellor's record of vacillating party loyalty—is the empirical evidence of an increasingly delegitimized democratic state wherein the *illusion* of real community and choice is imperiled.

But this is only part of the story. We may also see how the chancellor's responsibility within the college bears functional and structural similarities to larger political, economic, and educational systems. The thinking of Jürgen Habermas is helpful in understanding these similarities. Habermas sees late capitalism through a general systems model that has three sub-systems (Habermas, *Legitimation Crisis* 1975).[14] These are the economic, political and social/cultural systems. The state (i.e. the political sphere) works hand in hand with the economic system (i.e. the "privately owned capitalist enterprises" producing goods and services (Pusey 94)) to keep the latter robust. At the same time, both these systems—economic and political—require ongoing legitimation or rationalization from the social/cultural system; the latter functions, in short, to "maintain popular assent and mass loyalty" (Pusey 95). Without that legitimation, the entirety of systems goes into crisis. Our last example—the chancellor advising both democrats and republicans—illustrates a symptom of such crisis because it could imperil notions of "popular assent" and "mass loyalty."

It is notable, however, that this last system—the social/cultural—also requires maintenance. One avenue of maintenance arrives through money the state (i.e. political system) gets from the economic sphere (e.g. in taxes); this, the state invests in "social, educational and welfare services," all of which maintain the social/cultural system's ideological support of the state and economy (Pusey 95). Now, the university is one element of the social/cultural system, and by way of background, certain elements need emphasis. First, in the early nineteen-forties the U.S. government placed "scientific research and development in universities, *not* industrial installations [i.e. capitalist industry] or government institutes" (Poovey 2; italics mine).[15] Moreover, "government support for university science heavily favored *research over the development of specific products*"; this, along with looser rules governing "the use of federal funds, like the provision for indirect costs, enabled universities to support programs not directly linked to the sciences," which meant schools could allocate funds to other departments (Poovey 2; italics mine), like English, or in the fictional case of *White Noise*, Hitler studies. Thus, in Poovey's words,

> the combination of government support for university science and provisions that allowed universities to redistribute this wealth beyond the sciences enabled universities to acquire a remarkable degree of relative autonomy in modern U.S. society. This autonomy is signaled by the universities' ability to foster programs that do not pay for themselves [as in the case of the Humanities], to establish and maintain standards of academic freedom, and to successfully defend the institution of tenure, despite complaints that the latter violates the principles of a free market in labor. (2)

As a relevant aside, it is worth mentioning again that Jack's discussion with the chancellor about creating a department of Hitler studies occurs in 1968 (*White Noise* 4). Upon consulting Poovey's research, we find that between the nineteen-forties and roughly nineteen-sixty-four university funding in science "grew at an exponential rate," but grew no more after nineteen-sixty-four (Poovey 3). One can therefore surmise—given the loose allocation rules for university funding already noted—that there existed a relatively friendly climate for that department's creation. Indeed, though funding did not increase after nineteen-sixty-four, neither did it decrease for some time, nor were the majority of allocation rules changed until much later.

At the same time, as most currently employed academics know, the friendly climate did change, and it followed along the path very much like the one outlined by Habermas for advanced capitalism, as seen, for instance, in America circa nineteen eighties and nineties when the economic system increasingly infects the social/cultural system (in this case the university). By way of example, we may remember the Reaganomics of the mid-nineteen eighties. This is the very time *White Noise* is written and takes place. While the book's copyright date (nineteen-eighty-five) proves nothing on its own, if we add to it DeLillo's mention of numerous products present in the late seventies and early eighties (e.g. "Dristan Ultra," "Kleenex Softique" (*White Noise* 167, 39)), as well as the book's reference to "Acquired Immune Deficiency Syndrome" (*White Noise* 298)—a disease that first appeared in America and received popular press in the early eighties—we have some pretty convincing evidence of the rough date. It was during the early to mid-eighties governmental funding of universities diminished significantly as the former increasingly drew away from the public sphere. These cutbacks, of course, affected all elements within the university, but the financial blow to the humanities was—and continues to be—particularly striking, since of the billions in federal cash given to universities, "almost none . . . goes directly to humanities departments or professors" (Poovey 3).

However, it would be a mistake to view these changes too simply. They must be appreciated in the wider context of developing global capitalism. Together with this we must consider the way the state (as political system) retools the social/cultural institution of the university at both an ideological and material level to improve economic conditions, and thereby maintain legitimacy. In the economic realm, as Mary Poovey indicates, fear of "international competition . . . encouraged lawmakers to redirect funds from discretionary programs (like education) to programs thought likely to contribute to technological innovation and economic competitiveness" (Poovey 6).[16] In addition, such elements were augmented by corporate sponsorship, but corporations past and present operate within capitalist principles, so they make either explicit or implicit demands upon dollar hungry universities for this sponsorship; thus, as Sheila Slaughter and Larry Leslie note, "'faculty and institutions [have] *lost autonomy*. . . . The freedom of professors to pursue curiosity-driven research [has been] curtailed by withdrawal of more or less automatic funding to support this activity and by the increased targeting of R&D funds for *commercial research*'" (Slaughter and

Leslie qtd. in Poovey 6; italics mine). Let us reiterate that what we observe here is fundamental change at the level of both subject (individual academic) and institution (university). Moreover, this loss of autonomy is directly related to the economic sphere. As Slaughter and Leslie indicate,

> the center of the academy has shifted from a liberal arts core to an entrepreneurial periphery . . . : policies for academic R&D, . . . [have become] science and technology policies, more concerned with technoscience innovation and building links with the private sector than with basic or fundamental research that articulate[s] with learned and professional associations and less with the economy. For the most part, technoscience fields [have] gained resource shares while fields that were not close to the market, such as philosophy and religion, foreign languages, letters and performing arts, or fields that served the social welfare functions of the state, such as education and home economics, have lost shares. (Slaughter and Leslie qtd. in Poovey 6)

But what does this mean in terms of DeLillo's novel and my previous discussion of the chancellor? The answers are several and require some mental backtracking. First, as already mentioned, the chancellor's link with mystery and corruption follows a long tradition. But I have also remarked that DeLillo makes these links contemporary (e.g. "Nixon," "Ford," "Carter") as a subtle sign of the book's subject. Our above digression into Habermas and the present state of the real university serves as background for DeLillo's fictional picture of the contemporary liberal arts university in the nineteen-eighties. It also links, as we shall see, with mystery and the fear that mystery often invokes.

Reason's U-Turn and the Fully Capitalist Education

We may begin by locating a first link in the contemporary loss of university autonomy at both the subjective (individual academic) and institutional level (university level). As the situation now stands, *reason*—as practiced in and by the university—is chained in the manner noted above. That is, it exists solely to carve commercial products out of nature for the benefit of the "private sector," or to produce research geared toward that end ("technoscience innovation"). Reason put to critical and political purpose—loosely speaking, the humanities as "liberal arts core" striving ideally "to preserve, nurture, analyze, interrogate, and interpret [culture, which is] the human" (Poovey 8)—has been overwhelmed. It has been taken over; or, in the words of Slaughter and Leslie, it has been moved to the "entrepreneurial periphery" by a market driven model of education. Though Horkheimer and Adorno (1972) note the tendency of reason to turn against itself as early as Enlightenment, observing that it [reason] "recognizes no function other than the preparation of the object . . . in order to make it the material of subjugation," it is not until advanced capitalism that reason's u-turn accomplishes its highest form; here, "The true nature of *schematism*, of the general and the particular, of concept and individual case reconciled from without, is ultimately revealed in contemporary science as the interest of industrial society," wherein, we must understand, "being is apprehended under the aspect of *manufacture* and *administration*. Everything—even the human individual, not to speak of the animal—is converted into repeatable, replaceable process, into a mere example for the conceptual models of the system"(Horkheimer and Adorno 84; italics mine).

In short, the liberal arts university's mission, its very being, is in crisis because the elements valued (e.g. interrogation, analysis, interpretation of culture) no longer apply in a place where a market ideology forces institutions to view themselves as capitalist enterprises conducting efficient "manufacture" under equally proficient "administration." As we have already noted, DeLillo links the chancellor of College-on-the-Hill with the moral corruption of Hitler ("Hitler studies"), the political corruption of Nixon, and service to presidents Ford and Carter. This linkage foregrounds the *administrative* parallel between the chancellor as university functionary of the nineteen-eighties and these lofty, if questionable, political-administrative figures. Though the higher achievement of schematized and administrative procedures—as well as a matching globalized economic structure—do not occur until after the chancellor's death (i.e. during the Reagan presidency of the nineteen eighties), the retooling of the academic machine is well on its way in the nineteen-seventies; to see it we need only look at the number of undergraduates steered to the functionalist disciplines of business: "Since the early 1970s," remarks Poovey, "the enrollment and percentage of [undergraduate] majors in all liberal arts disciplines . . . declined relative to those in professional subjects, like accounting and computer science"(6).[17]

However, the corresponding shrinkage in liberal arts courses necessitated by these changing enrolment patterns probably tells us something about the kinds of college novels written in such crisis periods. Richard Sheppard, plotting the academic novel's changing status in England from the mid-nineteen fifties through the nineteen-seventies and eighties, notes that negative stereotypical depictions of professors or administrators—much like ones already mentioned—occur during periods marked by a crisis in faith regarding the university's mission (Sheppard 19–22).[18]

At the same time, this crisis may account for the college mystery's attraction in another way. Specifically, with rapid growth of functionalist disciplines (e.g. business, accounting, computer science) the college mystery's appeal may lie in the reader's own nostalgia for pre-functionalist education. Here, "attention to life-and-death issues in departments such as English and history"—though we could just as well substitute *White Noise*'s Hitler studies and American Environments—gives readers "an opportunity to revisit the prominence of the liberal arts, if only on the pages of a whodonit"; thus, besides offering crisis as symptomatic sub-text, the college mystery presents readers with an opportunity to engage in "nostalgia" (Kramer, "The American College Mystery" 14).

While such nostalgia might well attract readers to *White Noise*, it is nevertheless tempered by the negative schematization of the university and the liberal arts crisis. While I have primarily offered the chancellor as a key representative of this schematizing tendency, DeLillo's narrator, professor Jack Gladney, figures prominently as accomplice. Certainly, Jack is complicit in university schematization—the formalizing process of capitalist colonization of higher education—through both his lower bureaucratic responsibilities as "chairman . . . of Hitler studies" (*White Noise* 4) and as everyday teacher in the classroom. In order to address Jack as an academic, however, we should emphasize again how schematization represents an all encompassing proposition affecting all human activity; nothing escapes its touch. General schematizing of the university—indicative of larger social-economic schematizing—seems clear enough given our previous findings. Logically, however, we would also expect to find schematized organization applying to academic disciplines and professional life generally, as well as to discourses within individual disciplines (e.g. professional writing done by Jack Gladney within the discipline of "Hitler studies").

Unsurprisingly, capitalist schematization similarly controls and structures academic discourse in *White Noise*. Moreover, his cryptic references to schematized academic discourse connect directly with the previously mentioned humanities crisis, if in a somewhat different way. As will become apparent, this crisis relates in part to who reads and writes academic discourse. In terms of *White Noise* as a university novel, some have said that recent depictions of crisis in the genre are "manifestations of a loss of confidence in the central importance of literature" and the death of the Leavisite legacy (Schellenberger 46–47). This seems partly true, even if one does not necessarily mourn the Leavis legacy's death, if it is dead.[19]

However, the Marxist sociologist Ben Agger observes that such claims often seem a bit elitist in placing blame. In particular it accuses people not only of failing to read quality material—whatever that is—but also argues they are altogether incapable of reading such material. Moreover, Agger remarks that the popular and convenient position advanced places blame entirely on readers. As a solution, this version of the argument—as embodied, for example, in Allan Bloom (1987)—advocates "classics as castor oil" in an effort to better educate an ignorant public" (Agger, *The Decline of Discourse* 39).

But Agger views things differently. He sees it as both a *reading* and *writing* problem, but one that is institutional. On the reading end, he points to "the sheer absence of a reading public"; but his accusation is not elitist because this absence "*is effectively a product of particular social and economic arrangements of knowledge*" (Agger, *The Decline of Discourse* 33–34). Knowledge, as we all know, is power; so controlling access to it through particular "social and economic arrangements" enables domination. Those with the knowledge rule, have social control. Presently, capitalist interests maintain social control—dominate—by "determining [the] institutional forms intelligence is *allowed* to take," which is to say they institutionally manipulate relationships to knowledge (Agger 34; italics mine). In particular, "intelligence has been removed from a traditional literary culture into other realms, notably *popular culture* and *academia*" (Agger, *The Decline of Discourse* 34; italics mine). In this fashion "intellectuality is channeled to serve dominant institutions, thus losing the vitality of public life taken up with lively debate about larger social purposes" (Agger, *The Decline of Discourse* 34). In terms of the written word, intelligent writers are still among us, but because of capitalist social and economic arrangements, "they serve other masters, working in television, journalism, the university and the professions" (Agger, *The Decline of Discourse* 34).

Two things are important here. First, what we lose through this channeling of intellectuality is discourse within the "public sphere." Loss of this discourse equals loss of democracy. But what is the "public sphere" exactly, and how does its decline equate with loss of democracy? Agger, following Habermas and others, remarks that discourse, to be public—within the public sphere—"must embody public comprehensibility; that is, it must shun "narrow subservience to disciplines, within their highly differentiated argot" (Agger, *The Decline of Discourse* 37).

But as Agger notes, "public comprehensibility" *alone* does not make discourse part of the public sphere; after all, within the popular culture realm most of the public comprehends sitcoms like *Everybody Loves Raymond* or *Friends*. Instead, something else is needed. "To be discourse [in the public sphere]," argues Agger, "writing must solicit its own response by readers empowered to understand it and then engage with it" (Agger, *The Decline of Discourse* 37). Elements of response and engagement within the public sphere are critical for democracy because without them we have obedience rather than participation; or, put by way of example, without engagement in the public sphere, we have passive television viewers interpellated by advertisements or *Time* readers accepting magazine articles as unauthored, independent facts. Writers in both cases serve the channeling function for capitalist interests, at once reproducing status quo power relations within readers while also furthering an active ideology of consumption. What they write demands no response or engagement on the reader's part, but rather obedient *action*. It is writing for the highly schematized late capitalist mode, wherein virtually everything—including writing and reading activities—functions toward production and acts of consumption. In this respect all critical reading or examination is forgone in the public sphere and immediately shuttled into obedient behaviors.

Here, I follow Ben Agger's broadly defined idea of "reading" in his book *Fast Capitalism* (1989). For Agger, the late capitalist situation is one in which textuality (ideology) is dispersed into all environments. The dispersed textuality (ideology) becomes naturalized (*appears* natural) and is taken in by people without the conscious intermediary process of reading and engaged interpretation; the more this occurs, the more ideology gains material control. As he puts it, "The more texts are dispersed into an external environment in which they are not recognized as such and thus only enacted immediately as the agendas they really are—work, consume, marry, procreate, kill: GIVE IN—the more textuality, formerly Marx's ideology, gains material force" (Agger, *Fast Capitalism* 61). Obviously, such ideologized textuality is the opposite of communication in the public sphere, which *does* demand engagement and response, or a kind of writing-back.

But popular culture is not the only area into which dominant power shuttles discourse. Another area is *academia writing*, where we have a range of "narrow" texts displaying "subservience to disciplines" with "highly differentiated argot." This is exactly the textual landscape of DeLillo's academic specialist, professor Jack Gladney, whose discipline is "Hitler studies," a clearly narrow field, and one presumably having its own "argot." While this "argot" is nowhere present in the novel, Jack Gladney's atomized and highly compartmentalized professional life certainly suggests such things. While lack of argot in DeLillo's text prohibits specific analysis, we can make some generalizations about such specialized work.

A suggestion of disciplinary specialization comes early in DeLillo's book. Here, Murray Siskind, a fellow teacher, praises Jack for his entrepreneurial invention of "Hitler studies" and his ability to divide and subdivide it into other disciplines: "You've evolved an entire system around this figure

[Hitler], a structure with countless substructures and interrelated fields of study, a history within history. I marvel at the effort. It was masterful, shrewd and stunningly preemptive. It's what I want to do with Elvis" (*White Noise* 12). What, exactly, constitutes these "countless substructures and interrelated fields of study" is not at all clear, but one might jokingly imagine the existence of a "Goring studies" and "Von Rippentrop studies"; or, how about a narrowly defined "Mengele department" addressing only medical experimentation? The reference to "countless substructures and interrelated fields of study" surely points to exactly the sort of specialization we witness in universities today. And while Murray calls these fields "interrelated," a word seeming to imply cross fertilization and broad thought, I hope to show that is not the picture drawn in DeLillo's novel. In any case, Murray admires Jack's entrepreneurial spirit, noting its "masterful, shrewd and stunningly preemptive" character. However, Murray himself is not without entrepreneurial spirit; commenting on Jack's invention of "Hitler studies" Murray remarks, "It's what I want to do with Elvis." Of course, some such spirit is certainly more requisite in the nineteen eighties, when Murray makes this statement. Jack's invention (i.e. "Hitler studies") occurs in nineteen sixty-eight, a less fiscally stressful period for universities, relatively speaking. In leaner economic times like the eighties, it benefits a scholar to be skilled in self-promotion.

Murray's comments to Jack represent but one example of how DeLillo signals academic specialization. If we look at *White Noise* more closely, we can find other clues pointing to the singularity of the discipline and its hermetic nature. For example, though Jack mentions a "we" in reference to his department (e.g. "We [Hitler studies] are quartered in Centenary Hall" *White Noise* 9) and vaguely mentions others of his ilk ("The least of my Hitler colleagues . . ." *White Noise* 31), nowhere in the novel do we find another faculty member from his department. Though he does comment briefly on scholars attending the university's Hitler conference, he neither speaks with his colleagues at College-on-the-Hill, nor discusses them. Here, we draw our conclusion about the nature of his professional life not from what is in the text, but what is conspicuously absent, namely, Hitler colleagues. Instead of giving us a novel filled with heady discussions between Hitler scholars, the text makes it appear as though Jack has attained the ultimate in scholastic-capitalist atomization; his identity as disciplined worker (scholar), exhibits the height of divided labor. He is a virtual department unto himself.

Moreover, though he has associations with members of other departments, no substantive cross-departmental fertilization ever takes place.

While this is troubling enough, it is part of a larger problem in that Jack does not seem able to draw larger implications and connections with the specialized knowledge he possesses; it appears as though he has no ability to connect his isolated knowledge with present circumstances so as to *engage in public discussion* about future.

Admittedly, he does talk to Murray Siskind from "American Environments," which is the university's designation for the "popular culture department" (*White Noise* 9). He also speaks with Winnie Richards, a "research neurochemist," who does a chemical analysis of Dylar at his request (*White Noise* 184). While Winnie is from the hard sciences and might not have all that much in common with Jack's profession, Murray, as a thinker in what may loosely be termed "cultural studies," most certainly does. Thus, we would expect Jack to garner insights from him and use them to make other substantive claims. But exactly the opposite occurs.

As an example, we might look more deeply into the interesting co-lecture conducted by Jack and Murray. In this lecture the two teachers exchange numerous biographical parallels concerning the lives of Elvis (Murray's specialty) and Hitler (Jack's specialty). "Hitler adored his mother," says Jack; Murray responds in kind: "Elvis and Gladys [Elvis' mother] liked to nuzzle and pet . . . They slept in the same bed until he began to approach physical maturity" (*White Noise* 70). This banter continues, as Murray notes how "Elvis confided in Gladys [his mother]. He brought his girlfriends around to meet her"; Jack then responds: "Hitler wrote a poem to his mother. His mother and his niece were the women with the greatest hold on his mind" (*White Noise* 71). These are just a sampling of the parallels drawn between Hitler's and Elvis' life, but they illustrate the point.

However, these parallels reduce the two figures—namely, Hitler and Elvis—into a single phenomenon, the tragic pop-culture hero; for our purposes here, this seems an important point because Jack never registers the troubling implications of this even as it occurs. As evidence of the troubling reduction we can look at Murray's prefacing "monologue" before his joint lecture with Jack (*White Noise* 70). There, he observes how Elvis mirrored the mythic pattern of the pop hero's star-like ascension and tragic fall: "Did his mother know that Elvis would die young? . . . The life of a star of this type and magnitude. Isn't the life structured to cut you down early? This is the point, isn't it? There are rules, guidelines" (*White Noise* 70).

This stereotype patterns the entire series of equivalencies that follow, and the closing exchange between Murray and Jack serves to complete them in a similar evocation of pop-star death, which is self-induced and tinged with an almost heroic, romantic sensibility. Here is Murray Siskind's commentary on the untimely demise of the King: "Elvis fulfilled the terms of the contract. Excess, deterioration, self-destructiveness, grotesque behavior, a physical bloating and a series of insults to the brain, self-delivered. His place in legend is secure. He bought off the skeptics by dying early, horribly, unnecessarily. No one could deny him now" (*White Noise* 72). Jack's account of Hitler's last days is somewhat more extended, but it also transports us back to Elvis and pop-culture. It starts off with a picture of the *Führer* as lonely hero: "Hitler called himself the lonely wanderer out of nothingness" (*White Noise* 72). Then Jack's narrative moves toward a joining of Elvis and Hitler as we see the politician-totalitarian as a communicator of a magical language beyond this world: "He [Hitler] sucked on lozenges, spoke to people in endless monologues, free-associating, as if the language came from some vastness beyond the world and he was simply the medium of revelation" (*White Noise* 72). Hitler, though a politician, is like Elvis. Elvis, through his use of body, music, voice—i.e. rock-and-roll—communicated the secret and repressed libidinal life. Hitler communicated some mystical spirit—as from the *Volk*—through the power of his speeches, his "endless monologues," his acts of "free-associating" which seemed equally magical to many.

However, the pivotal death element joining the two figures comes via Jack's musing on Hitler's memories in his last days; these memories reduce both rocker and dictator into pop-culture heroes through place and audience. Here, it is worth quoting Jack's words at length to illustrate the point:

> It's interesting to wonder if he [Hitler] looked back from the *führerbunker*, beneath the burning city, to the early days of his power. Did he think of the small groups of tourists who visited the little settlement where his mother was born and where he'd spent summers with his cousins, riding in ox carts and making kites? They came to honor the site, Klara's [his mother's] birthplace.... In time the numbers began to increase. They took pictures, slipped small items into their pockets. Then crowds came, mobs of people overrunning the courtyard and singing patriotic songs, painting swastikas on the walls, on the flanks of farm animals. (*White Noise* 73)

At first glance, we have only Jack's imaginary wanderings to Hitler's childhood home, with no obvious connection to Elvis. But a little thought reveals the link, and it is one available, again, to a number of discursive communities. Using his imagined vision of Hitler's memory, Jack sees the *Führer* thinking about "the small groups of tourists" constantly plodding to his mother's early home, where Hitler had spent much time in his youth. Jack further imagines how these tourists "took pictures, slipped small items into their pockets," and how this small contingent became "crowds," "singing patriotic songs" and "painting swastikas on the walls" of Klara's home. But the parallels between Hitler and Elvis are unavoidable and easily drawn through these descriptions. Elvis, as a premier pop-culture icon, is well known to most Americans, and most of us have heard of Graceland, his famous home. Moreover, most of us know that many Elvis fans make something like religious pilgrimages to Graceland. They thus parallel the tourists paying homage to the home where Hitler spent some of his childhood. There are other parallels as well. Fans often write on the wall outside the King's home, offering messages of praise and love. The astute reader could easily link these with Jack's "painting [of] swastikas on the walls" at the house of Hitler's mother. Similarly, the tourists who "took pictures" and slipped small items into their pockets" could also extend to both Hitler and Elvis. The picture taking seems self evident; people take snapshots of stars. As for tourists taking "small items" placing them "into their pockets," that is an almost universal phenomenon amongst fans of celebrities today. Not only have people taken Elvis memorabilia from Graceland, as Jack imagines they did with items associated with Hitler, but there exists an actual market for such goods. Lastly, while Hitler's fans sang "patriot songs" we may observe a similar behavior on the part of Elvis fans, who not only sing his songs in front of Graceland, but also hold candle light vigils there to commemorate his birth and death.

The similarity of Hitler and Elvis is made complete as Jack comes near the close of his joint lecture with Murray. Though Hitler is his focalizing point, the unifying element seems to flow seamlessly from the easily inferred connections noted above; that element is the voracious and enraptured crowd seeking the anointed figure:

> Crowds came to hear him speak, crowds erotically charged, the masses he once called his only bride. He closed his eyes, clenched his fists as he spoke, twisted his sweat-drenched body, remade his voice as a thrilling weapon. 'Sex murders' someone called these speeches. Crowds came to be hypnotized by the voice, the party anthems, the torchlight parades. (*White Noise* 73)

Again, the description could as easily fit Elvis as it does Hitler. Elvis' erotic energy on stage was legendary; of course, his renowned sweaty gyrations at performances just contributed to the effect. Equally, the power of Elvis' voice commanded adoring screams from fans. While Hitler did not call forth exactly this sort of tribute, no doubt his followers assented to his words with cheers or some such response. Moreover, one can reasonably assume in Elvis a similar sense of betrothal to the loyal masses of fans at his concerts, not to mention those buying his records. Both the rock star and politician are nowhere without their following.

Now, Jack appears at first to appreciate the ramifications of these parallels, the gravity of extending Hitler's legacy to Elvis. After the above he says the following: "But wait. How familiar this all seems, how close to ordinary. Crowds come, get worked up, touch and press—people eager to be transported. Isn't this ordinary? We *know* all this" (*White Noise* 73). Jack feels there is some link between Hitler's crowds, crowds worshiping Elvis, and the everyday crowds he experiences ("How familiar this all seems, how close to ordinary"; "We all know this"). He even seems to draw out the commonality of crowds: they "get worked up, touch and press" in order to "be transported."

But Jack wants to make an *absolute* distinction between Elvis' crowds and Hitler's. As he puts it, "There must have been something different about those [Hitler's] crowds. What was it?" (*White Noise* 73). Jack finds his central difference in death; the singularity of Hitler's crowds comes from an obsession with death: "Let me whisper the terrible word, . . . *Death*. Many of those crowds were assembled in the name of death . . . Processions, songs, speeches, dialogues with the dead, recitations of the names of the dead. They were there to see the pyres . . . flags dipped in salute, thousands of uniformed mourners" (*White Noise* 73). But Jack asserts that the (Hitler) crowd's obsession with death is itself a means of evading death: "Crowds came to form a shield against their own dying. To become a crowd is to keep out death. To break off from the crowd is to risk death as an individual, to face dying alone. Crowds came for this reason above all others" (*White Noise* 73). Thus, what makes Hitler's crowds different, for Jack, is the concentrated effort to avoid death; individuals fight off death by gathering into crowds composed of equally death fearing people, who individually disappear in the vast ceremonies and rituals of National Socialism, but most especially in the figure and speech of its fascist leader, Adolph Hitler.

We may now turn to the issues at hand, namely, the confinement of Jack's professional life and the lack of broader thinking it entails. We may first observe that Jack draws his distinction between Hitler's and Elvis' crowds for several reasons. On the one hand, Jack's distinction is intended to keep his own field (i.e. Hitler studies) hermetically sealed off from others (e.g. the field of contemporary culture as seen in the figure of Elvis). As I will indicate momentarily, it also serves to elevate his specialty above Murray's.

Taken together, the points expose Jack Gladney as a scholar unable to connect his area of thought with wider contemporary society. Now, Jack does offer the insight that individual death—or aversion to it—is part of what feeds the desire to be within a crowd. But Jack applies this *only* to Hitler's crowds. Only Hitler's crowds carry the gravity of massive individual death in the fascist worship of the one, Adolf Hitler. Having made this first distinction, Jack draws two more through his elevation of Hitler and his crowds at the expense of Elvis and his: "I had been generous with the power and madness at my disposal, allowing my subject to be associated with an *infinitely lesser figure,* a fellow who sat in La-Z-Boy chairs and shot out TVs" (*White Noise* 73–74; italics mine). Calling Elvis "an infinitely lesser figure" obviously derides the study of the King, and by implication, his fans. The derision obviously shores up departmental distinctions. But it also does something else; by irrevocably splitting off Hitler from Elvis—and asserting a sensibility of taste between that which should be taken seriously (Hitler and his crowds) and that which should not (Elvis and his crowds)—Jack elevates his own discipline while dismissing Murray's study of popular cultural phenomena.

This is not to suggest an equation between Elvis' deeds and those of Hitler; that could hardly be supported. Rather, my intention is two fold. First, I want to indicate that popular culture, according to Jack's thinking, is not something to be taken seriously at the academic level. It has no connection with serious topics like Hitler. But as a second point I should immediately add that DeLillo renders this ironically to the extent that Jack cannot see how the university's thorough capitalist schematization—and his own activities within it—have in fact already leveled Hitler and Elvis to equal commodities. Both are equal commodities packaged for sale by the university. Here, parallel elements between entertainer and dictator do not so much indicate their unity as the fact that they are equal as commodities; it hardly matters that one, Hitler, killed six million Jews, and the other swung his hips to pop tunes. Moreover, and related in a related sense, Jack's seemingly total aestheticization of his subject matter appears to lessen the actual historical horror of Hitler and the holocaust he wrought. His subject, though evidently more high brow than work on Elvis, is ethereal, purely a matter of abstract intellection.

These points, one can imagine, speak to readers in various ways, some of which have already been mentioned. Certainly, it gives readers another chance to laugh at the folly and hypocrisy of the stereotyped academic. On the other hand, readers cannot help but feel a certain discomfort at placing Hitler and Elvis on the same level as commodities. Moreover, juxtaposing Hitler's crowds to Elvis'—even as Jack tries to separate them—might well make readers see certain similarities between them. Here, one need only think of fans at rock shows, where there can sometimes be an equal sense of selfless adoration for the star, whoever he or she is.

If we return now to Jack, we may see also that his blindness to these connections also makes him blind to the wider project of criticism toward liberation. Indicative of this failure, Jack makes the following revealing comment a few lines down as he is surrounded by "students and staff" who escort him from the lecture hall: "I realized we were now a crowd. Not that I needed a crowd around me now. Least of all now. Death was strictly a professional matter here. I was comfortable with it, I was on top of it" (*White Noise* 74). The word "denial" comes immediately to mind here. Though Jack understands that students and staff have made him part of a crowd ("we were now a crowd"), he denies his own desire to be part of that crowd as a means of denying death ("Not that I needed a crowd around me now. Least of all now. Death was strictly a professional matter here. I was comfortable with it, I was on top of it"). Yet, as I indicated earlier, Jack's fear of death is present throughout his narration of *White Noise*. He shies from doctors offices because of their "air of negative expectancy"; he prefers the hospital "emergency ward" where, in his words, "things have nothing to do with my own eventual death . . ." (*White Noise* 76). Of course, association with the gruesome figure of Hitler just magnifies this effect.

The wider social meaning evinced in the connection between Hitler and Elvis is directly related to death. Jack's claim that "death" is "strictly a professional matter" for him—only to do with topics covered within Hitler studies—partly reveals his blindness to this meaning. Since we have already noted his real fear of death, despite his denial, we may put Jack within the mass of Hitler worshipers, namely, those "crowds" assembled "to form a shield against their own dying." Interestingly, however, the fact that Jack commands a rapt presence in the crowded class—evinced by the immediate throng of "people gathered round" him at the lecture's conclusion—makes readers see a similarity between the Hitler professor and Hitler himself (*White Noise* 74). Moreover, his comments near the end seem equally indicative of the *Führer* ("I had been generous with the power and madness at my disposal"); both Jack and Hitler are men to whom one must listen and follow. At the same time, Murray's simultaneous lecturing about Elvis similarly links Jack and Hitler with Elvis' crowd, the King's death, and his power as pop-culture figure; this, despite the fact that Jack's narrative renders Murray more like a high ranking Nazi functionary as he leads Jack from the lecture hall: "Murray made his way to my side and escorted me from the room, parting the crowd with his fluttering hand" (*White Noise* 74). That Jack never really notices these mounting similarities seems particularly telling.

But even more telling in all this is Jack's failure to see the further implications, namely, connections between fascism and popular culture, as well as the subsumption of both more generally under late capitalist consumerism; indeed, it represents one of his greatest mistakes as a scholar, because it indicates his inability to see beyond his atomized subject matter (i.e. Hitler studies). DeLillo brings Elvis, the American popular culture figure adored by millions, into close proximity to Hitler, the German fascist dictator worshiped by millions. The two become one in respect to commodification. Moreover, as my earlier discussion of Jack and Murray's lecture reveals, the idols are worshiped by millions—their crowds—and they appear similar; both crowds pick up items associated with the particular hero worshiped; they write on things associated with that entity; they sing in praise of that person and gather in his name. In fact, it is the figure of the crowd—and Jack's hypocritical but nevertheless desirous longing for engulfment in it—that constitute signs of wider consumer culture and the schematized capitalism structuring it. To be explicit, crowds represent conditions of purchase wherein we exercise disciplined consumption. In Hitler's—or Elvis'—case "crowds come to be hypnotized by [among other things] the voice"; but when our two cult figures stand in for the general and leveled state of consumer culture, crowds gather for capitalist consumption. They gather to be "hypnotized" by endlessly similar products, created under capitalist schematization. Instead of death, crowds *seem* to offer preservation, as buying expands being itself; thus, reflecting on his own shopping Jack declares, "I felt expansive" (*White Noise* 84). This "expansive" element is essential for capitalism's survival—after all, given the shift from a supply side crisis to a consumption crisis, it is necessary for capitalism to penetrate every conceivable niche of human experience, to poulate the commodified self (consumer identity) with illusory dream worlds which fuel desire and consumption. Jack's failure to recognize this, and his general inability to think about his subject matter beyond its academically defined strictures and how that directly accords with capitalist schematization of universities and society more generally.

If we look closely at some of Jack's comments and read them in conjunction with his general behavior, as well as certain research on university trends, we may go slightly beyond our last point to discern how conditions of academia can more generally reproduce status quo social relations. We can begin on the first page of *White Noise,* where Jack witnesses parents helping their children move into school for the start of the Fall semester. By his own admission Jack has "witnessed" this ritual for some "twenty-one years" (*White Noise* 3). As the narrative continues, Jack lists a large number of items unpacked by these travelers, including "English and Western saddles" (*White Noise* 3). Jack also goes on to comment about the parents and their children. He notes how the parents look at each other and "feel a sense of . . . communal recognition"; he perceives in the fathers "something . . . suggesting massive insurance coverage" (*White Noise* 3). Still later in the narrative Jack tells us more about himself and his teaching attire. He remarks that "[d]epartment heads wear academic robes," and that he—as department chair of Hitler studies—is perhaps "the most prominent figure in Hitler studies in North America"; in his words, "I'd achieved high professional standing, because my lectures were well attended and my articles printed in the major journals . . ." (*White Noise* 31–32).

I have brought the above disparate elements together to make a number of points, the first of which is to indicate class status. We will notice that the students' possession of items like "English" and "Western" "riding saddles" signifies a relatively high class status; while some moderate income households could certainly have a horse or two at home, how many schools have stables full of horses for students to ride at will? This, of course, is not to mention the fact that while one might simply jump on a Western saddle and ride, the proper use of an English saddle takes some fairly extensive training, which is by no means cheap. Moreover, as writers like John Frow (1996) have noted, DeLillo means this scene to represent more generally the conscious enactment of a lifestyle not by one person but by many; "saddle*s*," after all, is plural. This would suggest to me we are talking not only many people, but also about people having sufficient capital to enact such a purchasable lifestyle. We may add to this Jack's reference to the fathers' "massive insurance coverage" and his remark regarding his teaching attire ("academic robes"), all of which would seem to confirm higher than average income level; "coverage" which is "massive" can't be cheap, and the tradition of "academic robes"—while obviously parodic and satirical—suggests the educational institution is rather exclusive and most likely extremely expensive. Again, we will recall here the earlier mention of College-on-the-Hill's tuition, which "is fourteen thousand dollars" (*White Noise* 41); in the mid-eighties—the apparent temporal setting of *White Noise*—that is no small sum for an education.[20]

Such suggestive economic elements ("massive coverage," tuition of "fourteen thousand dollars," "English saddles") mixed with the elitist cultural capital intimated by Jack's "academic robes" satirically indicates to readers how the academic and his/her academic institution may possess specific class loyalty and have a vested interest in reproducing the status quo. Here, we must remember that Jack is "the most prominent figure in Hitler studies in North America," and that his work has "achieved high professional standing" because his "lectures" are "well attended" and his "articles" published "major journals" (*White Noise* 9, 31). Of course, it helps that Jack "invented Hitler studies" almost twenty years before (*White Noise* 4), but that fact—taken in conjunction Jack's age and length of employment—suggest something further. First, we may connect jack's age—he says he is approaching "fifty-one" early in the book (*White Noise* 47)—with his own invention of Hitler studies in "March of 1968" (*White Noise* 4). While we cannot be certain of when Jack first arrived at College-on-the-Hill, if the book takes place in the mid-nineteen eighties and he proposed Hitler studies in "1968," he has been there at least seventeen years. Moreover, while it is possible a recently hired faculty member would propose a new department, as Jack does, it seems unlikely that such a new member would have that request granted. It is thus not unreasonable to suggest that Jack arrived at the school a little earlier, say, the early to mid-nineteen sixties. Thus, Jack might be in his mid-twenties to thirty upon arrival at College-on-the-Hill.

With this as a given, it would not seem unreasonable to consider College-on-the-Hill as Jack's first professional position. This, we may relate directly to the economic issues above and Jack's own class status as an academic. It has been shown, for instance, that a college academic's "career depends significantly upon the prestige or class standing of the institution at which one is first hired"; moreover, "advantages of one's initial job placement accumulate over the career" (Hogan, "Teaching and Research as Economic Problems" 20; McGinnis and Long qtd. in Hogan 20). Jack has, most likely, been at College-on-the-Hill his entire career and has thus accumulated exactly these benefits.

We may add to this a further related but unsurprising fact, namely, that "class position of faculty is continuous with that of students . . ." (Hogan, "Teaching and Research as Economic Problems" 20). That is, faculty and students have roughly the same class status. Put another way, Jack is well payed and has—at least to some extent—a shared class interest in maintaining the social-economic relations which produce his class privilege. This fact is equally confirmed by the single class Jack teaches, "Advanced Nazism" (*White Noise* 25). While such a light teaching load allows Jack time to research Hitler, it also indicates his class, since light teaching loads are typical of well paid professors at high prestige research universities.[21]

In this respect we may observe another fact which contributes to the preservation of the status quo. In particular, it seems important to register the "direct correlation between *institutional prestige* and *student family income*"; this relationship is evident in the university via an institutional process (e.g. systematic underenrollment) which blocks access to prestigious education for low income students (Hogan, "Teaching and Research as Economic Problems" 19; italics mine). As Alexander Astin explains, "public universities have consistently underenrolled low-income students . . . Moreover, the degree of underenrollment was greatest in the most selective public universities"; as a result, "the major public universities in most states are not as accessible to low-income and minority students as are the public four-year colleges and, more particularly, the community colleges" (Astin qtd. in Hogan, "Teaching and Research as Economic Problems" 19).

An important point here is how all this *reproduces* present class status and relations. For just as students' family income correlates with college prestige, so students' family income correlates with success in colleges of all kinds. Again citing his own research, Astin observes,

> freshman entering community colleges have a poorer chance of eventually completing the bachelor's degree than do freshman of comparable ability, motivation and social background entering public universities . . . In summary, the opportunities offered by institutions at different tiers in the nation's public systems of higher education are by no means comparable. (Astin qtd. in Hogan, "Teaching and Research as Economic Problems" 20)

In fact, students who are accepted in "major public research universities" on the whole have "better resources and greater career opportunities than do students who attend the four-year or community colleges" (Astin qtd. in Hogan, "Teaching and Research as Economic Problems 20). This indicates not only that "institutions catering to the underprivileged do not function to provide new opportunities," but also that such institutions "perpetuate the hierarchization which led to the underprivilege initially" (Hogan, "Teaching and Research as Economic Problems" 20). Of course, well funded universities or colleges would similarly reproduce "hierarchization," but as the argument implies, students lucky enough to attend would benefit from the hierarchy. If we apply this to the fictional College-on-the-Hill, we can discern DeLillo's satirical jab at how a particular sort of university preserves and perpetuates privileged class status by providing students with exactly those "resources" and "opportunities" which make for privilege. More to the point, College-on-the-Hill guarantees its students a future similar to their parents', namely, one of privileged class status. Opening his novel with a *ritualistic* event like parents accompanying children to college, and then consciously appending to that event myriad class indicators (e.g. "English saddles," "massive insurance coverage") suggests DeLillo wants to signal to readers—from the narrative's beginning—a systemic marriage between class and education. As seems obvious, such a reading is open to many sorts of readers, especially since it plays—at least to some extent—upon stereotype (e.g. "English saddles").

Jack, for his part, certainly aids in reproducing this system and its ideological cultural imaginary. He accomplishes this in part through his own research and thought which seem "academic" in the term's worst sense. Specifically, if his work on Hitler is not vacuous, it most definitely is compartmentalized. As already noted, while Jack will nod to Elvis and his legacy, he seems unable or unwilling to connect Hitler and fascism to the King as part of popular consumer culture. His Advanced Nazism class and his academic life more generally remain freestanding entities never connecting past to present in any significant way. In another related sense his discipline, Hitler Studies, stands in for so many highly specialized, compartmentalized areas of study which have no reference point outside themselves and as such remain completely removed from the public sphere.

It is easy to see the advantage of such compartmentalization to status quo social relations because—on this compartmentalized view—disciplines *discipline* themselves never to speak beyond their boundaries; troublesome relations between disciplines and individual discipline's relation to the world beyond academics is this avoided, which ensures the reproduction of the same. Thus, like a New Critical reader, the properly disciplined academic will never stray beyond preset boundaries of discussion, especially in *print*.

Now, considering this issue of print, it is obvious that—unlike mass market works which are disciplined for profit in the strictly monetary sense—academic works are disciplined to reproduce the hermetically sealed boundaries of the academic's area of study. But in both instances "the literary political economy" forces "conformity to the order of things (Foucault 1970) spelled out by . . . editors, producers, chairpeople, colleagues, readers (who are themselves products of the prevailing culture industry)" (Agger, *The Decline of Discourse* 52). In terms of academic writing, essential to such conformity are authors' complicit (if unconscious) entanglements "in political-economic relations of presentation and production largely conditioning the styles with which they compose themselves" (Agger, *The Decline of Discourse* 31). In this regard, while the profit motive separates mass market from academic work, both exist within the larger market driven ideology and logic, which necessarily effects the mode of presentation (e.g. how a book is composed, its style, syntax, etc.).

Here, editors and reviewers working for academic publishers of books and journals constitute part of a larger disciplinary structure which helps channel discourse. At the same time, and in a related sense, specific class interests support this disciplinary work. As regards editor's and reviewer's channeling function within the disciplinary structure, Agger states that,

> Unlike trade editors and producers constrained by a strict profit motive, academic editors of journals and university presses exist to *perpetuate the discipline—perhaps, better, just discipline itself.* They edit works that they believe both entrenches disciplinary boundaries (e.g. sociology as against non-sociology) and furthers the state of existing knowledge. (Agger, *The Decline of Discourse* 134)

At the same time, Agger's assertion that editors actually do select work which "furthers the state of existing knowledge" is perhaps too optimistic. As Hogan observes in the article cited earlier, "empirical studies" have actually shown "that acceptance of publication is not determined by evidence, rigor, significance of findings, etc. Rather it is determined by *conformity with disciplinary doctrine,* along with such factors as the author's *institutional affiliation* (in non-blind refereeing), triviality of focus, and prose style . . ." (Hogan, "Teaching and Research as Economic Problems" 22; second italics mine). Of special interest to us here is *institutional affiliation,* since, as Hogan further observes, "publication-determining bias toward disciplinary doctrine is the result of class interests, specifically the interests of those who represent the prevailing paradigm (including its special vocabulary and definition of 'normalcy'), and are situated at prestige universities" (Hogan, "Teaching and Research as Economic Problems" 22–23). Moreover, and perhaps "less obvious," is the fact that "these academic class interests are enmeshed in the larger economic structure and that it is this structure which most significantly determines those paradigms" (Hogan "Teaching and Research as Economic Problems" 23). While Hogan rightly asserts that this phenomenon is most clearly visible in the relationship between science and industry, it seems equally clear from all this that the liberal arts are not immune. This, then, brings us back to Jack's class status as a legislator and researcher within the very sort of prestigious university that underwrites paradigms of publication.

Of course, all this might make one rightly wonder exactly "*whose* discipline is being defended and advanced and *for what* reasons" (Agger, *The Decline of Discourse* 134). Here, we are talking not only about what exactly is *included in a discipline,* but also *what is not;* moreover, this has implications for what we customarily call mainstream journals and books, as opposed to the marginal ones. Mainstream publishers publish writing someone defines as "mainstream"; marginal publishers publish writing someone defines as "marginal." Thus, as Agger indicates, a hierarchy of value is established and maintained between the two; as for inclusion and exclusion from a discipline, defining also occurs whereby people (e.g. editor-scholars) systematically determine what submitted work counts as within the discipline and what remains outside of it (Agger, *The Decline of Discourse* 134). This, in short, displays the political and disciplinary power held by people like editors who, it should be remembered, are frequently from the individual disciplines themselves and also possess the class interests already noted.

While editors and other decision makers within academic publishing are not necessarily conscious of their actions in this regard, they nevertheless reproduce the "discipline of the disciplines," if you will, along Foucaultian lines. Thus, following Foucault, they "reproduce the social order to which they are attached through the relationship among higher education, the state and the economy. In particular, disciplines reproduce disciplinary discourse, the peculiarly private argots of academics constrained by the prevailing 'literatures' in their fields"; together, Agger writes, these elements work to "establish standards of publishability" while also prohibiting entrance to "general readers and writers as well as polemicists" (Agger, *The Decline of Discourse* 135). The intended audience for such disciplinary writing—namely, the sort Jack publishes in "major journals"—is narrow and versed in highly specialized codes; moreover, this increased specialization in subject and language contributes to the reproduction and schematization of the various disciplines themselves:

> Indeed, few academics outside the narrow ambit of one's own subfield of scholarship actually read academic journal articles and monographs, fragmenting the disciplines even further. Scholarly writings are to be entered into one's curriculum vitae and perhaps cited in the literature-review sections of future scholarly articles and monographs. They discourage their reading as essays, arguments, rhetoric . . . They exist merely to be counted as tangible proof of scholarly productivity, reflecting the bureaucratic Taylorization of academic life generally. If academic writing is read, it is only to instruct other academics (and student apprentices) how to write in the future, hence reproducing the discipline. (Agger, *The Decline of Discourse* 135)

Upon short consideration, the ramifications of all this appear fairly simple to understand and take us back to DeLillo's text: What public sphere speech might otherwise exist in academic writing (e.g. a sustained dialogical discussion of the relationship between Hitler's fascist thought and present social, economic, and political conditions) has been displaced into the realm of a disciplined academic discourse with its own increasingly narrow subject matter (e.g. the presumably arcane essays published in "major journals" by professor Jack Gladney, chair of "Hitler studies"). Displaced in this fashion by ideological and material discipline—much of which is driven by class interest—the myriad works produced in university disciplines (e.g. English) have little positive effect on the world, and instead remain comfortably ensconced in their compartmentalized fields outside the public sphere. Thus, in a real world parallel to our fictional academic Jack Gladney are poststructural-postmodern theoreticial texts which advocate liberation for the oppressed but remain safely imprisoned in the confines of esoteric academic journals, and are acted upon only in the form of more paper, namely, papers written by graduate students and professors. Successfully disconnected from the wider social-political landscape, such theories become politically ineffective and in that ineffectiveness reproduce the status quo. This point is, of course, beyond the further fact of their impenetrableness, which itself blocks access to the very people who they claim their work seeks to liberate. Lest we misunderstand the point here, I am not suggesting Jack Gladney writes inaccessible jargon laden texts like the poststructuralist authors above; there is no real evidence for that in DeLillo's text. Rather, I am suggesting a *disciplinary process* which results in the irrelevancy of such endeavors because of specialization, compartmentalization, and class interests.

The reproductive nature of all this cannot be over-emphasized. Academic writing, like writing in popular culture, is not designed for response, writing back. It exists to be consumed and *reproduced*. Indeed, nowhere is this more apparent than in the grueling pursuit of tenure, a matter very much about publication and writing "publishable" work. But the disciplinary apparatus of publishers, editors and department committee people comes directly into play here as the decisive elements determining whether a thinker will stay (be granted tenure) or go (be dismissed). Disciplinary requirements demanded of scholars seeking tenure are many. They span from a requirement to duplicate style, vocabulary, diction, and line of thought, to publishing in the correct journals as opposed to less favored outlets (e.g. textbooks, newspapers, or more widely read periodicals like *The Nation*)[22]. In the case of *White Noise*, homogeneity of academic writing is suggested in the monotonous physical appearance of scholars attending a Hitler conference at College-on-the-Hill; as Jack notes, "It was interesting to see how closely they [conference participants] resembled each other despite the wide diversity of national and regional backgrounds" (*White Noise* 274). Here, one may assume that the Hitler scholars' similar appearances ("they resembled each other") indicates a similarity of literary production, despite supposed differences ("despite their wide diversity of national and regional backgrounds").

Jack Gladney, as chair of Hitler studies, does not appear to have too much to worry about as regards job security, thanks to his rather entrepreneurial move to start Hitler studies in the first place. But I think there is little doubt his ability to form that department—and ultimately attain its leadership—was facilitated by such publication. In any case, because Murray comes to College-on-the-Hill in the eighties climate of declining liberal arts studies, he would be under extreme pressure to produce disciplined writing if he wants to, as he claims, duplicate what Jack has done with his own subject ("You've evolved an entire system around this figure [Hitler],. . . . It's what I want to do with Elvis" (*White Noise* 12)).

Now average readers—however broadly we define that discursive community—may have no knowledge whatsoever of Agger's disciplined discourse. But many people who have been to college, or have at least see academics represented on popular television programs, know about the high degree of specialization present today in departments (e.g. English) and their literary production. As an example from popular media, a 1994 episode of the highly rated television series *Law & Order* represents one murder suspect as a college professor and author of "The Whale was Red: A Marxist Reading of *Moby Dick*." Of course, at the title's mention in the show, the homicide detectives cannot help but trade derisive remarks. In fact, one of the cops even makes a snide reference to the ineffectuality of such academic work. The example illustrates both the general public's knowledge of such specialization, and at least one viewership's attitude toward it, though one hardly wants to shift the blame (or praise?) entirely to the victim. Indeed, besides reflecting audience awareness, the *Law & Order* example may indicate exactly how correct Agger is in asserting that much "intelligence has been removed from a traditional literary culture into other realms" like "popular culture" (Agger, *The Decline of Discourse* 34). If that is the case with our *Law & Order* example, it indicates how intellectual—if possibly *reactionary*—television writers are responding to contemporary academia. Of course, while such critiques of academia may possess genuine validity, linking them with things like murder, along with a general repudiation of the intellectual life, may in fact aid capitalist domination by dismissing universities as places occupied by useless sinecures.

DeLillo also judges academia's value by referencing popular cultural texts; the novel is full of them. However, his verdict is perhaps best summarized in the university's name, "College-on-the-Hill," which simultaneously marks similarities and differences between the English and American college novels. As regards similarities, with a liberal arts institution boasting "Hitler studies" and "American Environments," DeLillo's "College-on-the-Hill" surely supports many of the same liberal arts values as its English counterparts. Certainly they both work to preserve the Western canon through, among other things, the teaching of Shakespeare. This is true despite the university's encouragement

In terms of differences, the locales of English and American versions depart significantly, and invoke very different "cultural imaginaries," or "ensemble[s] of images and fantasies, thoughts and expectations, feelings and values" (Martin et al. 211). In this case, we are talking about culturally specific linkages or associations between university as place (e.g. "Oxford" or "College-on-the-Hill"). On a more superficial level, a good many English college mysteries take place in exclusive British schools (e.g. Oxford, Cambridge), while the cultural imaginary of American versions prefer "a state university or an undistinguished liberal arts college" (Kramer, "The American College Mystery" 5). This difference could indicate a deep ideological belief that American education operates more democratically than its English counterpart. However, Poovey's remarks and the sub-genre's mystery element—one frequently tied to crime—certainly temper such exceptionalist claims. Moreover, though College-on-a-Hill lacks the "exclusive" associations of Oxford, textual elements indicate a similarly prestigious hierarchical structure, but one based on American myths and bourgeois class exclusivity. The novel's representation of College-on-the-Hill as "internationally known" because of "Hitler studies" and explicit references regarding the cost of education indicate this class affiliation (e.g. "tuition . . . is fourteen thousand dollars" White Noise 11; 41). Such references suggest a school for upper-middle classes people at the very least, even if its faculty is rather eccentric or somewhat incompetent (e.g. Jack knows no German, though he is chairman of Hitler studies).

Consumerism and Purchasable Identity

Negative representation of academics in popular cultural artefacts like the television show *Law & Order* transports us to a crucial similarity implied throughout this essay. From the above discussion we can reasonably say that academic writing resembles its popular culture counterpart because it constantly offers "'new' products [which] are merely iterations of old ones that are packaged, composed, slightly differently. . . . The name 'new' passes for real innovation. That is why popular culture and academic writing both endure virtually as canons—bodies of knowledge with little room for innovation, let alone subversion" (Agger, *The Decline of Discourse* 39). With respect to DeLillo's Gladney, we may assume that "major journals" publishing his academic writing in the past, present, and future similarly repeat this process of iteration by providing nothing new, while at the same time offering a model of academic reproduction. Like the multi-national studio production of films like *Die Hard,* it repeats itself over and over again, if only by adding the numerals II and III to the title.

The model for this reproduction in the world outside academia is DeLillo's often cited example of "THE MOST PHOTOGRAPHED BARN IN AMERICA" (*White Noise* 12). In this short section professor Jack Gladney and Elvis expert Murray Siskind—representatives of high academia (Hitler) and popular culture respectively (Elvis)—travel to a barn frequented by tourists simply because it is the most photographed barn in America. When they arrive, the two find visiting crowds busily taking pictures of the barn. Murray comments, "Once you've seen the signs about the barn, it becomes impossible to see the barn" (*White Noise* 12). Later still, he says, "They are taking pictures of taking pictures" (*White Noise* 13). The barn "becomes impossible to see" because it is conditioned by so many earlier pictures of the barn; people are fascinated by these pictures—these images after the original—and so they take numerous photos of the original barn, hoping to duplicate the duplicate. But finally, of course, all are "pictures of taking pictures."

This early scene in the book announces the general state of affairs in postmodern culture; it is observable in both academia (as well as its academic writing) and so called popular culture. Others have equated this scene with Baudrillard's "simulacrum," and its picture of postmodern perception (e.g. Lentricchia 1996). Here, Steven Best and Douglas Kellner (1991) describe this supposed state of affairs:

> In a society of simulations, the models or codes structure experience and erode the distinctions between the model and the real. Using McLuhan's concept of implosion, Baudrillard claims that in the postmodern world the boundary between image or simulation and reality implodes, and with it the very experience and ground of the 'real' disappears. (119)

Thus, if we use DeLillo's most photographed barn as an instance of such simulation, we see the reality of the barn itself disappear into so many simulations of the barn (photographs) without an original. But there is another way of thinking about this. Ben Agger speaks of simulation not as the total disappearance of the real—what he considers a postmodern theoretical copout—but rather as "ideology . . . gone underground," wherein "the boundary between the textual and the material has virtually disappeared, disabling social criticism as a result" (Agger, *The Discourse of Domination* 80). From this viewpoint the barn is very much there (is real), but incessant exposure to images linked with interpellated habits of behavior—cognitive training in how to see according to capitalist ideology—results in obsession with the image and an apparent disappearance of the real. Though the "THE MOST PHOTOGRAPHED BARN IN AMERICA" is primarily a model of simulation here, the capitalist goal of such simulation, namely, purchase of images or ideals, nevertheless comes through. Thus, when Jack and Murray visit the barn, they note how "a man in a booth sold postcards and slides" of the barn (*White Noise* 12).

But the barn remains primarily a model. To get at its essence we need to remember some earlier comments in this essay. As we noted earlier, despite Jack's lack of insight on the matter, his joint lecture with Murray reveals similarities between Hitler's and Elvis' crowds. Moreover, I have tried to suggest how DeLillo displays a disturbing similarity between the Hitler-fascist phenomenon and the pop-culture phenomenon of Elvis. Here, fascism is popular culture, or more specifically, fascism is popular culture as *consumer* culture. This takes us to the actual roots of the barn model noted above.

To discover the roots of this model it seems useful again to consult Horkheimer and Adorno on reason's u-turn within advanced schematized and administrated industry; for in the figure of Hitler—and the course "Hitler studies"—we have a "science" by which to reproduce (teach?) "the subjugated mass society" (Horkheimer and Adorno 87). Its perfected nature in the schematized university and consumerism resides in its use of "reason" for "calculation," "planning," and "coordination"; its moral logic—akin to Hitler's logical and bureaucratic management of trains to Auschwitz—was sketched centuries ago in Sade's "sexual teams," which "employ every moment usefully, neglect no human orifice, and carry out every function"; in short, it represents "a[n] organization of life . . . which is deprived of any substantial goal" other than "its own 'organization,'" which is equivalent to saying "the schema . . . of activity" is "more important than its content" (Horkheimer and Adorno 88). Here, one might rightly ask, "reason, yes, but to what purpose?"

Reason, as practiced by the fictional university chancellor and "Hitler studies" professor Jack Gladney—but also, presumably, by most of us in real-life America—serves the seemingly invisible multinational corporations. Their market ideology, itself a kind of logic, speaks in "bright packaging," "jingles," and "slice-of-life commercials" designed to beckon us—construct us as subjects—telling us to buy (*White Noise* 51). Ghostlike, their machinations appear everywhere, but paradoxically seem unlocatable; hence, the previously noted persistence of seemingly authorless but commanding voices within DeLillo's text (e.g. "Kleenex Softique, Kleenex Softique"; "Dristan Ultra, Dristan Ultra" (*White Noise* 39; 167). This is further substantiated by Steffie's muttering in her sleep the words "Toyota Celica," which suggests unconscious knowledge Jack can only understand mystically as "the name of an ancient power in the sky, tablet-carved in cuneiform" (*White Noise* 155).

Presumably, the product of all this schematization and organization is exactly the reasonable consumer-citizen Jack becomes at one point in *White Noise,* an individual capable of saying, "I shopped for its own sake . . ." (84). This subject lives exactly the sadean futility noted above, namely, according to the logic of endless capitalist production and consumption, which exists for its sake. In this respect, DeLillo's early mention of the chancellor—as bureaucratic university administrator—and Jack Gladney (as functionary "Hitler studies" professor implementing the day to day procedures) appear emblematic of this mindless process.

But here we can return to our discussion of crowds and death. Because what dies in this process of consumption—a process which is itself the barn model lived out through buying images and lifestyles—is exactly the self. Other writers (e.g. Frow 1996) have commented on this death, noting how Lukács' theory of realism—one based on typicality—is undermined by DeLillo's persistent infusion of media images; in Frow's words, the "type is not a naive given, an embodied universality, but a self-conscious *enactment . . .*" (Frow 178; italics mine). That is, characters in *White Noise* merely act out, or take on media representations of a type (e.g. the typical college parent).

But it is also interesting to note that death of self often occurs in the shopping crowd, which is itself a figure brought together by assimilation of the fascist Hitler with the pop-culture hero, Elvis. A prominent place in which this occurs, of course, is the shopping mall. So it is that the Elvis guru Murray says the following about the shopping mall: "Here we don't die, we shop. But the difference is less marked than you think" (38). The mall represents a place which dissolves all sense of the human as we know it. As Jack says upon entering the mall with his family, "We went our separate ways into the store's deep interior. A great echoing din, as of the extinction of a species of beast, filled the vast space" (*White Noise* 82). The human becomes the crowd, the fascist whole of shoppers. It dissolves personal boundaries, and fits Elias Canetti's reading of the crowed sensation: "The man pressed against him is the same as himself. He feels him as he feels himself. Suddenly it is as though everything were happening in one and the same body" (Canetti 15–16). This explains the feelings of enlargement Jack expresses when shopping: "The more money I spent, the less important it seemed. I was bigger than these sums. . . . These sums in fact came back to me in the form of existential credit. I felt expansive, inclined to be sweepingly generous . . ." (*White Noise* 84). Jack is larger, because Jack shops; but Jack is also gone in terms of self. He simply represents the whole consuming population.

Don DeLillo's White Noise 155

Critiquing Readers and Hopes of Liberation

In the few pages remaining, I would like to indicate perhaps one of the most appealing elements of DeLillo's *White Noise*. In fact, this element relates to many of the points already noted. In particular, it has to do with the ways in which Jack exemplifies over and over again not only the consciousness of a disciplined academic, but also the consciousness of many contemporary consumers in late capitalist society. Readers cannot help but notice the intellectual disconnect between the avowed academic's role and its actual practice. Here, we may turn to Jack who, while discussing his "Advanced Nazism" course, remarks that it is "designed to cultivate historical perspective, theoretical rigor and mature insight into the continuing mass appeal of fascist tyranny . . ." (*White Noise* 25). Yet nowhere does the text show Jack connecting his own buying frenzies—or that of the Blacksmith citizenry—with the wider ideology of consumption, itself akin to fascism.

In this respect, he is like so many of the professors satirized in more recent college novels. Jack is perhaps blind, but he is also comical and even likable. John Schellenberger observes that while "it is true . . . that these [academic] characters are being satirized, . . . the type of satire does not suggest that these characters are seen by their authors as exceptional, pernicious, and requiring to be eliminated. On the contrary they are presented as absolutely normal, typical and acceptable . . ." (46). Jack therefore seems to have much in common with many middle class people in postmodern America, and this brings us back to the BOMC and its reading membership.

I earlier noted that BOMC selections were based heavily on commercial interests (selling of the book for profit). At the same time, however, this commercial pressure must be qualified because, traditionally, BOMC employs sales figures primarily to "structure new membership drives or to design initial-offer advertising"; hence, though projected sales figures "frequently dictate club choices, especially main selections, many alternate selections are made simply because individual editors like particular books and believe that they should be brought to the attention of other readers, even if that group potentially numbers no more than two . . . or three thousand" (Radway, "The Book of the Month Club and the General Reader" 265)[23].

This editorial freedom is most evident in BOMC's very nebulous category of "general fiction," which it further divides into "commercial" and "serious," with DeLillo's *White Noise* finding itself recommended by editors in the latter category (Radway, "The Book of the Month Club and the General Reader" 268; 275). According to Radway's research, it seems most likely that literary categories within BOMC (e.g. "serious," "commercial") operate like genres, and therefore act in the fashion noted earlier, namely, as "literary *institutions,* or social contracts between a writer and a specific public, whose function is to specify the proper us of a cultural artifact" (Jameson qtd. in Radway, "The Book of the Month Club and the General Reader" 268).

But what makes BOMC editors recommend works in the "serious" but "general" category? What determines these editor's feelings about works? First, by their own words we find editors indicating their tastes diverge from those of the membership. As Radway's interviews with editors indicate, "nearly all . . . replied that only a small segment of the membership shares their preferences" (Radway, "The Book of the Month Club and the General Reader" 263). Considering their backgrounds in literature and close reading, it would seem likely that BOMC editors' preferences include "complexity, . . . reflexivity, linguistic innovation," elements of "high" modernist aesthetic, even while they try to read like members (Radway, "The Book of the Month Club and the General Reader" 260).

The fact that editors feel a need to evaluate, judge, and guide in the category of "serious" but "general" (i.e. steers readers away from so called "trash") is interesting. Here, BOMC editors simultaneously express a certain "hostility toward the academy and the institutionalized teaching of literature, which the editors . . . believe transforms fascinating books into dry exercises in analysis" (Radway, "The Book of the Month Club and the General Reader" 269). The result is a contradictory situation, but one which is mediated. While they desire to judge texts for readers, "editors are also genuinely uncomfortable with arraying the categories along a simple hierarchy and prefer to view them as different sorts of books for different purposes" (Radway, "The Book of the Month Club and the General Reader" 270).

In terms of purposes, reader reports indicate editors desire in the "serious" category books with "relevance to the lives of contemporary readers" (Radway, "The Book of the Month Club and the General Reader" 275). Editors' "serious" selections, though they are still selections,

> serve club members in a way similar to the many self-help manuals, advice books, and reference volumes that make up the majority of the club's alternative list. Indeed literacy may still serve primarily as a tool or a technology for such people, which is to say a device for doing something, for bringing about change, for accomplishing some purpose. If this is true, it is understandable why fiction would be valuable to the extent that is readily applicable to one's own life, problems and concerns. No less relevant to daily life than self consciously didactic manuals, the artfulness of fiction is subordinated in the evaluative system to its pragmatic possibilities for application. (Radway 277)

Don DeLillo's White Noise

And indeed, that is what DeLillo's *White Noise* gives us. It is a book with molecular elements, as observed earlier. But it remains molar, namely, as a cohesive whole ruled over by the narrative voice of Jack Gladney. In doing so, it also speaks to many people who have little interest in experimental fiction concerned only with language. But equally important, its familiarity, its concern with the postmodern situation many people face everyday, gives mainstream (BOMC) readers a chance to ponder the meaning of it all, namely, the world of shopping and media, but also the powers behind them, as well as the affect such powers have on culture through the university.

We may add to these observations by noting certain possibly liberatory elements offered by recent technology; here, I refer to the internet and its possibilities for constructing communal dialogue and information exchange. Obviously, as Radway's essay on the BOMC was published some time ago (i.e.1989), it is unable to register fully the influence of culture industry marketers as regards areas of taste and related selection of literature in the year 2005. In particular I speak here of technological development in the areas of home and laptop computing, as well as the expansion of the internet. Like a good many other things, these elements have been developed and incorporated within late capitalist society, resulting in different modes of marketing and purchasing. As regards marketing, anyone searching for information on the internet cannot help but notice pop-up advertisements appearing at almost every search engine (e.g. google) and which hound the user relentlessly. Moreover, when one goes to a vendor's website, myriad other offerings of products appear, all of which can be purchased at the click of a few buttons and as long as one has a credit card.

Obviously, these changes affect the ways in which ideas of taste are transmitted and how products are purchased. However, the tech stock bust several years ago—an indication that we are *not* in a fundamentally new economy—and a glance at Amazon.com—one major internet purveyor of literature—would caution against hypothesizing an absolute break from the past. The first issue, fall of tech stocks, seems like prima facie evidence of this, though it is beyond the scope of our discussion. The situation of Amazon.com, on the other hand, is most enlightening for our discussion of taste, influence, and buying habits. While the following is by no means scientific proof of the similarity between practices of the BOMC and those of Amazon, it is nonetheless fruitful to look at some apparent similarities as regards influence and purchasing.

First, whenever one goes to Amazon's site (Amazon.com), one is given the option of searching for any number of products (e.g. electronic goods, music, books). Here, we are mostly interested in books. If a visitor to the

Amazon page types in "White Noise" under "books," s/he arrives at a page announcing its availability (usually within twenty four hours) and is also given the option of seeing reviews of the book in order to assist him/her in purchasing decisions. Interestingly, reviews are of two types: editorial reviews and customer reviews. The editorial reviews of *White Noise* were primarily summaries of the book's plot and its major issues; as regards the latter there was little use of postmodern theoretical jargon. In the case of customer reviews I read, most were written in non-academic language and expressed similar discussions regarding issues. Though one customer review actually used the term "postmodern," it took pains to put its descriptions of the novel's actions—many of which the customer reviewer saw as postmodern—in language clearly within the public sphere.

Another aspect relevant in all of this is Amazon's offering on the same page of an option to view other books and products ordered by individuals who purchased *White Noise*. Information I gathered from this option was particularly illuminating as regards readership and taste. First, some of the results fit expectations, especially given recent scholarship on DeLillo; in particular, William Gaddis and Thomas Pynchon were included on the list. Both writers are well known and much discussed among academics; they are also designated as postmodernists by many, if not most, in this reading community. This would tend to support the argument that readers of DeLillo are academics, but other anecdotal findings would throw this hypothesis into doubt. First, we cannot downplay the aforementioned reviews of *White Noise* which are clearly non-academic. These, however, are directly related to the explosive development of the internet as a taste-making or taste-transferring phenomenon. Amazon's rise as a distribution powerhouse is a case in point and instructive here. For any given book one finds on Amazon there is always the option of finding out what that book's other readers have read simply by clicking on the appropriate link. When I followed this path from *White Noise,* I discovered that readers of the novel had also purchased novels by Anne Tyler (*Back When We Were Grownups*), Anita Shreve (*The Last Time They Met*), Michael Chabon (*The Wonder Boys*), as well as Philip Roth (*Patrimony*). The first three of these authors fall well within the BOMC's "quality" works, but works we should remember are distinctly "middle brow," though the BOMC would not use that last phrase in its correspondence with readers. As evidence of this middle brow placement I might point to reviews of both Tyler and Shreve in *People Magazine;* the former was reviewed in the issue appearing May 21, 2001, and the second in the earlier May 7, 2001 edition. Also suggestive is the third novel, Chabon's *The Wonder Boys.* It has been made into a marginally popular film—subsequently released en masse by Blockbuster Video—starring, among others, the actor Michael Douglass. The video release was much touted, no doubt contributing to the novel's increased popularity—Michael Douglass graces the book's cover in its most recent edition—and will needless to say contribute to its sales in the future. The last author, Roth, is a canonical figure in American literature, and that fact would seem to illustrate the degree to which Amazon's mixed nature resembles that of the older BOMC, where a wide range of books are offered to a variety of readers and for "different purposes" (Radway 270).

At the same time, several points deserve mention here. Obviously, both Amazon and the BOMC exist within a capitalist system whose primary goal is profit; both companies want readers to buy their books. In fact, comparison of the BOMC to Amazon as regards internet capitalism is more applicable now than in the past, since the former is currently available online (bomc.com). We must understand the manipulative nature of this reader (shopper)/merchant relationship. While the BOMC makes plain its conscious selection of "serious" works, or those it believes "applicable to one's own life, problems and concerns" (Radway 277), Amazon is no less selective to the degree that it will categorize shopping/reading subjects and their desires (e.g. links taking readers to books addressing similar or related subjects). This, of course, is not to mention the barrage of advertising on every web page. Accordingly, both Amazon and BOMC are hegemonic and ideological in a Gramscian sense; the apparent freedom subjects believe they possess while clicking, searching, and buying conceals the degree to which dominant capitalist interests construct their desire and their subjectivity in an uneven cultural exchange.

At the same time, the news is not entirely bad. Following Janice Radway (1989) in her use of Kenneth Burke's "Literature as Equipment for Living," we might consider both DeLillo's *White Noise* and its commercial purveyors (BOMC and Amazon) in a somewhat different light. First, as already demonstrated, DeLillo's novel remains somewhat unconventional (e.g. its use of molecular elements), even while it appeals to readers demanding the coherent story, plotting, and character of traditional fiction, detective and otherwise. Moreover, the book demonstrates a concern for contemporary living conditions within a consumer society which commodifies everything, including education. DeLillo communicates this state, including the pervasive consumerist-simulation produced by such commodification (e.g. the individual's unconscious adoption of purchasable identity). As an unconventional book, but one which also speaks directly to present living conditions, we might consider *White Noise* "useful . . . to those searching for suggestions, models, and directions about how to live" (Radway 275). In this sense DeLillo's book is what Kenneth Burke calls "equipment for living" (Burke qtd. in Radway 275). The novel acts as a model of behavior to the extent that it is a sustained examination and critique of contemporary culture and society. *White Noise* warns readers about disturbing and dehumanizing trends within capitalist consumer society, but it also invites readers to reflect upon those trends. Contemporary readers may, for example, find some of themselves in Jack Gladney and his visits to postmodern malls and markets. The book thus invites readers to contemplate their own behaviors and motives. Additionally, DeLillo's surreal and uneasy rendering of contemporary life, which also suggests to readers that more is going on, much of it far from innocent. For these reasons the book invites readers to interrogate and critique contemporary social-political life. In this sense, White Noise must be viewed as positive. It is positive—or "emergent" in Raymond Williams' sense—precisely because the critique it invites offers "new meanings" as well as "new relationships" to the status quo (Williams, *Marxism and Literature* 123).

Certainly, set against this positive aspect are the more distressing, manipulative capitalist interests of our literary purveyors, BOMC and Amazon, among others. But as we have also seen, the power of these capitalist giants to pursue, capture, uniformly construct and control subjects is not limitless. Dominant ideologies—and let us call the disciplined book-consumerism of BOMC and Amazon just that—must always remain open. This is because, as Terry Eagleton remarks, "a dominant ideology has continually to negotiate with the ideologies of its subordinates"; this fact makes for its "essential open-endedness" and precludes "it from achieving any kind of pure self-identity" (Eagleton, *Ideology* 45). Hence, lack of self-identity is at the center of dominant ideology's power to control, but it is also its primary weakness. As Eagleton observes,

> what makes a dominant ideology powerful—its ability to intervene in the consciousness of those it subjects, appropriating and reinflecting their experience—is also what tends to make it internally heterogeneous and inconsistent. A successful ruling ideology . . . must engage significantly with genuine wants, needs and desires; but this is its Achilles heel, forcing it to recognize an 'other' to itself and inscribing this otherness as a potentially disruptive force within its own forms. (Eagleton, *Ideology* 45)

Or, to take an example close at hand, internet purveyors like Amazon—and now BOMC—must recognize the other, computing/reading subjects, in order to interpellate them into ideologically disciplined book consumers. Our booksellers' single-minded pursuit of ever greater profits leads them to construct perpetually changing arrays of on-line features to attract customers, among them the "customer review"; but in so doing, they fall prey to the Achilles heel of recognition, opening up a space for liberatory discussion and exchange.

While it would be naive to dismiss the toxic nature of alluring features designed solely to make people buy, it would also seem closed-minded and dogmatic to insist these features are entirely unified, that their consumer-logic is all-encompassing. Indeed, features like the "customer review" strike at the weak point of dominant ideology, acting as subterranean or alternative communication networks wherein people exchange information bearing on their "genuine wants, needs and desires," and isn't that exactly what Burke means by "equipment for living"?

Chapter Four
Repoliticizing Depoliticized Categories: Literary Inheritance, Textual Activism, and the Space of Reading

As I hope the preceding chapters illustrate, the novels of Reed, Acker, and DeLillo attempt to problematize—in various ways—traditional notions of author, text, and reading subject. While our study's focus has shown the respective texts to operate somewhat differently from one another and to relatively different ends, the three novels nevertheless possess a unity in the problematizing itself. The kinds of problematizing each accomplishes clearly associate them with artistic practices popularly labeled "postmodern." At the same time, I am convinced that any simple and single minded categorization of these writers, and a good many others, as "postmodern"—as against, say, "modern"—is itself wrong headed, perhaps motivated more by one's desire for clean theoretical categories than truthful description. Of course, we could not hope in this small space to analyze all the myriad complicated issues involved in such categorizations.

However, having said this, I would like to contribute modestly to such a discussion by looking at the ways Reed, Acker, and DeLillo's novels *converge* with and *diverge* from certain artistic practices and theories commonly associated with postmodernism. The result, I hope, complicates our understanding of the novels as postmodern artefacts, while also illuminating frequently encountered theories about postmodernism and postmodernity. In related sense, I believe it will also show how the postmodern texts addressed here refer to and interact with tradition (e.g. modernism), despite popular claims that such contemporary works remain absolutely different from their ancestors.

My intention in this chapter is to open up our discussion to wider issues, while still providing a degree of focus for clarity and precision. Again, what follows is not intended to definitively answer certain questions (e.g. is there an absolute schism between modernism and postmodernism), but to raise issues which complicate our obviously vague and over general understandings of terms attached to that now so popular prefix, "post."

Ishmael Reed: Traditional Postmodernist?

The second chapter of this study points out similarities between Reed's use of voodoo and postmodern and poststructural theory. Indeed, *Mumbo Jumbo*'s numerous subversions of unity (e.g. its dismantling of unified self, unitary authorship, textual unity, as well as singular visions of racial history and identity) would appear to concur with the theoretical proclamations of postmodern thinkers such as Foucault, Derrida, and even Lyotard. However, I believe we must temper such observations with others, namely, ones that criticize simple and unproblematic alignment of Reed's vision with those of postmodern theorists. For as often as Reed is called a postmodernist by writers like Fredric Jameson (1983, 1991) and Henry Louis Gates (1984,1988), he could just as often be cited as a traditionalist, a writer practicing within a coherent African-American heritage. In fact, the two claims (postmodernism and tradition) could even be combined into a contradiction, as they are in the second author above, Henry Louis Gates. Gates reads *Mumbo Jumbo* as signifying the undecidable poststructural nature of "blackness" and African-American literary tradition. But in so doing he constructs a grand narrative similar to the sort he would deny, namely, a coherent and identifiable African-American writing tradition.

While I will have more to say on this later, it is important here to register as significant Gates's position and that of the author cited before him, Fredric Jameson. They represent two highly influential though opposing views on Reed and his relationship to postmodernism. Furthermore, in the case of Jameson we have a scholar who seeks to theorize postmodern art more generally. For these reasons I would like to examine briefly certain claims offered by these thinkers.

As already remarked, the two thinkers stand in opposite corners regarding Reed's work. Gates, who is undoubtedly the most famous commentator on Reed, views Reed positively. Here, I refer to his well known essay on *Mumbo Jumbo* in *Black Literature and Literary Theory* (1984), but also the theoretical apparatus that book and others (e.g. *The Signifying Monkey: A Theory of African American Literary Criticism* (1988)) construct regarding

African-American literary tradition. Gates' exemplary essay on *Mumbo Jumbo* links Reed to the African/African-American trickster tradition. It also locates connections between Reed's novels and earlier canonical texts within African-American literary tradition. At the same time, Gates' wider project declares, by way of poststructural construel, that *Mumbo Jumbo* illustrates the absolute "indeterminacy" of "the text of blackness" (Gates, *Literature and Literary Theory* 305), which for him means the indeterminable nature of black identity and literary tradition.

Opposing Gates' theoretical depiction of the "postmodern" Reed is Fredric Jameson. Jameson's take on Reed is decidedly negative. Even so, his essay "Postmodernism and Consumer Society" (1983) and the highly influential book *Postmodernism, or, The Cultural Logic of Late Capitalism* (1991) clearly illustrate that Fredric Jameson is writer who thinks big; the expansiveness of his thought is illustrated in these two cases by the fact that his main target in both is not so much the individual artist and author as the general cultural milieu. In particular, both his works represent the larger effort to read present day (postmodern) cultural. One handicap in the two cases, however, is that while Jameson does offer extended discussions of certain artists and writers (e.g. Andy Warhol's art, E. L. Doctorow's book *Ragtime*) he does not give extended space to others, preferring instead simply to list them as participants in an all encompassing trend. Reed is one of these listed but neglected participants, and as such receives no treatment whatsoever; he is a mere name on a list.

Not surprisingly, membership on the list is no compliment. For Jameson novelists on this list—including the condemned Reed—suffer from an inability to envision our late capitalist conditions. Such writers cannot envision the present; nor can they represent history in any unfolding sense. Instead, such authors exhibit the central postmodern compositional characteristic of "pastiche."[1] For Jameson, "pastiche" is similar to "parody" in that it is "the imitation of a peculiar or unique style, the wearing of a stylistic mask, speech in a dead language . . ." (Jameson, "Postmodernism and Consumer Society" 114). But pastiche is also much less in that it is "blank parody," namely, "a neutral practice of such mimicry, without parody's ulterior motive, without the satirical impulse, . . . without that still latent feeling that there exists something normal compared to which what is being imitated is rather comic" (Jameson, "Postmodernism and Consumer Culture" 114; *Postmodernism, or, The Cultural Logic of Late Capitalism* 17). With "blank parody" no historical or outside reference exists for parody to criticize. Parody becomes empty in this sense; that is, it is a mere patchwork of imitations without reference to anything.

The concept of patchwork is central here. The feeling in postmodern culture, according to Jameson, is that everything has already been said and said in every possible combination. There is nothing new; contemporary artists are left to "imitate dead styles" and "speak through the masks and with the voices of the styles in the imaginary museum" (Jameson, "Postmodernism and Consumer Society" 115). This, it should be said, is historically significant for Jameson, since pastiche represented only a cultural "subordinate" within the artistic system of the past (e.g. the avant-garde art of *modernism*) and is now—in our postmodern era—the "dominant" form ("Postmodernism and Consumer Society" 123).

We should also note that Jameson's diagnostic closely links this dominance of pastiche within postmodernism to the poststructuralist disintegration of the subject, what he calls "the death of the subject" (Jameson, "Postmodernism and Consumer Society" 114). Of course, death of the traditional subject also implies the death of the individual author. Here, again, pastiche plays a role because the author is now nothing but the old masks and styles simply re-deployed. Moreover, the author *as subject* is similarly dispersed or fragmented into so many recapitulations of past discourses or utterances (e.g. subjective desire merely reproduces desire represented in commercials).

In terms of general validity, the most problematic part of Jameson's grand theory is his claim that pastiche is "dominant" within our culture (i.e. "postmodern culture"). This is itself an empirical question. Jameson's sample, however, is small, and thus far from convincing. Furthermore, one might easily launch a counter argument by noting just how many realistic novels are still written. Certainly, the pastiche style is rare in works selected by the previously analyzed Book of the Month Club, which we examined in the DeLillo chapter.

In terms of Reed specifically, Jameson classifies his work as postmodern precisely because he equates Reed's compositional techniques with the aforementioned regenerated masks or styles (i.e. with pastiche). As a result Jameson finds Reed dissolving identities in a manner similar to that noted above. This is particularly easy to see if we remember our earlier discussion of *Mumbo Jumbo* and its systematic undermining of singular authorship through employment of *loas* (spirits). There, we saw not only how the individual author is undermined by one or more of these spirits, but also how such spirits could embody larger ways of thinking (e.g. discourses), which themselves come to inhabit and speak through individuals.

Following this line of thought it is easy to see why Jameson thinks *Mumbo Jumbo* exemplifies the tendency he ascribes to postmodernism, namely, the poststructural disintegration of authorship and subjectivity. Reed's notion of *loas* would *seem* to correspond, at least roughly, with certain ideas held by poststructuralists such as Foucault, Derrida, and Lyotard. In Foucault's case we might think of the disappearance of a text's author into the "author function," or the idea that autonomous subjects disappear into so many disparate discourses which speak through them. Here, Reed's loas would perform similarly, though within the voodoo/hoodoo system. In the case of another poststructuralist, Derrida, we earlier observed affinities between his concept of "dissemination" and Reed's loas. Here we may remember how, within Reed's authorial vision, texts become inhabited "by other texts, or other genres or topics of discourse" (Norris 25–26), and in so doing spread out infinitely. In a third poststructuralist comparison not yet mentioned, we might think of Jean-François Lyotard, who triumphantly calls an end to all "grand narratives." If Reed were interpreted in this way, he might claim the demise of any singular African-American literary tradition; the alternative, I suppose, would be numerous small narratives of African-American tradition, with each claiming equal validity. Of course, such a Lyotardian position would itself be ironic, since it reinstitutes a grand narrative, if one whose grand claim is the existence of only small narratives. In any event, all these similarities would seem to affiliate Reed with the very poststructuralist theories so often associated with postmodernism.

But is such an alignment all that simple and straightforward? Moreover, given its negative cast, at least in Jameson, is such an alignment entirely fair? In many ways, our own examination would say otherwise. First, though we did find apparent similarities between Reed's concepts and many poststructural ideas—ideas often associated with postmodernism—we also interpreted him in ways that would appear to contradict Jameson's appraisal. Though I will momentarily set aside contradictory evidence regarding Reed and subject disintegration, we can list a few pieces of evidence contradicting Jameson's view. We may, for instance, remember that our discussion of *Mumbo Jumbo* was both political and critical. We interpreted *Mumbo Jumbo* as positive, historical, and undermining of dominant ideology (e.g. dominant white western versions of history, dominant white ideology in the press). Here, we interpreted Reed as consciously playing on past texts, namely, offering parodic representations in order to criticize. Jameson, on the other hand, clearly considers such usages mere "blank parody," and thus empty of the very political and critical import we analyzed.

In a related sense, we also saw a critical interrogation of those who would pretend to author a singular narrative of African-American identity and tradition. As seen in Chapter One, Reed's black nationalist editor, Abdul

Hamid, could represent one such author. He is meant, at least in part, to stand for similar attempts by black critics past and present who attempt to author and authorize a singular African-American literary and cultural tradition (e.g. past critics of the Harlem Renaissance and more recent critics such as Houston Baker and Amiri Baraka). At the same time, that chapter also showed us similar attempts at singular authorship by white hegemonic interests. For example, we saw the white racist Hinckle Von Vampton and his group, The Knights Templar, attempt to narrate African-American history and cultural tradition.

If this is not convincing, there exists other counter evidence to Jameson's diagnostic. There is, of course, the already mentioned listing of "postmodern" authors without adequate—indeed, without any—explication. But what this implies regarding Reed is worse yet. To be specific, Jameson's listing of Reed without explication would seem to suggest his own unawareness of African-American literary history.[2] In particular he appears unaware of the enormous influence of voodoo (American HooDoo) as an historically inherited practice within Reed's work—something Reed has admitted to time and again.[3] Beyond this he also seems unconscious of numerous other inherited African-American literary practices informing Reed's novels.

One primary and inherited element is Reed's syncretism. Syncretism, we will remember, refers to the tendency of cultural practices to rub up against one another and mix; the resulting mixture implicitly destroy claims of cultural purity or the purity of a tradition. In *Mumbo Jumbo* American, European, Haitian, and African cultures intermarry to produce American HooDoo practices. Hence, just as Haitian voodoo practitioners (e.g. Houngans) conjure by mixing inherited cultural practices with those of the colonizer (e.g. mixing of sacred Haitian voodoo spirits with Catholic saints), so too do American HooDoo practitioners create within their historical circumstances by authoring or conjuring with familiar inherited African-American material, which is similarly mixed with other less familiar elements (e.g. jazz musicians use trace African ingredients, such as a particular rhythm, along with ingredients present in the American cultural context). Jameson, however, seems entirely unaware of this syncretic lineage and Reed's use of it.

Such facts imply a different history, as well as different theoretical foundations from those of western poststructuralism. More to the point, whatever their similarities, voodoo and western poststructuralist theories are not really based on the same beliefs. Postmodern poststructuralism is a kind of anti-metaphysical thinking founded in reaction to epistemological questions directly related to European history, philosophy, and linguistics.

Voodoo practices are rooted in African and Haitian religious practices which were themselves products of specific historical circumstances like colonization and slavery. American Hoodoo represents those inherited practices, if in different circumstances and syncretically mixed. Thus, unproblematically equating poststructural postmodernist practices with syncretic Hoodoo practices seems wrongheaded, whatever their commonalities.

But these elements are not all that Jameson seems to neglect. In fact, briefly sampling well known and canonical African-American literary practices throws further doubt on Jameson's claims. In particular it demonstrates that Reed's compositional method follows earlier African-American texts. Some readers might reasonably retort that this hardly refutes Jameson since, according to him, it is a mark of postmodern authors to borrow from earlier texts, using them to don stylistic masks. But such a rejoinder fails to understand a central difference between this sort of usage and Reed's. Reed has read African-American works of the past and believes he can discern in them a compositional tradition. Right or wrong, he believes his novels follow that tradition. In an interview with John Domini Reed states as much, observing "no matter what my contemporaries may say, there is tradition for me" (Domini 141). With this and other evidence in mind, we should consider his methods (e.g. intertextuality) and content (e.g. voodoo) as representing something more than a *bricolaged* use of masks or guises.

To get some idea of this we need only look at his use of the African-American literary past. In terms of inherited content, we may note voodoo as a prominent feature of past African-American canonical texts such as *The Conjure Woman* by Charles Chesnutt, first published in 1899. This work offers as a main character an African-American freeman, Uncle Julius McAdoo, who tells stories about hexing and "conjur women" strongly suggestive of voodoo (e.g. "The Goophered Grapevine," "Po' Sandy"). Furthermore, as the part-time but mostly dominant narrator, Uncle Julius cleverly uses tales to control the behavior of the whites around him, namely, those ostensibly in material control. Thus, as so many other black writers have done, Reed invokes the African inherited trickster figure. Though to my knowledge Reed has never announced the influence of Chesnutt's text on *Mumbo Jumbo*'s composition, in a nineteen sixty-eight interview with Walt Shepperd he explicitly states Chesnutt's influence on an earlier work, *The Freelance Pallbearers* (1967) (Shepperd 3). In any case, the prevalence of conjuring along voodoo lines seems evident enough to illustrate the point.

Furthermore, Reed has also inherited other elements from canonical African-American sources. Speaking with Al Young in 1972, Reed notes that "some of the same satirical thrusts" in his *Yellow Back Radio Broke-Down* (1969) are found in his predecessor William Wells Brown's 1858 play *The Escape; or, A Leap to Freedom*. Specifically, Reed remarks that his satirical jabs against "doctors, and the church," as well as against "Christianity," are quite similar to Brown's (Young 46). Much the same is illustrated in Chapter One, where we saw Reed's *Mumbo Jumbo* making similar satirical attacks on a bullying and corrupt Christianity which uses reason—in the form of the medical professional "health department"—to diagnose the African-American spirit as illness. Here, as with Chesnutt's *Conjur Woman*, we have what Reed calls a "non-Western form of satire," namely, one representing "the way the persecuted get back at their exploiters" (Henry 213). Interestingly, Reed also isolates this same type of satire in very old "Afro-American masks," the likeness of which he hints at and updates in the figure of the singular African-American vaudevillian, Bert Williams, who he states has "captured the Afro-American mask with Northrop Frye's inverted ∪ lips" (*Mumbo Jumbo* 96). This statement at once interdiscursively references Frye's archetypal analysis of comedy's use of masks (Frye 1957), but in so doing also connects African-*American* descendants—represented by Williams and his renowned gestural abilities—to the ancestral humor intrinsic in African masks.[4]

Interestingly, another of Browns works, *Clotel; or, The President's Daughter* (1853), provides further evidence that Reed follows inherited practices. For those unfamiliar with Brown's achievements, *Clotel* is the first African-American novel and describes the fate of the mulatto daughter of one of Thomas Jefferson's consorts, Clotel. What is striking about this for us is the conjunction of the work's age—it was produced in eighteen fifty three—and its author's conscious use of plagiarism and borrowed themes. Furthermore, and equally important, Brown freely incorporates news clippings and other publicly printed announcements into his book.

As the first chapter demonstrated, Reed's *Mumbo Jumbo* employs news items and announcements. *Clotel,* a much older work, does the same thing. Indeed, Reed has asserted the inheritance of this practice directly from Brown (Nazareth 183). A similar observation can be made about Reed's plagiarism and borrowed themes. To see the connection we need only consult the actual source of Brown's work and how he adjusted it for his own purposes. It is well known that Brown took large sections of Lydia Maria Child's tale "The Octoroons" and placed them verbatim within *Clotel* (Zafar 133; Yellin 172).[5] What proves interesting is not just the historical precedent of verbatim plagiarism—something Reed clearly practices in *Mumbo Jumbo*—but also what both Brown and Reed do with thematic borrowing. Specifically, Brown's *Clotel* refigures the plight of Child's mulatto

Repoliticizing Depoliticized Categories 171

heroines. As opposed to Childs, who represents her mulatto females "dying of broken hearts," Brown gives them "imagination, ingenuity, and courage to outwit their oppressors" (duCille qtd. in Zafar 133). This obviously demonstrates the tricksterism noted above, but it also shows Brown's reworking of a dominant textual representation—in this case Child's portrayal of helpless and passive mulatto heroines—for political and ideological purposes. It is thus quite similar in method and purpose to Reed's textual manipulations whereby the author refigures the history of western civilization, culture, and religion.[6]

But Reed follows another canonized work of the past which also refigures, though somewhat differently. Here, I speak of the canonized Harlem Renaissance poet James Weldon Johnson who, with the help of illustrator Aaron Douglas, composed *God's Trombones* (1927). That book—itself a paean to the African-American folk sermon—offers numerous drawings between its sections of verse. In fact, Reed affirms Johnson's influence on his drawings in *Mumbo Jumbo* and even credits his predecessor for that book's use of "jes grew" (Gaga 55). Interestingly, Johnson's book—similar to Reed's—attempts to counterbalance dominant white representations via refiguration, though in Johnson's case he focuses on Biblical representation. Moreover, both use pictures. Specifically, Johnson insinuates blackness into biblical narrative, suggesting "an alternative means of representing blacks . . ." (Carroll 74). The effect, only fully realized in the interaction between Douglas' illustrations and the black preacher's narrating dialect, is to "suggest an African context for the narrative, and . . . perhaps . . . encourage readers to question the accuracy of assumptions in the 1920s that Biblical characters were white" (Carroll 72). Such refiguring of dominant ideology through pictures and words is thus quite similar to Reed and again illustrates coherent inheritance of African-American artistic practice.

Finally, there are Jameson's claims regarding authorial disintegration and the related disintegration of the subject (i.e. the death of the subject). Here, again, I believe Jameson combines theoretical overreaching with a forgetfulness of cultural-historical context; this, however, I must infer since Jameson nowhere fully explicates his claims regarding Reed. In any case, my point here is that Jameson's desire to associate contemporary cultural artefacts with poststructuralist theoretical claims makes him insist that these same artefacts all embody the death of subject and author. But in Reed's case such a global claim again forgets African-American artistic history and its connections to the larger culture and community.

Though I must be brief here, in terms of African-American history and wider cultural connections, it is helpful again to examine Reed's own statements. In one interview, for instance, Reed comments directly on the anonymity of African-American authorship and its relation to community. As he remarks, that "Afro-American art has usually been anonymous" (Shepperd 11). As an example, he points to the genre of "field chants," and comments upon one such instance, noting that "we don't know who did 'Stagger Lee.' . . . He [the artist] didn't put his name to it. . . . He didn't sign his name to it" (Shepperd 11). According to Reed, this anonymity is inherited from Africa and relates directly to art's communal function for both Africans and African-Americans; in both, remarks Reed, "art is a function of the society" (Shepperd 11). In other words, according to Reed, African-American art—as well as African art—play central roles within the community and are not separate from it. Positioning art intimately within community and communal practices not only robs the art work of total autonomy; it also weakens autonomy of the artist, since the artist functions so closely within and for community. The romantic image of the sole and isolated creative genius is here replaced by an image of the artist in intimate dialogue with community.

This African rooted authorial vision is present as subtext in the aforementioned *God's Trombones,* James Weldon Johnson's homage to the African-American sermon. In Johnson's collection of poems the preacher delivering the sermon is an artist of sorts; he has a message and holds the church crowd's attention; but his art work—the sermon—is communal rather than purely autonomous. This is true not only because the preacher wishes to instruct the church community, but also because a central aspect of the sermon is its "call and response" format (Huggins 229), namely, its two way (communal) speech. That is, the preacher delivers the sermon and is met with "a chorus of responses" by the congregation, which gives the sermon "an antiphonal quality . . ." (Johnson 11). Such responses, it must be said, are in fairly sharp contrast to the rote responses of most Western Christianity, since they play off of the reverend's words—much like the jazz player off of a central theme—and are not always the same. Hence Johnson speaks of the impossibility of rendering precisely the existential experience of the congregation's "fervor," its "amens and hallelujahs," or even "the undertone of singing which was often the accompaniment to parts of the sermon" (Johnson 10).[7] Such improvisational interaction is, of course, exactly what we saw in our chapter on Reed's *Mumbo Jumbo*.

In terms of African-American emphasis on community over self, we should perhaps consider the issue more complexly. We might, for example, view emphasis on community over self—or self as author—as resulting partly from transported African or Haitian practices. But it is probably also the case that community valorization results partly from historical exigencies specific to the American context. Here, stress on the communal might be due in part to a racist culture which refuses to admit blacks into the (white) American mythology of self. That is, perhaps African-Americans have had to find alternative sources for self definition, since dominant white culture has until recently controlled the availability of narratives about the self—and this extends from early Puritan religious visions welcoming the (white-European) self into the American "New Covenant" to much later autonomous visions like Ben Franklin and Horatio Alger's myths of capitalist self-creation.[8]

At the same time, American myths of self are based largely on the autonomous self produced by European Enlightenment and its social-economic conditions (e.g. rising bourgeoisie). Unquestionably, such visions must have affected African-Americans. Nevertheless, it seems important to recognize that whatever their similarities, the African (or Haitian) senses of self and community are born of different circumstances and may well emphasize different elements to different degrees.

But does this emphasis on community mean that Reed totally denies the self and the self that writes, namely, the author? Asserting so would, I believe, be a mistake. Specifically, diminution of subject and author does not necessarily entail their absolute disappearance. Indeed, much of the above would seem to suggest that the subject still exists but is defined in close relation to community. For example, Earline, once possessed for not feeding the loas, does regain her selfhood. Similarly, an author might be possessed by the loas of previous writers or their techniques but use them to her own advantage, thus creating her own style, much like the jazz great John Coltrane did with the material of artists before him. Here, loss of authorial identity is neither entire nor permanent. Instead, it looks more like the author consistently engages with the past, namely past writers and their practices. In any case, all this hardly matters in terms of Jameson's argument because his condemnation—his assertion that Reed dissolves the subject and author—is based on a linkage between Reed's art and poststructuralism; but this, as our foray into African-American literary history shows, is far from accurate or fair.

Having demonstrated some of the weakness of Jameson's generalizations with regard to Reed, I want now to briefly return to Henry Louis Gates, a critic who not only views Reed more favorably, but also more throughly and insightfully. Gates' *The Signifying Monkey*, as well as his essay in *Black Literature and Literary Theory*, are penetrating and offer some of the best criticism of African-American literary practice. Indeed, a good case in point are the remarkable connections he makes between Reed's *Mumbo*

Jumbo and other African-American works. Unfortunately, as my agenda involves troubling postmodern categories, much of what I have to say is critical despite my admiration of Gates' insights.

As I said earlier, the two works by Gates have a larger project, and it is that larger project that I want to criticize. Gates' project involves the use of poststructuralism in analyzing the operation of African-American literary tradition and identifying black identity. Poststructuralist theory, it will be remembered, is often closely associated with postmodernism. As our umbrella topic is postmodernism, this is one reason Gates's work on Reed is important. Gates' position is roughly this: Gates bases his analysis of Reed on certain poststructural tenets, some of which I will elucidate further below. These tenets lead him to declare the absolute "indeterminacy" of "the text of blackness" (Gates, *Literature and Literary Theory* 305), which means the indeterminable nature of black identity and African-American literary tradition. Moreover, for Gates, Reed's *Mumbo Jumbo* is emblematic of this in that it formally represents this "indeterminacy" and is about "the nature of writing itself" (Gates, "The Blackness of Blackness" 307).

Though I agree with Gates on a number of points here, I disagree with his larger theoretical underpinning. In particular, I disagree with his poststructural reading and all that it implies.[9] One objection has already been noted, in that in the process of claiming the absolute "indeterminacy" of African-American literary tradition he systematically maps out just such a tradition. That is, he constructs the grand narrative of African-American tradition he said was impossible. Here, he makes numerous, insightful connections between, say, Reed's work, and other African-American writers of the past (e.g. Reed's *Mumbo Jumbo* playing off of and revising texts like Ralph Ellison's *Invisible Man* (1952)). He also accurately claims that *Mumbo Jumbo* is about writing and its social-political ramifications. Of course, these important insights prove neither his poststructural base nor his claims regarding the absolute indeterminacy of African-American identity and literary tradition. In fact, I would assert that it is not necessary to associate many of his important insights with such theory at all. We may instead simply read them as interesting and textually based assertions which fit with the social and historical facts.

One important problem in Gates' theory is its self-contradiction. This self contradiction results from Gates' poststructural dissolution of both race and African-American literary tradition. While his procedure operates similarly with African-American literary tradition, in terms of race Gates' poststructuralist theory—namely, his holding to popular deconstructionist beliefs spanning from Saussurean linguistics to principles of *différance*—

compel him to eliminate the very notion of race, so that discussion of it in real world terms becomes impossible. To quote the man himself, "There can be no transcendent blackness, for it cannot and does not exist beyond manifestations of it in specific figures" (Gates, "The Blackness of Blackness" 316).[10] Similarly, of course, African-American literary tradition is dissolved into a poststructrual indeterminateness.

What seems interesting, however, is that this move to dissolve race, African-American literary tradition, and identity itself ultimately end up reinstating it, if in a hidden way; this produces logical problems for his theory, but also results in troubling ethical and political positions. The form of this reinstatement—popular among poststructural theorists like Gates—is called a "hybrid." In typical application, this "hybridity" usually "comes down to a combination of European tradition with some ethnically-defined tradition—often given in the first term of a 'hyphenated' identity category (African-American, Irish-American, or whatever)" (Hogan, *Empire and Poetic Voice* 36). Interestingly, a "standard assumption in discussions of hybridity is that hybridity is opposed to identity categories. Thus to be hybrid is to reject identities; to celebrate hybridity is to cast off regulatory regimes" (Hogan, *Empire and Poetic Voice* 4). This, of course, perfectly describes how Gates believes his African-American non-identity category operates for both African-American identity and African-American literary tradition. But as Patrick Hogan indicates, claiming hybrids are outside identity categories is false. As he puts it,

> Hybridity is no less an identity category than 'authentically indigenous' or 'westernized.' It [hybridity] has the same function in defining and opposing groups and in setting out norms. It simply defines groups differently and establishes different norms. Instead of adjuring us to be authentically African, Indian, Hindu, Igbo, Irish, or whatever, it adjures us to be hybrid. (*Empire and Poetic Voice* 8)

Thus, even while Gates claims his theory exists outside "regulatory regimes," and that African-American hybrid identity does not constitute an identity category, he nevertheless ends up reinstating both identity and regulation.

However, we should also note that associated problems exist within the reinstatement of (hybrid) identity. While Gates and believers in hyphenated identity often insist such categories merely designate the fluidity of cultural traditions (e.g. Gates' undecidable African-American tradition), a number of commentators have indicated serious political and ethical problems for such conceptions (Said 1993; Kuenz 1997; Zafar 1997; Hogan 2004). For one, such a hyphenated identity remains bound to nationhood, namely, the second half of the hyphenated identity (e.g. African-*American* tradition).[11] Such a definition of cultural identity focuses attention on the dichotomy and hierarchy which places "self" against "other," or, put another way, it fixates upon "our nation" and "our literature," while xenophobically excluding all others as "foreign."

In a related sense, and equally troubling, is the fact that hybridized formulations like Gates' tend to fixate on the first half of the hyphenated term (e.g. *African*-American tradition). This tendency, which Patrick Hogan calls "ethnic confinement" (Hogan, *Empire and Poetic Voice* 7–8), results in a fixation upon ethnicity, but one which ironically "tend[s] to treat European traditions as universal and non-European traditions as ethnic" (Hogan, *Empire and Poetic Voice* 36). We should register here a further consequence of *ethnic confinement* of tradition, namely, that it is troubling precisely because it *dissolves tradition to ethnicity*. Speaking on such reduction in reference to Gates, Jane Kuenz observes that "like racial nationalisms grounded in romanticized versions of difference," Gates' "multiculturalist formulations assume an unbroken sequence of cultural transmissions, qualified by specific circumstances, but loyal finally to the integrity and continuation of an originary conception of racial identity and a form for its expression" (Kuenz 205). In short, Gates "grounds" his "claims in a theory of race as identical to 'culture' unaffected in any great way by what's outside of it . . ." (Kuenz 205).[12]

In doing this Gates unintentionally plays into the hands of racists since he gives them precisely the grounded absolute difference they seek. As Kuenz observes, "the rhetorical elision of race and culture allows racist writers to continue spouting the same [racist] beliefs under the less egregious heading of 'cultural difference'" (201). Indeed, part of what this shows is that the "elimination of 'race' as an essential category does not alleviate the need for its preservation as a practical political one" (205). Gates' position, which does not recognize this necessity, may in fact lead to a variety of political quietism since his poststructural reading eliminates race as a category of discussion. As far as this goes, we could add to Kuenz's remarks and observe that Gates' quietism must also extend to issues of class, since his poststructural doctrine similarly demands we obliterate the identity called "class"[13]. Such a position thus advocates a kind of simplistic acceptance of differences without deeper and complex critical interrogation.

This fact is interesting in terms of the social-historical context Reed sets for *Mumbo Jumbo,* namely, the Harlem Renaissance.[14] That period saw intense "debates" among black thinkers "about whether or how black experiences in the U.S. affect the cultural inheritance of Africa presumably available to African-Americans through the exigencies of race" (Kuenz 198). As it happens, one prominent participant in those debates was Langston Hughes, who fiercely endorsed the idea that blacks remain in touch with their uniquely African spiritual and racial roots, what he called "the eternal tom-tom beating in the Negro soul" (Hughes qtd. in Kuenz 198–199).[15] Of course, there was an opposing argument, and on that side was W.E.B. Dubois, who considered Hughes' position "naive and politically dangerous" because of its romantic vision of racial and cultural roots (Kuenz 197–209). Interestingly, Henry Louis Gates' position affirming indissoluble racial difference appears similar to Hughes' position in this sense, his poststructuralist dissolution of race not withstanding. Thus, in a curious way Gates reenacts one side of this important Harlem Renaissance argument.

What also seems worth noting, as Kuenz points out, is that very similar debates continue today, if in slightly differing versions (e.g. Gates' multiculturalist perspective verses Molefi Asante's Afrocentricity) (197–198). Not surprisingly, what is at issue in such debates is African-American identity and the identity of African-American tradition. In contemporary terms, we may observe that while Gates is no Abdul Hamid—Reed's fictional African-Nationalist critic—his work nevertheless seems to imply a limitation on the boundaries of African-American identity. While Hamid wants to rid African-American identity and tradition of all past traces of the "lewd, nasty, decadent thing[s] . . . depicted" in Reed's ancient Book of Toth, Gates, who desires to construct an authentic (hybrid) African-American tradition, must act similarly. Here the aforementioned regulation and irony return in moments of inclusion and exclusion. In specific, Gates says that "the implicit premise of this study is that all texts signify upon other texts, in motivated and unmotivated ways" (Gates, *The Signifying Monkey* xxiv qtd. in Adell 133). Yet Gates also says that the shared nature of the "text of blackness"—its specific tradition—is found in "the process of revision that tropes and topoi undergo when they are seized by writers as they read each other's texts" (Adell 133). So if all texts signify similarly, what, exactly, makes signifying in the African-American tradition (its shared "text of blackness") so different from other traditions? Gates' only answer is to elide the problem by secretly—if unconsciously—reducing tradition to race. Here, his situation seems similar to the one Patrick Hogan isolates in postcolonial adherents of hybridity (Hogan, *Empire and Poetic Voice* 2004). Speaking on the postcolonial hybrid thinker Homi Bhabha, Hogan observes a "tension" between the assertion that "everyone is hybrid" and logically problematic assertion that "a particular group" is "specially hybrid" (6). Indeed, this is strikingly similar to

Gates' problem with regard to the special sort of signifying supposedly enacted within African-American tradition. Moreover, we may add to this the irony that Gates' distinctly African-American tradition is throughly saturated with western, specifically, French, poststructural theory; indeed, as Sandra Adell remarks, for Gates it is the only sort of theory that *can* explicate African-American tradition.[16]

In a different sense other critics have performed similar exclusions and inclusions, by categorizing certain literary works as within African-American literary tradition or outside of it. As a primary case in point, just because an author is African-American does not necessarily mean critics will categorize that author's work as part of African-American literary tradition. This fact alone reveals how tradition is itself a construction and a function of power relations. Indeed, whoever wins the power struggle regarding inclusion and exclusion will be the one(s) to determine tradition.

Illustrating this point and also relevant to Reed's *Mumbo Jumbo* is Rafia Zafar's recent work, *We Wear the Mask: African Americans Write American Literature, 1760–1870* (1997), which discusses this inclusion/exclusion tendency. As Zafar observes, before the "last third of the nineteenth century African American writers adopted many of the ideas and genres of the white dominant culture in order to declare themselves part of it." (Zafar 7). Not surprisingly, however, the works of these writers are often not included within African American literature, which is to say African-American literary *tradition*. While I will offer only one example here, Zafar cites numerous others, among them the Christian and African-American writer John Marrant. Though he is rarely if ever mentioned as part of so called African-American literary tradition, Marrant wrote numerous sermons (e.g. Sermon for "The Festival of St. John the Baptist" (1789)) and a captivity narrative based on the Puritan model (*A Narrative of the Lord's Wonderful Dealings with John Marrant* (1785)) (Zafar 1997). But the fact that many critics consider captivity narratives and Puritan sermons—as genres—the sole property of white dominant culture prohibits them from including Marrant's work in the ranks of African-American literary tradition. Moreover, one would assume that in terms of the author's individual identity the evidence used for exclusion from literary tradition automatically condemns Marrant—as writing subject—to the position of mimic, and therefore brands him an inauthentic African-American.[17] Theorists of hybridity (e.g. Gates) may, in a move of supposed non-identitarian inclusion, incorporate such writers, but they will nevertheless construct identity categories through a regulatory process of inclusion and exclusion (e.g. through ethnic confinement) in order to attain tradition.[18]

Zafar—herself a hybrid thinker of sorts—considers writers like Marrant "not witless imitators" but African-Americans attempting to offer "a positive attitude about themselves" (Zafar 7). According to Zafar, their works represent an attempt at "literary 'trasnculturation,' whereby they as individuals become part of the host society" (Zafar 7). Zafar, working with Mary Louise Pratt's definition, calls "transculturation" a method by which "subordinated or marginal groups select and invent from materials transmitted to them by dominant or metropolitan culture" (Pratt qtd. in Zafar 193). Here, one cannot help but be struck by the similarity between the Pratt-Zafar vision and Reed's own syncretism seen in Chapter One, where voodoo and Neo-Hoodoo borrow from available resources.

While these observations seem positive, the idea of a distinctly African-American *tradition* and *identity* remain problematic. Given such problems we might want to replace a term like "tradition" with some variation of "inherited artistic practice," though even that substitution remains beholden to the notion of "inheritance"; such a formulation therefore begs the question of who, exactly, is the just beneficiary of such inheritance. I would like, then, to close this section by discussing identity and tradition, especially as they relate to Reed, whose position is in some large sense hybrid as is indicated by his gumbo approach.

Reed's notion of hybridity involves its own internal tension, in this case one between descriptive and normative accounts. Specifically, I am talking about the tendency to slide between description of a tradition or culture and the tendency to favor that tradition or culture. As analyzed in Chapter One, part of Reed's goal in *Mumbo Jumbo* is to offer and explain a hybrid counter-tradition to the hegemonic western one. In that sense, it could be called descriptive. At other times, however, Reed clearly seems to advocate that same counter-tradition as preferable (e.g. his sarcastic critique of Christianity and its cultural pilfering of ideas from marginalized cultures), while also isolating it as specifically African-American (e.g. tracing African-American tradition through specifically Haitian and African practices).

But here a cautionary note seems advisable. Reed, unlike Gates or Bhabha, is not a theorist; he is a poet, novelist, and essayist who has never formally written a theory of tradition, even if he does have one. Rather, it is left for us to construct such things from evidence in his works. Moreover, and possibly more troubling for those who desire consistency, is the assertion that Reed will demonstrate consistency in such matters. But as most of us know, artists often fail to demonstrate consistency in this respect.

With this in mind I believe other evidence should temper the correspondences drawn between Reed, Gates, and Bhabha. In particular, we should observe that portions of Reed's narrative appear so heavily ironized that it is difficult to separate legitimate statements of authorial conviction from humorous remarks; or, put another way, it is often difficult to tell where the author stands in regard to the above issues of description and valorization. More directly still, while much of *Mumbo Jumbo* condemns hegemonic white western culture and its version of history, the African-American voice(s) speaking its counter-version are themselves highly ironized (e.g. LaBas' outrageous claims regarding time periods and his inaccurate characterizations of Freud). The resulting irony jeopardizes the singular authority and veracity of the counter-version. In short, the counter version's description and valorization are undermined by the narrative's irony. What we end up with is an African-American counter-version which perhaps balances the scales of oppression by telling an other's tale, but which is by no means trustworthy. In so doing, Reed may be suggesting that claims asserting a singular authentic tradition—African-American or otherwise—are suspect. Of course, this would be ironic since Reed has always claimed he follows African-American tradition.

In fact, the search for an authentic African-American *tradition* may itself be the central problem. If that is so, it must be linked to the accompanying issue of *identity*, since identity is clearly implied in the terms "African-American." Hogan's recent work (*Empire and Poetic Voice* 2004) seems instructive here because it suggests how poststructuralism's definition of "tradition" (e.g. in Bhabha and Gates) and a contemporary artist's definition (i.e. Reed's) might result from very similar philosophical principles, even if theorist and artist operate from different viewpoints. Specifically, if Reed's irony does not signal the impossibility of authentic tradition, he might well operate on a definition of tradition very similar to that of Gates and Bhabha; that definition, it must be said, is essentially Platonic. That western classical philosophy—and poststructuralism's adoption of it—should define African-American tradition is itself ironic, but no matter. In any case, this Platonic view holds that meaning is autonomous. In terms of tradition, it means that something called "tradition" exists beyond *extension* and *definition;* that is, the abstraction ("tradition") is itself real outside of its actual instances in the world.[19]

But as Patrick Hogan (1990; 2004) observes, such a view flies in the face of modern linguistics, which denies such autonomous meaning. Rather, it considers language an abstract system with no real existence beyond "individual grammars" existing in the world; there is no autonomous, Platonic superlanguage (Hogan, *Empire and Poetic Voice* 245–246). Hogan's perspective on "tradition and culture is identical with this view of language" (Hogan, *Empire and Poetic Voice* 246). As he puts it, "traditions, literary or otherwise, exist only in individuals"; that is,

> Traditions are entirely and solely a matter of 'idiolect,' personal systems of belief, expectation, preferences, and the like. These systems overlap from one person to another, but they never entirely coincide. One consequence of this individuality of tradition is that it makes no theoretical sense to refer to a tradition as belonging to one group more than another. Traditions belong equally to everyone, or to no one. Like a language, it only makes sense to say that some persons have greater or lesser communicative ease, fluency in shared idioms, that their idiolects are, as a contingent, changeable, empirical fact, more similar to one another than to the idiolects of some other persons. Moreover, that ease, fluency, etc., in no way imply convergence in opinions or attitudes. In that sense, too, traditions are individual. (Hogan, *Empire and Poetic Voice* 28–29)

That individuals' "idiolects" are "contingent" and "changeable" is important, as is the fact that "ease" and "fluency" do not necessarily "imply convergence in opinions and attitudes." First, such ideas are important because they suggest the complex and conflicting nature of interactions among different individuals. At the same time, individual identity is itself complex, which is reflected in Hogan's division of identity into "categorial" (i.e. one's "self-concept," which "is defined by a set of categories, prominently including gender, race, ethnicity" etc., which make for "in-group/out group divisions"), and what he calls "practical identity" (i.e. the whole range of "competences" and "expectations" one operates on in everyday life) (Hogan, *Empire and Poetic Voice* 12). As part of such complexity, categorial and practical identity do not always correspond with one another; they may, in fact, contradict one another in many and numerous ways. Moreover, as categorial identity primarily constructs and encloses one's ethnicity—it constructs "in-group/out-group divisions"—it is deeply political-social and by no means exists in some Platonic and autonomous sense.

The categorial move of ethnic division is thus much like the construction of tradition in that it is strictly idiolectal; that is, ethnic division and enclosure are more a function of individual social-political categorization (e.g. construction of in/out groups) than anything else. The theorist or novelist trying to find an essential link between *ethnicity* or *race* and tradition (e.g. "African-American literary tradition") will therefore confront problems similar to the above. Thus, Hogan, addressing the problem in terms of post-colonial thinkers seeking to discover and valorize either an authentic "Hindu" or "Muslim" culture or tradition, observes the following:

> [O]nce one eliminates the idea of a supra-individual culture or tradition, once one sees culture and tradition as sets of partially overlapping but partially divergent individual idiolects (beliefs, skills, etc.), then the reason for privileging such categories as "Hindu" and "Muslim" disappears. Moreover, the entire argument applies *pari passu* to the racial and ethnic groups themselves. For they too exist only as individuals, who could be gathered and categorized in many different ways. (*Empire and Poetic Voice* 230)[20]

Hogan's idiolectal view of tradition and ethnic division opens a space for what he calls "common cultural ownership," wherein "no tradition or culture is the special property of a particular ethnic or racial group"; instead, "every tradition belongs only to humanity; it is collectively owned" (Hogan, *Empire and Poetic Voice* 248).

Reed's highly ironized narrative might signal something like this collective ownership. Such a reading would jibe with his own personal comments regarding a syncretism which breaks down identities. However, as we have already seen, identity categories are easily reinstated, if unconsciously. Moreover, it is difficult to overlook Reed's explicit declarations that he writes according to African-American *tradition*. For these reasons it would seem that Reed, like many artists, refuses to deliver the definitive statement on his position, or to demonstrate within his work the consistency and coherence we might demand. Nevertheless, it also seems clear that Reed's work does not follow the postmodern pattern set by Fredric Jameson. *Mumbo Jumbo* is anything but surface or mask; it confronts the political and social spheres Jameson denies it. Moreover, it continually invokes history and the authors behind it in order to interrogate history. Finally, for Reed neither the author nor the subject has disappeared; rather, they have become less ideologically autonomous and more integrated in history and community.

Of course, some readers might respond that my earlier treatment of Reed's place within *tradition* contradicts my later idiolectal critique of the term. To this I can only respond by holding myself to that same idiolectal reading; that is, there is nothing in what I have said about Reed and tradition that requires anything beyond an idiolectal conception of tradition. In this sense my earlier examination of Reed's relation to past works and writers was nothing more than an analysis of the author's own idiolectal reading of African-American tradition. That examination demonstrates that Reed's idiolectal tradition is not that of postmodernism or poststructuralism.

While such observations by no means constitute the last word regarding Ishmael Reed's difficult relationship to postmodern art, they nevertheless demonstrate problems for anyone wanting to unproblematically categorize his vision of authorship or African-American identity as uniformly postmodern. As we will see in the next section, similar objections apply to those who would unproblematically declare Kathy Acker's *texts* postmodern. This is due, at least in part, to the fact that Acker's own idiolectal tradition is that of postmodernism and poststructuralism.

Kathy Acker and The Practical Postmodern Text; Or, Can Poststructuralist Theory and Textual Activism Coexist?

Kathy Acker is, like Ishamel Reed, a novelist. However, as Chapter Three shows, Acker is unlike Reed in that she has explicitly stated her own indebtedness to varieties of postmodern poststructuralism, including Lacan, Derrida, and Kristeva. Though we did not exhaustively investigate Acker's connection to these theorists, we did see how her work reflects their influence, even if her interpretations of them are idiosyncratic. Such findings might at first lead one to believe her work susceptible to Jameson's postmodern diagnostic. But here, as with Reed, the issues of consistency, as well as political and historical engagement handicap any universal application of Jameson's theory. While some of Jameson claims regarding postmodern writing would seem to apply to Acker, I would like to show that the universal applicability of his claims to her work are more problematic. In particular, I affirm that Acker uses poststructural postmodern elements within her text; however, I would argue that her use is highly problematic, at least from the standpoint of theoretical consistency. In particular, Acker's novel exhibits a conflict between her obvious political-ethical position and the various theories informing her textual production. The result, for better or for worse, is a text whose theoretical underpinnings are at odds with Acker's own ethical-political project. What follows is, I hope, an explication of this, but also a demonstration how Acker's work is, nevertheless, different from other less politically oriented texts of so called postmodernism. In this respect I hope to suggest a few of the difficulties with classifying her work solely as "postmodern."

We will recall that Chapter Two examined Kathy Acker's generalized disruption of *traditional realistic narrative,* and one of its prominent forms, the *detective* genre. Through a series of Lacanian and Derridian like strategies, including *interdiscursivity*—the technique whereby a "singular narrative voice" utters a "mix of different discourses" (Bal 65)—and *intertextuality*—the use of words or phrases directly "traceable" to previous texts (Bal 65)—Acker conducts an all out assault on the unified text as model for unifying and reifying reading subjects, their conditions, and history. In terms of reading subjects this is made especially clear through frustration of one primary realist mode guaranteeing identity, namely, the *identification of narrators*. Here, Acker splits or hopelessly fragments narrative voice so that identity seems entirely unstable (e.g. Toulouse as narrator). In terms of historical conditions, the aforementioned techniques of intertextuality and interdiscursivity serve to reintroduce elements of actual history (e.g. class war as evident in the Paris Commune; the actual plight of oppressed women in Montmartre brothels) within the confines of the aestheticized fictional text. Moreover, Acker adds devices like *iteration*, which heighten all this by undermining senses of time, place, and identity to the extent that reality itself becomes difficult to identify. Difficulty of identification, while not exactly indicative of a less reified view of reality, would at least seem to invite its possibility, since the text representing reality refuses the usual "descriptive residue" guaranteeing its validity (e.g. iterative moments opening up duration and frequency of women's denigration and oppression).

In connection with this, we will also recall that Acker uses the detective genre precisely because its structure—in terms of hermeneutic and proairetic codes—is the very model of the traditional linear narrative. For Acker such narratives are *lisible* (readable) and offer, in the form of character and plot, models for identity and world view, which situate and constitute individuals as subjects. Such linear and well formed texts naturalize and reify contingent circumstances into frozen or permanent realities, so that reading subjects reproduce status quo social relations. Among these, of course, are the relations of patriarchy and capitalist exploitation.

At the root of patriarchy and capitalist exploitation Acker finds a rigorous logic. The detective narrative—as a quintessentially readable (*lisible*) genre—is intimately tied to this logic. As the most readable (*lisible*) of genres, the detective narrative embodies the logic and law of genre itself ("the law of genre"). For Acker, who seems to follow Derrida, the "law of genre" is similar to "The Law of the Phallus," in that both are marked by a rigorous logic of exclusion demanding purity, wholeness and stability of identity. The exclusionary logic of both ostracizes woman as "other," as outside reason and representation. Hence, Acker, again echoing Derrida, sees our culture as essentially "phallogocentric" (phallically hierarchized and ruled by a "metaphysics of presence" or wholeness).

For her part Acker uses the phallogocentric genre of detective fiction to construct a *scriptible* (writable) text that formally interrupts and undermines the readable (*lisible*) text's reified vision of the world and its social relations (e.g. gender and class relations). She constructs this writable text by systematically violating the implied narrative contract of the realist detective tale through the strategies noted above.

Much of this evidence suggests Acker's *ALTL* suffers from exactly the textual symptoms Jameson diagnoses in postmodern art. Using our previous discussion of Jameson, it is easy enough to see how her work fits his diagnostic. First, we will recall that Jameson designates "pastiche" the primary marker of postmodern art. Acker's *ALTL* would seem to qualify as just this sort of thing. Indeed, if we look at Acker's parodic employment of the detection formula, her use of intertextuality (e.g. her actual quoting of the anarchist Charles Gallo's protesting cry ("Long live dynamite")), as well as the formative role interdiscursivity plays in her work (e.g. interdiscursive employment of Henri Toulouse Lautrec, Vincent Van Gogh, (Henry) Fielding; interdiscursive use of Gallo and anarchism, Sophie Perovskaya and the Russian "Land and Liberty" movement; the historical narrative of the Paris Commune), such a conclusion appears very sound. In this case, Acker's work would be exactly "the imitation of a peculiar or unique style" that Jameson asserts; it would, indeed, be "the wearing of a stylistic mask, speech in a dead language . . ." (Jameson, "Postmodernism and Consumer Society" 114).

But central to any such derogatory categorization is the aforementioned idea of blankness ("blank parody"). That is, for Acker's text to submit to Jameson's diagnostic it must be "blank parody"; it must constitute "a neutral practice" of parody, namely, it must be without "parody's ulterior motive, without the satirical impulse . . . without that still latent feeling that there exists something normal compared to which what is being imitated is rather comic" (Jameson, "Postmodernism and Consumer Culture" 114; *Postmodernism, or, The Cultural Logic of Late Capitalism* 17). However, the question of whether or not *ALTL* is an instance of such blank parody is far from a settled issue. Indeed, our analysis in Chapter Three indicated that Acker's text is fueled by a politics of gender and class; its methods—including parody, interdiscursivity, and intertextuality—as well as its goals—changing of gender and class relations—are far from neutral. Moreover, her references, interdiscursive and otherwise, are far from a patchwork of imitations without reference; she is referring to a real world and a history, but as things she believes should change. Acker envisions textual construction as part of that change.

It should be clear from much of what has preceded that Acker's texts have straightforwardly political and ethical goals. Moreover, while I have not made this point, her own writings and comments also indicate that Acker considers textual production not just a matter of ethical purity on the part of the author, but also of practicality; that is, she sees her texts as informed by ethical beliefs but constructed in very practical ways so as to achieve the desired political-ethical goals, whatever they are. In this sense, she also believes—rightly or wrongly—that texts can perform social change.

To understand these points we must consider the degree to which her work is fueled by present social and economic conditions. For Acker, these conditions present a particularly *acute* phase in the process of monopolization, or that process Marx called in *Capital* a "constant decrease in the number of capitalist magnates" (Marx qtd in Miller 82). Today, this "constant decrease" results from ever more powerful and consuming multinationals. Acker echoes this thought in "Postmodernism" when she asserts that, "ownership is becoming more set: The rich stay rich; the poor stay dead. Death-in-life" (5). At the same time, these conditions are markedly different from earlier capitalist phases. For Acker the situation is *capitalistic* but also distinctly *postmodern,* as can be seen by her reference—one sentence later—to "appearance" as the controlling ideological reality. As she puts it, "The only social mobility left occurs in terms of appearance: things no longer change hands. . . . There is no more right-wing versus working class: there is only appearance and disappearance, those who appear in the media and those people who have disappeared from the possibility of any sort of home" ("Postmodernism" 5).

This commentary relates directly to the reciprocal relationship between media and economic conditions. Media are funded by and incorporated into political economy, but they also have a powerful capacity to reproduce that economy through representations. Media and capitalism therefore hold hands, supporting one another. But what seems so unusual about this (postmodern) situation, and Acker is not alone in believing this, is the way an all-saturating media has helped form a new foundation for society, "one in which," to quote Stuart and Elizabeth Ewen, "the human subject has been expelled from history" (Ewen and Ewen 75); in such a situation, "[p]rogress" is equated with the degree to which "social relations . . . become . . . a 'mirror of production'" (75). Here, people have disappeared from view, and what replaces them are the media generated identities attainable only through consumer culture. In this sense, "Only goods and images seem really to be *there*" (Ewen and Ewen 76).

Our responsibility remains only to pick among these products and available identities, and these—media tell us—are available to *all*. But of course, even as the *image* or *appearance* may have become available—at least in part—to all, the *real material circumstances remain the same.* Thus, for example, the issue of actual material conditions—real class conditions—is veiled by mass marketed fashion. So, for instance, even the poor may be seen wearing Nikes.[21] All of this is certainly what Acker implies when she says, "The only social mobility left occurs in terms of appearance . . ." and again later when she insists there exists only "appearance and disappearance" within the media.

Of course, in all this talk of "appearance" we cannot help but be reminded of Baudrillard's conception of "simulation," a concept we discussed briefly in the DeLillo chapter. It is that supposedly predominant condition within postmodernity wherein all signs have "no relation to any reality whatsoever" but are merely their "own pure simulacrum" (Baudrillard qtd. in Conner 56). Here, in Steven Conner's words, "the cult of immediate experience, of raw, intense reality, is not the contradiction of the regime of the simulacrum, but its simulated effect" (Conner 56). In this vision, "It is no longer a question of a false representation of reality (ideology), but of concealing the fact that the real is no longer real . . ." (Baudrillard "Simulacra and Simulations" 172). In short, for Baudrillard the real is reduced to simulation, as is the experience of that real.

Baudrillard's vision, however, is not exactly what Acker has in mind. Certainly, her position bears *some* similarity to Baudrillard's, but there remain decisive differences, and I would maintain the most important difference has to do with Baudrillard's steadfast assertion that in postmodernity simulation alone exists. To put the objection bluntly, this assertion flies in the face of Acker's philosophy of writing and her vision of the text. First, Acker's texts clearly have worldly goals, if by "goals" one means the changing of *real*—not simulated—social and economic conditions. Here, Acker—similar to Reed—sees the writer's task as communally based; for her the writer composes texts to lift the culture's "past up out of senselessness" in order to envisage "possibilities of action" in the present (Acker, "Postmodernism" 4). That "action," she believes, can change the aforementioned *real* conditions. In this sense the text's job is essentially political and pragmatic, remaining tied to the here and now of lived experience.

But if this is Acker's take on writing and the text, what is her relation to Baudrillard? A brief excerpt from Acker's nineteen ninety essay "Critical Languages" (1997) gives some hint of the relation, while also offering insight into Acker's general attitude concerning much so called "postmodern theory," especially deconstruction. Here, Acker begins by talking about her own methods of constructing texts, but quickly moves to the theories behind their construction as well as accompanying political and ethical concerns:

> I had been writing in certain ways due to certain theories about deconstruction and decentralization. . . . When I had first read Foucault and Deleuze and Guatteri and met Felix Guattari, I knew that those philosophes were working as they were working for cultural and *political* reasons and purposes. At that time, Deleuze and Guattari were deeply involved with the Autonomia in Italy.[22] The Anglo-Saxon adoption and adaption of deconstruction had depoliticized the theories. It seems not by an act of chance that Jean Baudrillard, out of all those French theorists, became the theoretical idol of the New York art world, Baudrillard whose politics, unlike Deleuze's and Guattari's, are, at best, dubious . . .
>
> Suddenly and ironically, in this Anglo-Saxon climate, deconstructive, now known as postmodernist, techniques became methods for applauding the society and social values composed by American postindustrialization. Freed of Nietzchean *sovereignty*, any value or text could be equivalent to or substitute for any other value or text; meaning became a black hole and frivolity instead of humanism reigned . . . (85)

Here, Acker makes several important points. For one, she clearly believes theory should never be disengaged from (political) practice, a thought evident in her statement that "those philosophes [Foucault, Deleuze, and Guattari] were working as they were working for cultural and *political* change." Acker then moves on to condemn cheerleading "deconstructive" and "postmodernist" "techniques" which have disengaged from politics and implicitly given unconditional approval to "the society and social values composed by American postindustrialization."

Acker clearly accuses Baudrillard and the "New York art world" of exactly this sort of theoretical cheerleading which goes hand in hand with the American depoliticizing of both deconstruction and French theory more generally. In terms of depoliticized deconstruction her targets are—among others—artists of the nineteen eighties like David Salle and Thomas Lawson. Within their deconstructive art, as Hal Foster observes, "there is a basic inversion . . . of deconstructive practice: for rather than comply with a form (like painting) in order *to make visible* its conditions and operations . . . , artists such as Lawson and Salle seek *to be made visible* through such complicity. They are, if you like, double agents whose 'sabotage' becomes proof of their good standing" (53). As regards Baudrillard's complicity in depoliticizing theory, we need only remember the nineteen eighties, when the New York art scene conducted a brief fetishistic love affair with his concept of "simulation." Here, I speak of the short lived Neo Geo movement, which included artists such as Peter Halley, Meyer Vaissman, Heim Steinbach, and Jeff Koons. Their works supposedly represented perfect examples of what the new "postmodern" art of the eighties had to be, namely, pure "simulations," as witnessed in, among other things, Koons' production of, "or causing the production of, stainless steel simulacra of plastic bunny rabbits . . ." (Danto 40)[23]

Beneath these artistic practices resides a belief in the inevitability of simulation and the impossibility of reference. This, as I have already noted, flies in the face of Acker's clearly pragmatic and worldly goals. But equally, Baudrillard's position flies in the face of materialist (postmodern) theories developed by the aforementioned figures of Deleuze and Guattari, who sought, as Acker indicates above, to develop theory in concurrence with practice. Indeed, as Steven Best and Douglas Kellner have pointed out, Deleuze and Guattari's theory—at least in *Anit-Oedipus* (1983)—rejects the idea that reality is inevitably wholly subsumed by simulation. In that work Deleuze and Guattari assert that "the real is not impossible; it is simply more and more artificial" (Deleuze and Guattari qtd. in Best and Kellner 121).

If we return to Acker's critique of Baudrillard in "Critical Languages," we also find that she is disturbed by his absolute rejection of "Nietzschean sovereignty." Instead, Baudrillard's world contains humans who merely "internalise the media and thus become merely terminals within media systems" (Sarup 112). Not too surprisingly, such a position leads to a theoretical throwing up of hands, namely, the cynical ideological stance whereby no liberation is possible, and any thought of it becomes absurd. Symptomatic of this, Baudrillard's works over the years have become increasingly riddled with talk of "the masses, the silent majorities, who passively consume commodities, television, sports, politics and information to such an extent that traditional politics and class struggle have become obsolete" (Sarup 112; Baudrillard, *Jean Baudrillard: Selected Writings,* especially Chapter 9). As an aside, one would imagine that Baudrillard's position regarding human sovereignty would also influence textual production such that texts produced by human "terminals" would merely reflect the present state of simulation referring to no reality whatsoever.

But the attitude behind this kind of textual production—as well as depoliticized deconstruction—is problematic for Acker because it refuses individual freedom and responsibility. In her words, both "techniques" were "[f]reed of Nietzschean *sovereignty,*" which lead to a situation wherein "meaning became a black hole and frivolity," thus eliminating chances for human liberation. Here, we must understand Acker's appeal to a specifically Nietzschean sense of "sovereignty" in her condemnation of Baudrillard and depoliticized deconstruction. She considers both reactionary and negative precisely in the Nietzschean sense. For Nietzsche the sovereign person is a "legislator," and this quality of "sovereignty depends on the measure to which the will has the power to determine and fix its own future, to give its word and keep it, to stand security for its own future" (Lingus 55–57). Equally important is the fact that the sovereign person (*souveräne Individuum*) has a "proud knowledge of the extraordinary privilege of *responsibility*" [*das außerordentliche Privilegium der Verantwortlichkeit*], and this sense of responsibility "has gone down to the deepest depths and become instinct" within the sovereign; this instinct Nietzsche names "conscience" [*Gewissen*] (Nietzsche 303). For Acker, Baudrillard and practitioners of depoliticized deconstruction have given up the highest parts within their humanity, namely, the free power to "legislate" and that "extraordinary privilege of responsibility," otherwise known as "conscience."

But if Acker's condemnation of Baudrillard stands, what do we make of her apparently contradictory relation to his simulation theory, namely, her tendency see simulation as reality—and therefore the place where texts operate—while simultaneously seeming to deny this very claim ("there is only appearance and disappearance")? The answer to this question lies in Acker's early educational and personal relationship with Herbert Marcuse, a leading member of the Frankfurt School. Thinkers associated with that school, most notably Adorno, Horkheimer, Fromm, Marcuse, et al., were very much involved in discussing and investigating ideology, while working to construct a "'materialist' or 'critical' theory of the general process of social existence" (Wiggerhaus 2). In addition, Marcuse, above all the other members of the school, steadfastly supported direct political action and civil disobedience performed by students in the nineteen sixties. This support was directly linked to earlier work by other Frankfurt School members (e.g. Horkheimer and Adorno's *Dialectic of Enlightenment* 1972), but most especially to Marcuse's own influential *One Dimensional Man* (1964), which pictured a society entirely enslaved by the culture industry (e.g. media).

In relation to this Frankfurt connection and simulation, I would submit that Acker regards Baudrillard's concept as something akin to "ideology." If we look at Acker's textual production, and *ALTL* is a good example, we see numerous attempts to unveil and criticize *ideology* within texts. Acker does this by, among other things, exploiting common textual conventions (e.g. genre of detective fiction) in order to assemble parodic and critical texts designed to unearth the hidden ideology beneath texts, and wipe away their seemingly naturalized content and structures.

Acker links her Marcuse inspired critical theory and idiosyncratic postmodernism to her concrete practice in the last sections of "Postmodernism":

> In such a society as ours the only possible chances for change, for mobility, for political, economic, and moral flow lies in the tactics of guerrilla warfare, in the use of fictions, of language.
> *Postmodernism*, then, for the moment, *is a useful perspective and tactic.* If we don't live for and in the, this moment, we do not live. (5; italics mine)

For Acker, the writer represents, among other things, an artistic combatant, which doesn't mean she's left the Seattle streets to the W.T.O. or Scotland to the G8. She conducts "guerrilla warfare" through "the use of fictions" and "language" to facilitate "political," "economic," and "moral" change. But what, we may ask, is this convenient "perspective and tactic"? Acker states it bluntly; it is "postmodernism" which uses "fictions of language" ("Postmodernism" 5).

In terms of Acker's textual activism we may say, then, that there exists a tension between her morally committed artistic vision—a vision concerned with "right" and "wrong"—and a poststructural epistemological vision concerned solely with, as Jochen Schulte-Sasse puts it, questions of "true versus false" (Schulte-Sasse xxii in Bürger). Or, more to the point, Acker's morally committed textual activism is directly at odds with the very theories she idiosyncratically employs. This, of course, might explain the contradiction we find in *ALTL* between a distrust of realist narrative and a simultaneous employment of that same narrative to introduce history (e.g. her interdiscursive introduction of anarchist history or the Paris Commune). In any case, all of this would suggest that Acker's work does not perfectly fit within the "postmodern" category; this is true whether we accept her provisional and strategic view of poststructuralism or not. Right or wrong, Acker believes postmodern writing strategies (e.g. deconstructive, Lacanian) are useful within texts because they facilitate liberation from patriarchy and capitalist oppression in the conditions of postmodernity.

However, I must reiterate that poststructural theories cannot accommodate such ethical-political purposes. In fact, they stand in direct opposition to them. Acker nevertheless bases her *formal* postmodern interventions—her art—upon those poststructural theories, though idiosyncratically. But it is here that a slightly different issue arises, namely the question of whether or not formally radical art can transform reality and change the political status quo. I would submit—against Acker—that it cannot; but to say so is not to admit "the impossibility of challenging contemporary social structures," but rather to assert "the vapidity of claims that this challenge is most effectively undertaken by experimental art involving radical formal innovation"

(Hogan, *Philosophical Approaches* 216). More to the point, art cannot substitute for political activism as it is more traditionally understood (e.g. grass roots organizing, demonstrating, etc.). Acker, of course, is an easy target here, not only because she has explicitly asserted the power of art to make such changes, but also because her work represents a higher degree of formal experimentation than either Reed or DeLillo. In any case, to the best of my knowledge neither Reed nor DeLillo have ever made such revolutionary claims on behalf of art.

At the same time, even in Acker's case ideological critique is present as depth, not surface. While this is opaquely demonstrated through Acker's Lacanian and deconstructive moves, both of which point to gender oppression, Acker demonstrates it most clear in her contradictory employment of interdiscursivity and historical reference. Such use implies her own belief that historical reference is possible and ethically necessary, even if the theories borrowed deny that position. Thus, Acker recounts elements of the Paris Commune and anarchist history to force the past back into consciousness. In another sense her book, though written in the seventies, is the perfect ideological corrective to postmodern phantasmagorical cinematic blizkriegs like Baz Lurman's *Moulin Rouge* (2001), which effaces actual history with exactly the glitzy and chaotic surfaces Jameson diagnoses as postmodern. Lurman's film presents a sybaritic Lautrec among beautiful and vivacious prostitutes, all of whom love their exploitative jobs and live one never ending party. Acker, on the other hand, gestures to the historical figure of a miserable Lautrec and the impoverished living conditions of the real female prostitutes in Montmartre. It is at moments like these that Acker's ideological work surpasses so many of the surface instances of postmodern art, despite her idiosyncratic use of theory.

In a related sense Acker's idiosyncratic textual activism displays an obvious concern for audience, namely, it raises the issue of how a writer might speak to readers and alert them to certain vital issues within contemporary society. Similar concerns with audience and contemporary society focused our discussion of DeLillo. But here one might be tempted to ask if DeLillo's treatment of audience places him more securely within postmodernism than Acker. The answer to this question, I sumbit a resounding, "No."

It's White Noise, But Whose White Noise?

If we consider DeLillo's readership, a related concern for the real emerges, despite the fact that many critics consider DeLillo a postmodern writer. As Paul Maltby notes, "this assessment rests on readings that focus on his accounts of the postmodern experience of living in a [Baudrillardian] hyper-reality" (260).[24] In terms of disintegrating (poststructural) subjects and their world, one might even make the case that *White Noise* does in some sense transform both into simulations. Certainly, DeLillo gives our experiential world a Baudrillardian face of simulation in numerous ways. Among these we may list "THE MOST PHOTOGRAPHED BARN IN AMERICA," an actual barn whose image has become realer than the thing itself. We can also think of the "airborne toxic event," which causes an actual evacuation that authorities treat as less real than the simulated one they had planned for the future.

On the level of the subjects themselves, we may remember that DeLillo paints a picture of individuals ruled by the logic of market ideology; they do not act autonomously via reason in its more positive sense, but follow the ideological demands of "bright packaging," "jingles," and "slice-of-life commercials," all of which beckon them to consume but also construct them as subjects in that consumption (*White Noise* 51). Such a process thus reduces the subject to the futile sadean consumption machine predicted by Horkheimer and Adorno, namely, a reasonable consumer-citizen living according to the logic of endless capitalist production and consumption. This inhabited subject is not the Lukácian subject of realism—namely, one based on "type" as "a naive given, an embodied universality"—but is rather a "self-conscious enactment" of so many media representations (e.g. the typical college parent) (Frow 178).

All of this would appear to make the subject fit Jameson's general diagnostic as already discussed. Seen in this way subjectivity has entirely disappeared into so many re-enactments of commercials, television shows, etc. . Indeed, the whole of reality—at least as it is suggested—is merely production and reproduction of the same. If read in a Jamesonian manner, the sameness is exactly pastiche to the extent that personality and reality are mishmash of past images or representations that are now substituted for depth. DeLillo's book thus represents the subjective experience of this condition.

But characterizing *White Noise* solely in this way seems overly simple and problematic. One central problem for such a simple view is *White Noise*'s social-political critique, which refers not to a simulation, but to a real and recognizable world organized under capitalism.[25] A second difficulty, however, are the structuring principles which facilitate DeLillo's critique; these not only enact the critique, but in the process attract myriad sorts of readers to greater and lesser degrees. The net result of all this is positive, in that it suggests a readership and text not entirely suffused with the terminal postmodern maladies Jameson diagnoses. That is, though the patients—text and reader—may be ill, they are not necessarily terminal.

To appreciate this we should briefly review how DeLillo organizes his critique. In particular, we should remember—as noted in Chapter Four—that he employs the genres of the college novel and college mystery. As his book is generally organized by such conventions, the unsuspecting reader tries to read according to rules of convention, one of which demands terminating the process of hermeneutic question and answer. In mystery—college and otherwise—termination usually occurs with revelation of a killer or criminal. *White Noise* as part college mystery exhibits this tendency through professor Jack Gladney's sleuth-like endeavor to discover who, exactly, supplies his wife with the mind altering drug called "Dylar," a substance said to rid the user of the fear of death. Per convention, he finds the drug dealer, Willie Mink.

This basic hermeneutic closure, which DeLillo constructs within the college atmosphere, appeals to readers fond of the college mystery genre. In a general sense it appeals to such readers because it gives them what Fredric Jameson calls *"molar unities* (constructions produced by the reader to create plot, personality, coherent character, and so on)" (Radway, "The Book of the Month Club" 271; italics mine). In this sense we may say that part of the book's appeal to this group is its presentation of Jack Gladney as a fairly consistent and coherent narrator throughout the book, and the one who ostensibly closes hermeneutic question and answer.

In a related sense, *White Noise*'s general structural coherence, as well as its associated invocation of the college mystery's element of enigma (e.g. the chancellor's puzzling death "on a ski lift in Austria" (*White Noise* 4); the death of Murray's academic "rival. . . . in the surf off Malibu"(*White Noise* 168)), enable DeLillo to offer readers the university as a microcosm of the greater world, but one which is troubling because of the answers it also refuses to give to the enigmas just noted. Such use is, in part, how DeLillo delivers his political-social critique to the audience.

There are, however, additional formal elements which add mystery but in a different way; interestingly, these draw in readers of another sort, enabling them to access DeLillo's critique. These elements occur at what Jameson calls the "molecular" level; these molecular elements are evinced through the "individual sentence, [or] the electrifying shock of the *individual word or the individual brush stroke*" (Jameson qtd. in Homer 87; italics mine). Such elements we isolated in a number of instances where DeLillo uses language outside the structuring force of the sentence (e.g. "Krylon, Rust-Oleum, Red Devil" (*White Noise* 159)). This molecular tendency appeals to readers fond of "high" modernist literature, which is known, according to Jameson, for pushing language to its limits through molecular moments.

At the same time, readers captivated by the invitation of DeLillo's college novel/mystery will not reject the novel on account of its molecular moments because the book—as a whole—is overwhelmingly molar in character. This, perhaps, accounts for the book's popularity and its status as an alternate book choice within the Book of the Month Club (BOMC), which has a broad membership. Indeed, the BOMC's favoring of molar wholes— and DeLillo's delivery on that for the most part—must account for this book's fairly large readership. Nonetheless, its smaller molecular moments still speak to a smaller group of readers demanding high modernist experimentation. It is in this sense that we noted in Chapter Four how DeLillo's book speaks to a larger "discursive community," and one that is a "socio-rhetorical 'discourse community'" to the extent that represents how "we all belong to many overlapping (and sometimes even conflicting) communities or collectives" (Hutcheon, *Irony's Edge* 92).

There are, however, more general difficulties with unproblematically categorizing DeLillo as postmodern in Jameson's sense. First, categorization of DeLillo as unproblematically postmodern would seem to neglect the fact that some readers are attracted to elements within *White Noise* which are *traditional*. While there are elements of simulated subjects along the lines noted by Jameson, we cannot ignore the fact—as indicated by the BOMC's wide readership and selection policy—that a significant number of readers believe *White Noise* offers exactly the molar elements (e.g. coherence of character) Jameson himself isolates within more traditional work. As I have already suggested, Jack Gladney—as subject—is a case in point; he is a relatively stable narrating figure throughout the novel, a far cry from Acker's Toulouse. In a related sense, of course, the closure of hermeneutic question and answer could equally point to traditional narrative structure, which is also appealing to many readers.

As a second point, we may think of a different readership's affinity for the molecular elements in *White Noise*, which are, by Jameson's own accounting, not postmodern but *high modern,* and thus traditional in a different sense. Then there is the general appeal to readers of the college novel and college mystery, both of which—as we saw in Chapter Four—have a rich and lengthy tradition addressing numerous issues regarding academics and their place in society.

It might be objected—as with Acker—that DeLillo's employment of the college novel and its mystery subgenre constitute only "pastiche." In this case his supposed parody of academia and society is reduced to "neutral practice" namely, one "without parodies ulterior motive" or its "satirical impulse"; it refers to nothing and is "without" a "feeling that there exists something normal compared to which what is being imitated is rather comic" (Jameson, "Postmodernism and Consumer Culture" 114; *Postmodernism, or, The Cultural Logic of Late Capitalism* 17).

But this, as I have already said, is far from an accurate description of DeLillo's work. For one, DeLillo gives readers *reference* in terms of actual historical figures (e.g. Nixon, Ford, Carter, Hitler) and the fictional figure of the academic who stands in for actual liberal arts academics and academic institutions in the nineteen eighties. Moreover, DeLillo contributes further reference through real consumer items (e.g. "Red Devil," "Toyota Celica"). These, he situates within the contemporary by using the formal elements already noted (e.g. molecular elements and clues without answers). On one level such elements create discomfort and a sense of mystery within both the molar and molecular reader (e.g. clues without answers and a surreal world in which products seem to speak). On another level still, the interdiscursive use of historical figures (e.g. Nixon, Ford, Carter) linked with fictional ones (e.g. the chancellor, Jack Gladney) and employment of quotidian consumer objects (e.g. "Toyota Celica") impel readers to interpret what they are reading in some coherent way. If they read according to parody, which would seem to make sense in terms of the narrative contract of the college novel more generally, then many readers would indeed see *White Noise* as parodic and as parodying *real* academia, as well as academics and their links—whatever they might be—to *real* society and consumer culture of the nineteen eighties and now. This seems true even for readers relatively unfamiliar with the college novel as parody, simply because of DeLillo's rather comedic representations (e.g. the idea of Hitler Studies; the Department of "American environments" wherein Elvis is a serious scholarly topic). As an instance of parody, then, *White Noise* is a sustained critique of contemporary social conditions, if in novel form. This is true, *regardless of the degree to which individual readers understand it in all its complexity.*

This brings up another central point. It is the variety of readers attracted to *White Noise*—something made evident in Chapter Four's discussion of the BOMC's wide readership—that assures DeLillo's critique is not in vein. Clearly, not every reader will make the same connections as we made in Chapter Four; some readers may ignore the Nixon and Hitler references, never invoking the former's unfortunate legacy and later's terrible deeds. But readers of a different sort will invoke these ideas. Similarly, DeLillo's critique of academia and academics (e.g. education reduced to the logic of capitalism;

the vacuity of some scholarship) may be ignored by certain readers, but not all. The same holds true of his sustained critique of consumer ideology and its effects. To this extent DeLillo's book has made at least some readers reflect upon issues within contemporary society. As such, *White Noise* is not pure surface or mask, but engaged critique.

Beyond these observations, we may consider other evidence suggesting we grant *White Noise* and its readership a bit more credit than Jameson's diagnostic might. As I remarked earlier in Chapter Three, capitalist-consumerism as "a dominant ideology" can never be absolute and all controlling; it always retains an "essential open-endedness" precisely because it must "negotiate with the ideologies of its subordinates" (Eagleton, *Ideology* 45). It must speak to subjects' genuine needs. As a capitalist entity, Amazon.com is no less subject to such rules; it must speak to its subjects, potential consumers, but in so doing it opens a space for liberating practices. It offers prospective readers reviews written by people who have purchased and read books. Thus, one may read a customer's review of *White Noise,* as well as reviews of a good many other books. These reviews, which range in sophistication from very erudite to the securely middle brow, offer a kind of short tutorial on the work's content (e.g. *White Noise*'s). To that extent, potential readers may find themselves informed of elements within a work before they ever buy it (e.g. Nixon's function or place in *White Noise*). Thus, it is difficult to account for the possible effects such elements have in readers' approaches and interpretations of a book like *White Noise.* We may add to this the fact that when one visits the Amazon web page offering *White Noise*—or any other book—there is a section listing other books purchasers have found of interest. These, like the reviews, may range in taste and sophistication. But again, the possible pedagogical effects—in terms of influence—cannot exactly be determined, at least not without empirical study. All this suggests a more liberatory vision of the reading public than Jameson seems to propose, regardless of how capitalist interests might also use such technological innovation for non-democratic purposes.

These elements, along with those already discussed, make DeLillo's *White Noise* more than just a pleasant read. It is a book carrying important messages regarding contemporary life and may disseminate these widely, thanks to the logic of capitalism itself (i.e. competition between internet book retailers). At its heart the book critiques consumerism and the fascist market logic of late capitalism. Yet in another sense, *White Noise* investigates the university to show how that same logic operates within academia to similarly schematize and discipline what is often thought of as the last bastion of free thought. Part of what facilitates its appeal to a wide variety of readers—and thus its influence on them as ideological critique—is its employment of popular genres (e.g. college novel; the college mystery) and high modernist technique (e.g. molecular level elements). At the same time, the book's sheer popularity—as evinced by its presence on the BOMC's list of book selections—would seem a convincing retort to those claiming absolute and total cooptation of art by capitalism. Many readers have bought DeLillo's book, and many will buy it in the future; while some will miss his critique, others will not. The evidence regarding the possible uses of the internet only further supports this point (e.g. individual book reviews on Amazon.com).

In conclusion, I would like to turn from these particular cases to the more the general idea of postmodernism. While doing this we can also address political problems within certain theories grounding various postmodernisms.

To begin with the more general, we must certainly affirm that, As C. Barry Chabot remarks,

> 'Postmodernism' . . . is a broad term and has been pressed into service to describe developments throughout the arts; it is even said that we live in a postmodern society. Any number of people obviously believe that a cultural rupture of some moment has occurred, and that its mark is discernible across the range of our cultural activities. There seems to be little agreement, however, about the precise nature and timing of the supposed break, and even less about how we can most adequately characterize its effects upon culture. (22)

Moreover, because we "lack . . . an adequate and widely accepted understanding of literary *modernism*" itself, it appears all the more easy to accept an equally vague *postmodernism* (Chabot 22; italics mine). This tendency continues, observes Chabot, despite the fact that "much of what has been termed postmodern derives quite directly from the work of earlier writers" (22). These complex questions, as well as those above, have yet to be fully explored, and we certainly have no space to address them here. Nevertheless, they deserve adequate answers before anyone can make such global claims about "postmodernism" and its supposed break from the modern

However these issues are resolved, I nevertheless remain convinced that the *critiquing* aspect of Reed, Acker, and DeLillo makes their works qualitatively different from much that is currently called "postmodern" writing, if for no other reason than that their works exhibit reasoned critique of today's culture which, in its current state, appears as if it worshiped the opposite, the irrational.

Here, rationality of critique is directly related to both real world reference and historical remembrance as opposed to a conscious—often poststructurally based[26]—embracing of various irrationalites which erase history and reality, as well as the subject. In the case of reality and history we have pure fabulation, namely, the construction of various equally legitimate narratives, no one holding any more truth than another. In this respect we may remember, among others, the influential poststructural theorists Jean-François Lyotard, Michel Foucault, Jean Baudrillard, and Jacques Derrida. In the first theorist's case, Lyotard, we witness a renunciation of all metanarratives (Lyotard 1984); here, all totalizing structures explaining social phenomena (e.g. systematizing historical change, class, racism) are dismissed as oppressive metanarratives. In the second case, Michel Foucault, we have a reduction of knowledge to power and its construction of discourses (Foucault 1972, 1973, 1980, 1984). In the work of Derrida, we have a deconstructive philosophy that seems to reduce all of reality to indeterminate texts (e.g. Derrida 1976, 1978). In total, as Terry Eagleton remarks, this version of postmodernism says there simply is "no such thing as truth [and thus history]; everything is a matter of rhetoric and power; all viewpoints are relative; talk of 'facts' or 'objectivity' is merely a specious front for specific interests" (*Ideology* 165).

A related plight applies to human subjectivity. Foucault, for instance, joins with thinkers like Jean Baudrillard to virtually annihilate the subject in and of history. The former thinker's analysis reduces all subjects to discourses (Foucault 1972, 1973 1980, 1984),[27] while the second, Baudrillard, remains equally reductive by dispersing subjectivity; that is, subjects simply "internalise the media and . . . become merely terminals within media systems" (Sarup 112; Baudrillard 1988).

Writers like Alvin Rosenfeld claim that fiction seeming to embody these theories can easily be seen as similar to literary works considered classics. Rosenfeld points to the mixing of history and fiction in works like "Shakespeare's history plays and the fiction of Scott and Tolstoy," all of which would seem to blur the historical real (Rosenfeld 107). But while these similarities exist, Rosenfeld considers recent works built upon (poststructural) postmodern theory to carry unacceptable "epistemological risk" with reference to history and the real.[28] For Rosenfeld it is a question of historical context. As he puts it, questions regarding epistemic risk might exist in older works,

> but in recent years they have assumed a greater degree of seriousness and even taken on a certain urgency. They have done so at a time when "reality" itself has become a more extreme and elusive concept, when our ability to represent it within language has been called into question, and when the political will to misrepresent has become blatant and unrestrained. (107)

This is important because it increasingly appears as though certain forms of poststructural postmodernism have taken hold with a vengeance in political culture and rhetoric. (Again, I do not pretend to define and differentiate between postmodernism/postmodernity and modernism/modernity, but only remark on how the wider political culture appears to have absorbed some theoretical tendencies from that which is frequently labeled "postmodern.")

The authors addressed in the present work—however they are finally categorized—remain committed to propositions about the real and history. Despite their textual manipulations—and their sometimes contradictory claims (e.g. Acker's epistemological skepticism combined with a clearly ethical position)—the authors discussed remember and reference real history in order to critique it and the present it produces. Or, put somewhat differently, they seem to affirm reason in a manner similar to the Frankfurt School thinkers, in that they affirm "critical, substantive rationality—the rationality of values, ends and possible attitudes towards life" (Held 67).

This rationality, it seems to me, is particularly important now as it stands in stark contrast to our current president's frequent political language, which we may justly call irrational. In fact, I would say that president George W. Bush's recent statements concerning America's justification for the Iraq war—namely, Iraq's supposed possession of W.M.D.s, its links to Al Qaeda, and its importation of uranium from Niger—embody elements strikingly similar to what I have been calling "poststructural postmodernism." In particular, we are talking about an administration whose (ideological) interpretation of the world seems governed by an almost textualist vision, wherein language games may be mutually exclusive, but each is equally legitimate (e.g. Lyotard), and where absence is indicative of presence (Derrida). The result is an abiding Baudrillardian simulation of reality, though not in the manner that thinker intends, since I would still insist that the real exists.

For our purposes, it is especially important to recognize that our president's political rhetoric goes hand in hand with (capitalist) media's power and ubiquity, as well as its associated ability to structure signification. In terms of signification, media's language constitutes a "signifying practice" Derek Briton terms "marketspeak" (Briton 19). As Briton observes, its sole purpose is to act as a "language of rationalization . . . that seeks to hasten the commodification of culture . . ."; moreover, its operating characteristics appear strikingly similar to "contemporary theories of language," by which Briton means poststructuralism (19).

Briton's analysis concerns the way the new right employs nostalgic terms or "signifiers" (e.g. the word "equality") to get audience approval or consent. However, in order wheedle the citizenry's consent, the right disconnects these signifiers from their particular sociohisorical context—what they once "signified'—and refigures them accordingly (Briton 22). Hence, when the right wing uses a word like "equality"—which, among other things, reminds us of the founding fathers and the American constitution, as well as people like Martin Luther King, who sacrificed for its principles—it refigures the term to mean a particular kind of "free market" capitalism. Media imagery (e.g. televised images of waving flags, president Washington, blacks and whites working together harmoniously) assist in the rhetorical trickery.

In its detachment of signifier from signified—with consequent loss of social-historical context—such cynical rhetoric seems to affirm many poststructural tenets. In particular, we might notice that the conscious playfulness with signifier/signified relations betrays a tendency to reduce reality to interpretable text. Reality has disappeared; all that exists are the interpretations of that textual world.

Interestingly, Bush's statements about reality (e.g. the presence of W.M.D.s in Iraq) follow this thinking closely, and in so doing harken back to a major innovator in linguistic, image-driven shenanigans, Ronald Reagan. Like Reagan, who said in his autobiography that "I've always believed in the *teller who* locates himself, so the audience can see the game through his eyes" (Reagan qtd. in Saul 532), Bush interprets reality for the audience. He asserts the existence of W.M.D.s and offers his interpretation—regardless of reality—to the public. For example, before the war, the Bush Administration said unequivocally that the "Iraqi government possessed weapons of mass destruction [W.M.D.s]" (Schell 8). As of the date of this writing, no such weapons have been found. Yet not long after declared the war over, he insisted that the "United States . . . 'found weapons of mass destruction'" (Schell; Bush qtd. in Schell 8). This declaration about reality—i.e. the statement that weapons of mass destruction were "found"—referred to "two vans discovered in Iraq that may or may not have been built to produce biological weapons" (Schell 8). For his part, Jonathan Schell calls such rhetorical-interpretive moves "cognitive torture." Translated in poststructural postmodern terms, it is a cynical willingness to assert presence where one finds absence; inconclusive results about the manufacturing of W.M.D.s become definitive evidence. Rationality is bemused, for as Schell further remarks, "If someone states to the world that he has a black dog when he does not, he is lying. But what do you call it if, in full sight of all, he says he has a black dog while pointing to a white dog?"(8). Indeed.

Here, Bush has out-Reaganed Reagan, but like Reagan who "placed himself in a *chosen position* vis-à-vis reality," Bush "told people where he thought he was and then described in simple but mythological terms what he saw. If you accepted that he was where he said he was, it was difficult to reject the description that followed" (Reagan qtd. Saul 532; italics mine). While Bush and Reagan are somewhat different—Reagan was certainly mythologist extra ordinaire—their mutual and conscious wrenching of language and its relationship to reality stand. But as I've said, Bush deserves extra praise here. Despite so many truths (e.g. the apparent non-existence of said weapons, the evident fabrication of the Iraq/Niger-uranium connection, as well as a dearth of evidence linking Iraq to Al Qaeda linkage)—Fourty Three continues to produce innovative readings of reality beyond even Ronald Reagan. The earlier president was mostly a paranoid visionary employing images with B-movie acting skill, while our current president seems able to bend reality to his interpretive will.

I do not wish to risk misunderstanding here. I am not suggesting that George W. Bush has ever read Derrida, Foucault, or Lyotard, much less any other poststructuralist. Rather, my point is that Bush's political rhetoric follows a logic similar to poststructuralism, with terrifying real world consequences far beyond any produced by cloistered academics. As such, my observation is merely an extension of arguments made by others much smarter than myself, who have remarked that poststrcturalism's inclinations to see the world as text, to eschew any and all totalities, and to annihilate the subject's agency make it anathema to progressive politics. (I refer here to critiques by, among others, Barbara Epstein (1999), Terry Eagleton (1996), Steven Best and Douglas Kellner (1991), and Patrick Hogan (1990)).

In closing, we might return to Jonathan Schell, who observes that at the moment a "'lie' is out in the open," when "any fool can see that the dog is white," we "must shift attention from the deceiver to the deceived"; otherwise, "the corruption threatens to spread from the teller to the hearer—from administration to the country, from them to us. . . . What is needed now is not so much more investigation as an awakening of the will. . . . Cognitive torture calls for cognitive indignation. And indignation should lead to action" (8). Indeed, as the present study has tried to suggest, it is action-directed cognitive indignation that inspires the political critiques of Reed, Acker, and DeLillo. If scholars should ever definitively place these novelists in the postmodern category, honesty demands that placement include a recognition of these political goals.

Notes

NOTES TO THE INTRODUCTION

1. It is worth noting that academic writers sometimes contribute to this obliquity and conceptual vagueness through a less than rigorous use of terminology. This is most evident in the appending of the prefix "post" to the noun and adjectival forms of "modern," which are then suffixed with either "ism" or "ity." The problem here is not the appended prefix or the use per se (e.g. "postmodernism," "postmodern," "postmodernism," "postmodernity"), but rather the careless mixing of nouns, adjectives, and suffixes. A particular glaring example is the interchangeable use of "postmodernism" and "postmodernity," two words with entirely different meanings. For a definition and discussion of these terms, see Chapter Four.
2. It is important to note that Habermas' characterization of poststructuralism and postmodernism is decidedly negative and represents one pole in late seventies and eighties arguments regarding poststructuralism's legitimacy and its political implications. For Habermas' assertion regarding poststructuralism's unequivocal connection to postmodernism see Habermas (1981). Andreas Huyssen (1986) offers an insightful explication of Habermas' position and its problems, including difficulties concerning his fusion of poststructuralism and postmodernism. Among other things, Huyssen observes that it is illogical to claim that a temporal confluence between theoretical practice (e.g. New Criticism) necessarily corresponds to actual artistic practice (e.g. Modernism); hence, it is also wrong to assert that the simultaneity of poststructural theory and postmodern art indicates a necessary correspondence. Moreover, he convincingly argues that Habermas' own reading of (politically progressive) modernism expurgates that movement's "nihilistic and anarchic" aspects—its (politically reactive) and aestheticizing tendencies—in much the same way as poststructuralism—in the name of its aestheticized vision—seeks to eliminate reason as a cultural

inheritance of Enlightenment (Huyssen 200). Huyssen further remarks that finding aestheticism within modernism—a quality Habermas associates with poststructuralism and postmodernism—further problematizes the supposed absolute difference between modernism and postmodernism (208). This section is heavily indebted to Andreas Huyssen's observations and analyses.

3. Here, a cautionary note seems in order. Construction of "modernism" and "postmodernism" is always a theoretical matter. In this respect, I am not claiming that differences in epistemological doubt are definitive markers of "modernism" and "postmodernism"; rather, I am addressing poststructuralism's theoretical construction of "postmodernism" (and, implicitly, "modernism").

NOTES TO CHAPTER ONE

1. Voodoo is also known as "Voudoun." Throughout this essay I will use the former spelling unless quoting sources using the later variant.
2. Reed's work and its relation to Voodoo has been explored in several very influential and probing investigations. These include Henry Louis Gates' early work (Gates 1984) and his now canonical book *The Signifying Monkey: A Theory of African-American Literary Criticism* (1988). The groundbreaking Bakhtinian work on Reed by Sämi Ludwig (1994,1996,1998), as well as Robert Fox Elliot (1987), James Snead (1990) and Patrick McGee (1997) are also requisite reading for Reed studies. Indeed, my arguments here are informed by these writers, but my goals and methodology are somewhat different. Moreover, while many of these works offer important insights, some are grounded in poststructuralism and therefore represent, at least for this writer, highly problematic formulations of African-American culture (e.g. Gates 1984, 1988; McGee 1997).
3. Though I will examine Reed's *Mumbo Jumbo*—as well as some of his poetry—to prove my points regarding satire, cursory perusing of his novels makes this equally clear. *Yellow Back Radio Broke-Down* (1969), for instance, offers satire of America's class and race problems, as well as addressing aesthetic mandates Reed finds disturbing. Similarly, we may cite Reed's satire of American life and habits in *The Freelance Pallbearers* (1967). For an interesting and exhaustive discussion of the history of African-American satire see Darryl Dickson-Carr's *African American Satire: The Sacredly Profane Novel* (2001).
4. Jarrett's excellent book even analyzes Reed in these terms, though its focus is almost exclusively on jazz, and he primarily uses Reed's *Freelance Pallbearers* (1967). Moreover, Jarrett's primary goal is somewhat different than mine in that he desires "to show how one might employ popular culture—actually

representations of popular culture—as a means to invention and innovation" (Jarrett xi).

5. Jarrett points to Petronius' indictment of rhetoricians "concocting 'great sticky honeyballs of phrases, every sentence looking as though it had been plopped and rolled in poppyseed and sesame'" (Petronius qtd. in Jarrett 26). Jarrett notices food tropes in other early writers as well, including the Roman Marcus Terentius Varro writing after the style of Menippus of Gadara [the Cynic philosopher] (Jarrett 26; on this see also M. H. Abrams 188–189).

6. For a discussion of Menippean satire as Bakhtinian dialogical practice, see Julia Kristeva's *Desire in Language* (1980). In that work Kristeva refashions the traditional notion of "genre," and envisions "the novel as a narrative texture, woven together with strands borrowed from other verbal practices such as carnivalesque writing, courtly lyrics, hawker's cries, and scholastic treatises" (Roudiez, Introduction (Kristeva 1980) 2).

7. On Reed's use of humor to undermine African-American singular identity see also Jesse (1996).

8. The black detective prototype, as noted by Sämi Ludwig, we first find in Rudolph Fischer's *A Conjure Man Dies* (1932) (Ludwig 1998). For an illuminating discussion of Reed's anti-rational HooDoo detection, the detective genre's allegiance to western metaphysical beliefs and its ideological complicity in maintaining strict class and racial boundaries, see Swope (2002).

9. Interestingly, Reed's utilization of "Jes Grew" remains indebted to previous African-American utterances. However, while this chapter makes some reference to Reed's borrowing from traditionally cited African-American literary sources, much of its content relates specifically to the occasionally neglected Caribbean (e.g. voodoo) and African sources (e.g. Youruba). Certainly, "Jes Grew"—in the sense of "spirit"—remains connected to these sources, as does Reed's usage. But Reed's use also relates to a more recent and specifically American context. Thus, Darryl Dickson-Carr is partly right in asserting Reed borrows "Jes Grew" from James Weldon Johnson, a hero within African-American literature, who used the term to signify "the earliest ragtime songs" (Johnson qtd. in Dickson-Carr 152). But such an assessment is still only partly right, since Reed demonstrates an ironic tension indicating a refusal to perfectly define authorial voice or grant it ultimate authority. We might, for instance, wonder if Reed uses the terminology as an oblique reference to the earlier Harriet Beecher Stowe's *Uncle Tom's Cabin* (1852). When a white owner asks Stowe's black slave girl, Topsy, "who made you?" she refuses both parental and divine creation, stating "Nobody, as I knows on. . . . I spect I grow'd" (Stowe 1907). This possible reference—and an anomalous one in terms of literary inheritance, since

Stowe was white—troubles both ultimate authorial delineation as well as a unified sense of African-American literary tradition and identity. Though this general point will become clearer through the course of this chapter, it will also be expanded and explicated further in Chapter Four. For further study on related issues see Hogue (2002).

10. For a lucid narratological discussion of displaced narrators see Snead (1990), Ludwig (1994, 1998), and Jesse (1996).
11. It is interesting to note that "Return of Julian the Apostate to Rome," another poem in *Conjure*, in presents an alternative and less complimentary view. This poem is but one illustration of the difficulties inherent in classifying Reed's poetic and political position. Even so, in the present context Reed's intent is clearly signaled by his positive characterization of Julian.
12. Logically, of course, the "Moses" reference also most likely refers to Freud's *Moses and Monotheism* (1939).
13. Henry Louis Gates' important essay (1984) on *Mumbo Jumbo* states that Reed is here practicing the African-American tradition of "signifying" (315). In particular, for Gates, Reed is signifying upon Ralph Ellison's "gesture of closure . . . , and that of the entire Afro-American literary tradition" (314). That closure, according to Gates, is most famously exhibited in Ellison's prologue to *Invisible Man* (1952), where Ellison himself signifies upon Melville by, among other things, using the phrase the "Blackness of Blackness," which Gates says refers to "Melville's passage in Moby-Dick on 'the blackness of darkness' . . ." (315). In Gates' poststructural reading, *Mumbo Jumbo* is a work which signifies upon the closure present in both black authors (e.g. Ellison) and African-American literary tradition. In Gates' view, *Mumbo Jumbo* does this in order to signify the openness of blackness and African-American literary tradition, namely, to mark them as a non-identities. For Gates the identity of African-American literary tradition is found only in its difference and deferral in the poststructural linguistic sense.

    While Gates' essay is important and illuminating, I make little reference to it for two reasons. First, the present essay addresses authorship somewhat differently. Second, and probably more important, I find Gates' poststructural foundation highly problematic. For more on this see the fourth chapter of the present work.
14. Patrick McGee's book *Ishmael Reed and the Ends of Race* (1997) notes that Wintergreen's paranoid comments regarding black interpretations of *Moby Dick* actually refer to "Trinidadian Marxist T. L. R. James," whose counter-hegemonic examination "withdraws Moby Dick from the codified space of the Western canon and inserts it into the incommensurable space of symbolic change" (98). According to McGee, James envisioned Melville as a writer who rejected capitalism's foundations, including "profits and the rights of private property"; instead, Melville's work saw

humans as part of nature—not separate from it—and refigured human relationships in more communal terms, which also necessarily altered attitudes to technology.

15. In a remarkably astute essay which, in part, examines nationalism within the New Black Aesthetic, Phillip Brian Harper (2001) observes the prevalence of the pronoun "you" as a shifter within much (nationalist) Black Arts poetry in the nineteen sixties. As he remarks, the use—if viewed along the lines outlined by Emile Benveniste (1971)—has a tendency to call in readers/audience at the same time as it establishes a clear oppositional relation to the speaking "I"; this does show "a desire to appear to engage their audience [African-Americans] directly . . . , but because the *you* references also," there emerges within such phrasing "implication of *intraracial division* within the Black Aesthetic's poetic strategy" (Harper 466–467; second italics mine). The problem is that the aforementioned opposition "is thematized in the poetry, not in terms of the 'us verses them' dichotomy that we might expect, . . . with *us* representing blacks and *them* whites; rather, it is played out along the inherent opposition between *I* and *you*, both of these terms deriving their referents from within the collectivity of black subjects" (Harper 467). In short, the call of much Black Arts poetry of the sixties is one that implicitly makes some blacks blacker than others; that is, some blacks have black consciousness—are genuinely black—while others possess a white consciousness, and are not black, but toms to the white system. Moreover, in the hands of writers like Amiri Baraka (e.g. his essay "American Sexual Reference: Black Male" in *Home: Social Essays* (1966), this call to real blacks, according to Harper, is based on a desire to avoid a "failed masculinity," which can be found in homosexual male writers like those of the Harlem Renaissance (e.g. Wallace Thurman, Countee Cullen, Alain Locke) (Harper 469). Harper also notes a virulent anti-white bias, which is related to this failed masculinity, in that the condemnation of failure in the black writer is based on his resemblance to the (white) "Euro-American intellectual" (Harper 469). The hatred of whites more generally can easily be found in any number of (nationalist) Black Arts poems (e.g. Amiri Baraka's "Poem for Half White College Students" (1965) and "Black Art" (1966); Nikki Giovanni's "The True Import of Present Dialogue: Black vs. Negro" (1968)).

As an aside, while a limited version of Harper's diagnostic concerning "failed masculinity" seems persuasive, he and others have elsewhere painted a hyperbolic picture of real African-American males and their fictional counterparts as misogynistic and hyper-masculine (Gilroy 1993; Harper 1996; McGee 1997; Fraiman 2003). Critics claim these misogynisitc traits are historically related to black oppression by dominant white culture. One could hardly contest the fact of oppression; however, these characterizations appear, not coincidentally, in rough temporal proximity to an emerging right wing pop-sociology and dominant white media's creation of the violent black (male) predator. Following the rich tradition of dystopic representations of the city as "other," Charles Murray's works in the nineteen eighties and his later coauthored pseudoscientific and racist book *The Bell Curve*, published in 1994, "disseminated and popularized the notion of a dangerous urban underclass that became hooked in a culture of crime and poverty and that was to be blamed for much of what was going wrong in the city" (Baeten 108). William Bennett, Dan Quayle, and Bob Dole fanned the flames in the early nineties with their indictments against rap and Tupac Shakur (Glassner 125). Given television news' ratings driven logic—"if it bleeds, it leads"—the networks offered skewed coverage of racialized crime, wherein "night after night, black men rob, rape, loot, and pillage in the living room. . . ." (Rivers qtd. in Glassner 109). Barry Glassner's *The Culture of Fear* (1999) outlines the creation of this predator and America's irrational fear of black men.

For an expansive and materially grounded reading of the city's place in African-American modernism and postmodernism see Dubey (2003).

16. "*Mu*" is the Arabic prefix for "one who"; so, by this word play Reed might mean "one who" fucks. Alternatively, "Mu'tafikah" also means "Mother Africa." Finally, as Robert Elliot Fox observes, "Mu'tafikah" is somewhat similar to the Arabic word "*muthaqqafin*," which "refers to the cultured class"; this, as Fox astutely notes, makes sense because it emphasizes "the fact that these 'thieves' (thieves in the same sense that Twain's Nigger Jim is when he 'steals' himself) are representatives of peoples with their own valid cultures that had no need to borrow from others in the same rapacious manner that Western culture 'borrowed' from them" (Fox 89).

17. Sämi Ludwig's Bakhtinian analyses of this conversational element is particularly interesting (Ludwig 1994,1996,1998).

18. Generally, Voodoo does not practice sexism in this regard. That is, there exist both male Voodoo priests (houngans) and female priestess (mambos), and their functions/abilities remain roughly equivalent. Any hierarchy regarding the two is rare and strictly regional. See Deren p. 46.

19. Hogan (2000) observes that Foucault's notion of "discourse" has several necessary elements: For one, a discourse must have "a set of ideas" (Hogan 270); so, if one were postulating about Voodoo in this regard, one might suggest that Voodoo has "a set of ideas" which locate loas as part of a larger cosmology wherein they may alter circumstances but not "create." Secondly, Hogan notes that Foucault demands every "discourse" have a "vocabulary" (Hogan 270); so, in the case of Voodoo, we might list "loa" as a "legitimate category" within Voodoo, and "loa possession" as a legitimate possibility; while on the other hand, contemporary psychiatry (as a discourse) would not admit "loa" as a category and would likewise deny "loa possession." Foucault also requires discourses have

"rules of authority," by which he means "criteria determining who can speak authoritatively . . ." (Hogan 270). In the instance of Voodoo we might list an authority as the houngan (male priest) or mambo (female priestess). Thus, we could construct what Foucault calls a "discursive formation" of Voodoo.
20. Deren defines the "maît-tête" as "'master of the head,' or the loa which is dominant above all others in the psyche of an individual . . . It may also refer to the particular aspect of the loa which is carried in the head of a person" (Deren 31).
21. The example here is male (i.e. "houngan"), but the writer/priest could just as easily have been female (i.e. a "mambo"). See endnote 5.
22. For a penetrating study of these musicians and their relation to Reed see Jarrett (1999).
23. Deren translates "langage" as "sacred language, probably African words, used in ceremonials" (331).
24. Gates (1988) has, of course, addressed Reed's references to Ellison and other African-American writers and discerned—at least to his mind—that a kind of suspension occurs in terms of authorial attribution.
25. Reed has been unjustly attacked by certain factional elements within feminism for his purportedly negative representations of women; his depiction of Earline is an example of one target for such attacks. These vitriolic assaults, however, neglect Reed's equally negative portrayals of men. Joyce Joyce (1994) offers an important and informative analysis supportive of this position.
26. I consulted two editions of the novel, and in both it proved impossible to tell which was "correct."

NOTES TO CHAPTER TWO

1. The novel was originally published in 1975, but has since been reissued together with two earlier works (*The Childlike Life of the Black Tarantula by the Black Tarantula*, 1973, and *I Dreamt I Was A Nymphomaniac*, 1974) to form a trilogy entitled *Portrait of an Eye* (1998).
2. The present chapter is indebted to Siegle's discussion of "literalizing," or what he calls "desublimation"(Siegle 1987; 1992); his use of the term "literalizing" simply means making visible what is usually repressed, and is more useful than his handling of the word "desublimation," which is easily confused with Marcuse's employment of the term. (See Marcuse's *One Dimensional Man* 1964).

  In a related sense, this chapter's analysis is also indebted to Rob Latham's brief but lucid reading of Acker's collage as *Verfremdungseffekt* (Latham 1993). In the case of Siegle, while his earlier discussion of Acker's *ALTL* (1987) is very illuminating, it remains somewhat limited in that it

is a short essay written for the journal *Literature and Psychology* and designed to discuss not only Acker's work but that of Walter Abish. Siegle's later significant and well argued book on Acker and many other postmodern writers, *Suburban Ambush: Downtown Writing and the Fiction of Insurgence* (1992), reprints the aforementioned earlier essay on *ALTL* with minor changes. While this chapter works very loosely with some of Siegle's ideas, it investigates in depth issues either not addressed by him or issues he covers in a cursory manner. As for Latham, while my reading of Acker has affinities with his work, he addresses Acker primarily in terms of "collage."
3. For a recent extended analysis see Pitchford (2002). Pitchford's analysis is insightful but based in the poststructuralism my argument disputes.
4. Acker has admitted influence in numerous interviews (e.g her interviews with Ellen Friedman (1989), Karl Schmieder (1991), Sylvere Lotringer (1991), Beth Jackson (1996), Larry McCaffery (1996), and within *Apparatus and Memory* (1999)). We may also note her mention of such influences in her book *Bodies of Work: Essays* (1997). Moreover, her longstanding relationship with the poststructuralist philosopher Sylvere Lotringer, a writer publishing extensively on Foucault and related poststructuralists-who by Acker's own admission, taught her about Derrida and Foucault-serves as further evidence of the point (Acker, *Bodies of Work* 1997).
5. I feel obliged here to explain my use of terminology. First, there is my categorization of historical narrative and detective fiction as specific instances of "realist narrative text." This follows if one defines the three terms in the following way: They are all instances of "realism" if by that one means—as do structuralists—writing in "accordance with literary conventions and codes which the reader has learned to interpret, or naturalize, in a way that makes the text seem a reflection of everyday reality" (Abrams 174). I wish to stress, however, that I do not draw a hard and fast distinction here between narrative "realism" and some forms of "naturalism" as seen, for example, in writers of the nineteenth century (e.g. Balzac, Eliot). While my use of the term "realistic" could be said to include such writers, it extends beyond them because I use the term more loosely. Thus, the structuralist codes still apply, even if I am not referring *only* to "realism" as a genre.

Second, they all represent examples of "text" if by that one means "a finite, structured whole composed of language" (Bal 5); third, they all constitute the distinctly "narrative" text if by that term one means "a text in which an agent relates ('tells') a story in a particular medium, such as language, imagery, sound, building, or a combination thereof" (Bal 5). This definition still applies to so called "*historical narrative*" since, as Hayden White has argued, our contemporary notions of history are very much inherited from a (Hegelian) nineteenth century vision of history as *story* (White 1973, 1996).

This brings us to the term "genre." "Genre," of course, means "type" or "kind" in French; but as Jane Feuer observes, the term—be it used in "literary, film, or television studies"—"takes on a broader set of implications" which imply "that works of literature, films, and television programs can be categorized; they are not unique" (Feuer 113). Thus "genre theory deals with the ways in which a work may be considered to belong to a class of related works" (Feuer 113). Because I need to use the term "genre" itself, I will at times set aside a number poststructural claims. In particular, I will occasionally set aside the claim that genres never exist in uncontaminated form—or, somewhat differently, that they are subjected to the pernicious effects of Derridian supplementarity—in order to define my genres in fairly commonsensical ways. The individual genres will be defined and elaborated upon in individual sections. For this reason I feel comfortable extending definitions of individual genres beyond those classically outlined by Aristotle (i.e. epic, tragedy, comedy, etc.).

6. These comments on genre mixing are much indebted to Shari Benstock's theoretical reading of Derrida and Lacan in *Textualizing the Feminine* (1991).

7. There are, of course, certain problems with this idea because no one can really "possess" the Phallus. It is merely the initial marker of difference, from which all differences flow. Some have suggested that the theory's base is sexist because the Phallus marks the primary moment of meaning; that may well be. I take no position on this here, but only wish to indicate the subtlety of Lacan's theory. Moreover, Acker's employment of Lacan may be contradictory or problematic in other ways. For a detailed examination of these issues see Chapter Four.

8. Acker has stated that her "favorite models" for writing are based on reading she did as a child; as it happens, Agatha Christie's detective fiction provided one such model for her, as did pornography (Friedman Interview 1989 20). Indeed, besides the early *ALTL,* we can see Acker's interest in detective stories showing up in her later published novella *My Life by Pier Paolo Pasolini* (part of a collection entitled *Literal Madness* (1988)), as well as subsequently published first novel, *Rip-Off Red—Girl Detective* (Acker, *Hannibal Lecter* 2). *Rip-Off Red* parodies the detective genre in a similar manner to *ALTL.* Like *ALTL* it offers a detective narrative which combines mystery with political critique. It also employs similar references to real life political figures. I have chosen to analyze *ALTL* rather than *Rip-Off Red* because the former work is more explicitly parodic of formulaic detection's fetishized phallogocentrism.

9. I have been referring to the detective genre as "realistic." I do so because the vast majority of popular detective fiction follows realist tenets. I therefore

ignore examples of non-realist—often called "postmodern"—detective fictions like Alain Robbe-Grillet's *Erasers* (1964) and Jorge Luis Borges' "Death and the Compass" (1998). Obviously, my use of Acker's anti-traditional detection story implies her membership in this category.

10. Barthes' term *"le lisible,"* Dennis Porter (1981) translates as "readable" (Porter 83). I adopt Porter's translation.

11. "Interdiscursivity" is sometimes referred to as "intertextuality." But Bal possesses an astute narratological sensibility and therefore draws a sharp distinction between "intertextuality" and "interdiscursivity." In particular, Bal "reserve[s] the term 'intertextuality' for . . . traceable cases," by which she means cases where one can actually trace words themselves back to a previous source, namely, a text of some sort (Bal 65).

    As an aside, while Bal never invokes Jameson's name in the course of making her distinction, she does note that "interdiscursivity" is nothing new, and cites *Don Quixote* as an example. This, of course, reminds us of the problematic nature of Jameson's claim that postmodernism is something absolutely new, a claim he vaguely defends by calling practices like interdiscursivity culturally dominant. This might be debatable, though I'll not bother to address it here.

12. What has been said about Fielding's relationship to Aristotle's concepts (e.g. unity of action) applies even if the latter never anticipated the development of complete or secondary subplots as seen, for example, in Elizabethan drama and the novel. This is because traditional narrative texts (e.g. novel) still retain the notion of a unified plot, even if within a central plot there exist smaller complete plots. How is this the case? Well, taking the example of the traditional novel, we may observe that despite its use of complex—but complete—subplots it nevertheless adheres to Aristotle's notion of unified plot because it always has the essential elements of *beginning, middle,* and *end.* Speaking on Aristotle, Abrams observes that "The beginning initiates the main action in a way which makes us look forward to something more; the middle presumes what has gone before and requires something to follow; and the end follows from what has gone before but requires nothing more. We are satisfied that the plot is complete" (161).

13. While I will not dwell on it here, the not so subtle mention of "Fielding" and his self contained unity of action may well be an act of self-irony on the part of Acker. Certainly, in one way Acker's use of Fielding points to the classic unified construction of beginning, middle and end, as well as her belief that such a model is phallic in nature, a point we shall discuss when we get deeper into Acker's anti-detection. But her inclusion of Fielding may also be an act of interdiscursivity pointing to Acker's belief in the always already mixed nature of texts and genres, the fact that they are always shot through with other discourses. As others have remarked (e.g. Cohn 1988), a text like *Joseph Andrews,* also written by Fielding, betrays clear affinities to

postmodern texts in this regard. To bring up Fielding and his supposed unity invites thoughts not only of *Tom Jones* but also *Joseph Andrews,* and thus also the fact that the author who thought he created singular works actually created mixed ones containing discourses from elsewhere, much like Acker's own text which claims no autonomy for either itself or its supposed author.

14. I adopt these terms from Mieke Bal. For Bal, any time there is language there is an "I" speaking that language: "As soon as there is language, there is a speaker who utters it; as soon as those linguistic utterances constitute a narrative text, there is a narrator, a narrating subject. From a grammatical point of view, this is always a 'first person.' In fact, the term 'third-person narrator' is absurd . . ." (Bal 22). Bal also says, however, that this criticism "does not imply that the distinction between 'first-person' and 'third-person' narratives is itself invalid" (22).

15. For a fascinating discussion of Poe, detective fiction, and police surveillance techniques (e.g. photography, assigning of addresses as means of identification) see Walter Benjamin's insightful work, *Charles Baudelaire: A Lyric Poet in the Era of High Captialism* (1973).

16. Porter cites as evidence Christie's use of "well constructed sentences" and literate turns of phrase (Porter 133).

17. In fact, such language use is even outside the seedy world of its Americanized urban descendent, namely, the "hardboiled" species of detective fiction (e.g. Raymond Chandler).

18. Mike Davis' extraordinary book on the history of Los Angeles (*City of Quartz* 1992) discusses Chandler's references to locations within the metropolis. As a history of L.A.'s culture, politics, and development the work is unmatched.

19. Their agreement is rough indeed, because Barthes in *Le Plaisir du texte* says that detective fiction has *no* digressive moments or delays. Acker would buy that there exist delays but would assert that these make no difference because the detective narrative is still overwhelmingly end or goal oriented.

20. I must credit much of this interpretation on Acker's rhythm to Mieke Bal (1999). She actually makes this point about Acker's *Blood and Guts in High School* (1978) though she does not connect it to Lacan as I implicitly do.

21. For those unversed in his career, Herbert Marcuse was a leading member of the Frankfurt School. Thinkers associated with that school, most notably Adorno, Horkheimer, Fromm, and Marcuse et al. were very much involved in discussing and investigating ideology, while working to construct a "'materialist' or 'critical' theory of the general process of social existence" (Wiggerhaus 2). In addition, Marcuse, above all the other members of the school, steadfastly supported direct political action and civil disobedience performed by students in the nineteen sixties. This support was directly

linked to earlier work by other Frankfurt School members (e.g. Horkheimer and Adorno's *Dialectic of Enlightenment* 1972), but most especially to Marcuse's own influential *One Dimensional Man* (1964) which pictured a society entirely enslaved by the culture industry (e.g. media). The use of Marcuse in this portion of the essay, however, is mostly indebted to an extension and development of his thought in *Counterrevolution and Revolt* (1972).

22. While it is well known that the emergence of Foucault's genealogy is most explicitly stated in his later essay "Nietzsche, Genealogy, History" in *Language, Counter-Memory, Practice* (1977), a work which predates *ALTL*'s writing and publication, its central historical elements are clearly evident in *The Archeology of Knowlege* (1972). As Barry Smart observes, "in both archaeological and genealogical analysis a comparable conception of history is to be found in which dispersion, disparity, difference and division are conceived to lie behind the historical beginnings of things rather than a singular point or moment of origin" (55). For his part, Peter Dews dates Foucault's take on history as a phenomenon of the seventies more generally; Dews remarks that, "For most of the 1970s," Foucault holds that "the autonomy of discourse is entirely dissolved, and epistemic structures are seen as entirely moulded by proto-social forces" (232).

23. To be fair to Kofman, while I use her here to describe Freud's position, she seems to hold that Freud's notion of "penis envy" is the ultimately a saving moment for males because it causes the fear of castration, but in so doing really affirms the male in his own position of not being castrated. Citing Freud, she points to the male reaction to seeing Medusa, which causes "stiffening (*Starrwerden*), which signifies erection" (85). Thus, for Kofman, Medusa produces fear of castration but also reassurance in the "stiffening" excitement it arouses in males.

24. I am indebted to Hutcheon's *A Poetics of Postmodernism* (1988) for observations regarding Jameson, nostalgia, and the postmodern text.

25. As an aside, though it is probably inappropriate to equate Acker's critique of history with Hayden White's, it is nevertheless interesting to see how she too critiques history as linear, coherent and closed narrative. White, it will be remembered, critiques history which proclaims objective "Truth" in terms of a fixed and linear narrative as outlined by Hegel. On the problems with the Hegelian notion of history as narrative, as well as implicit moralizing within historical writing, see Hayden White's *Metahistory* (1973) and *The Content of the Form* (1987).

26. *Alexander and His Times* is Moss' updated web version of his recently printed work on Alexander II entitled *Russia in the Age of Alexander II, Tolstoy and Dostoevsky* (2002).

27. I must say that because of time and space I have only investigated three instances of Acker's employment of historical narrative. In fact, *ALTL* is

filled with many others worthy of investigation. For example, Acker's book also includes sections on the Haymarket riots as well as Henry Kissinger life and role within the Nixon administration. Moreover, and in direct relation to issues of feminism, some recent work has investigated women's pivotal role in the Paris commune and the popular representation of those women as fear inspiring—almost Medusa like—figures (e.g. Gullickson 1996). This sort of investigation would certainly connect with what Acker is attempting to communicate in *ALTL*. In a different but related sense, Acker's references to artists of this period must interdiscursively correspond to artistic representations of the horrors of the Paris commune; recent studies on artistic representations of the rebellion would seem to bear this out (e.g. Boime 1996; Milner 2000). Moreover, Acker's historical references to real artists like Van Gogh, Toulouse Lautrec, et al. also appear to critique the place of artist and art in capitalist society (e.g. artist as whore in the art market).

NOTES TO CHAPTER THREE

1. This is a statement about the general tendency of research on DeLillo and is not intended to deny credit to writers who have, if only briefly, made insightful comments about DeLillo's readers. Here, I refer not only to Frank Lentricchia (1996), but also to Daniel Aaron (1996), and last but not least, Tom LeClair (1987), all of whom have made very interesting observations on DeLillo's readers. In fact, this chapter is indebted to LeClair's brief comments on the reader and DeLillo's genres in *White Noise*.
2. Given my comments regarding interpellation in the last chapter it goes without saying that likes and dislikes concerning types of literature are, at least to some extent, a function of social conditioning, which is to say, we are frequently "taught" what to like and dislike.
3. The internet article "Underworld Media Watch" chronologically lists *Underworld*'s location on the "Bestseller list," and notes the book's ranking within the top twelve from late September to mid November (<http//perival.com/delillo/underworld_media.html>).
4. My use of Hutcheon's concept is intended to open up or broaden the definition of reader. Of course, broad definitions can become useless if they are too broad. But as I hope the rest of my argument shows, my use of literary history and broad reader categories (as "discursive communities") does not fall prey to this criticism to any alarming degree. Obviously, as we are all aware, definition is part of the larger problem regarding the place of the reader. I refer here to the troublesome areas of "reception theory" or "reader response." As some writers have reminded us these theories have some very real problems, stretching from the logical to the politically dubious. For example, in the first case we have Stanley Fish's *Is There a Text in this Class?*

1980), which has difficulty in defining what exactly makes for an "interpretive community" (Hogan, *Philosophical Approaches* 145–146). The difficulty does not totally invalidate Fishes' theory, but it does make for problems. As for politically dubious theories, Terry Eagleton in the early nineteen eighties remarked that a good many of these theories were emblematic, embodying "nothing less than the central contradiction of the dominant textual economy" wherein "the reader must be ascribed certain quasi-autonomous capacities at the very moment that he or she is subdued to a mere function of the text" (Eagleton, "The Revolt of the Reader" 449). In that same essay Eagleton goes on to remark that no matter what slight freedom these theories grant the reader, s/he nevertheless remains stuck within a range of unpleasant choices, ranging from the hard right—in figures like Roman Ingarden, who gives readers "localized indeterminacies" which they must "dutifully . . . fill in"—to the further left but "bourgeois-liberal" position of Jonathan Culler, who allows readers "access to the closely protected secrets of the boardroom—to the codes, blueprints, paradigms, and technical know-how which govern the manufacture of commodities" (Eagleton, "The Revolt of the Reader" 449–450).

The issue of agency is crucial here, and nowhere is that clearer than in a number of other "popular" postmodern theories of the reading subject and text which go beyond Ingarden's (reader) constraints, Culler's consumer guide book or Fish's "discourse communities." Here, I speak of the positions held by Barthes, Foucault, Derrida, Baudrillard, and Lyotard—this representing just a short list of our most famous postmodern "stars"—who, to different and varying degrees, reduce textual meaning either to absolute relativity (i.e. no one reader's interpretation is the "Truth") or, in some cases, reduce world and reader to texts or confluences of texts. Thus, in some of these theories readers are not traditional consumers of texts, but in their acts of reading actually write (e.g. Barthes), even if the texts they produce in reading possess no truth with a capital "T." Or, in other variations, readers—even if they can be said to "write"—merely write what has already been written in them, namely, the discourses, codes, or whatever the culture inculcates (e.g. Foucault). And in the last instance, many of these theorists (e.g. Derrida) treat the external world not as reality but as mere text to be interpreted at will.

As seems obvious, this essay does not pretend to resolve issues brought up by these theories. But an analysis of DeLillo's *White Noise* from the contemporary reader's perspective would seem to require occasional reference to these "popular" theories since, as I have already noted, many writers view the book as offering a representation of the subject in present social and cultural condition, namely, postmodernity, and specifically postmodernity within America. Therefore, I will make reference to some of these theories where deemed relevant and necessary.

5. It goes without saying that terms like "genre" and "tradition" are themselves problematic, as is shown in Acker's deconstruction of genre and Reed's earlier rewriting of tradition. Nevertheless, the present essay follows the previous chapter's usage of the term "genre"; for explanation of terminology see endnote three, Chapter Three. In the case of the last term, "tradition," use of it begs the question and invites us to ask, "Of whose tradition do we speak?" I therefore use these terms with caution and mean them only to stand for the *dominant* ways in which artefacts of American literary tradition have been categorized. My adoption of Hutcheon's constraining "discursive communities" is an attempt to recognize this.
6. See Zinn 1995, especially 462.
7. In the sixties and seventies Nixon used COINTELPRO to surveil, delegitimate, intimidate, and otherwise destroy a wide variety of social activists spanning from the Black Panthers to the National Council of Churches. On this see: Chomsky (1990); Powers (1988); Davis (1990).
8. On this count, one need only think of somewhat recent disclosures surrounding, among other things, the Iran-Contra arms-for-hostages scandal and supposed links with it, namely, C.I.A. drug dealing in central America. These are but two examples, though it would be easy to construct a laundry list of such secret activities. On this see also Zinn's (1995) exhaustive discussion of governmental secrecy policies and lowered voter turnout after Nixon years because of general public disillusionment in the electoral process.
9. Using Jameson in this way may appear to do some injustice to the theory he articulates in *Fables of Aggression: Wyndham Lewis, the Modernist as Fascist* (1979). His is a complicated play on the work of Gilles Deleuze and Félix Guattari in *Anti-Oedipus: Capitalism and Schizophrenia* (1977). But my sin is a small one because I use his remarks, like those of Bal in the previous chapter, to pull out something which is visible at the level of the text and does not require using his theoretical system.
10. Lest we misunderstand his meaning here, Jameson's analysis seems diagnostic and not overtly evaluative; that is, he seems to be explaining an aspect of the category (modernist literature) itself, not declaring it as superior to this or that form of art. My use of the phrase "high art" is meant, however, to signal the usual or typical evaluative usage.
11. Of course, much the same thing has taken place with British college mysteries (see Nover 1999; Bevan 1990).
12. This is a short list; if one thumbed through the pages of Kramer and Kramer's extensive annotated bibliography (1983), one could find many more.
13. A number of writers have expressed this phenomenon in different ways (e.g. Harvey, *The Conditions of Postmodernity* 1990). While I find Habermas' theory helpful here, it does not necessarily contradict theories like Harvey's

(i.e. Harvey's notion of "flexible accumulation"). Both Harvey's and Habermas' theories find problematic those claims that a "Chinese wall" exists between the private and public sectors (i.e. the fact that the private sector can make profit, while the public sector cannot). While they recognize that the state may not be able to make a profit—though this is increasingly not the case, as witnessed with U.C.L.A.'s distance learning program (Poovey 3)—both understand, though somewhat differently, the reliance of the state on the economic sphere, be it through taxes (Habermas) or through complex investments (e.g. bonds) in the government itself (Harvey); moreover, and this is the important part, both acknowledge that such reliance effects state action.

14. While I am indebted to Habermas' theoretical reading, the majority of my remarks on university funding are drawn from Mary Poovey's incisive analysis entitled "The Twenty-First-Century University and the Market: What Price Economic Viability?" (2001).

15. Efforts "to enhance this redirection of priorities, including the "Bayh-Dole Act" of 1980, "which allows universities to patent the results of federally funded research," is a primary instance offered by Poovey (6).

16. While it may be true that the pinnacle of the schematized does not occur until Reagan's era, it would perhaps be wise to appreciate Howard Zinn's commentary on the Carter years:

> Whatever Carter's sophistication . . . , certain fundamentals operated in the late sixties and the seventies. American corporations were active all over the world on a scale never seen before. There were, by the early seventies, about three hundred U.S. corporations, including the seven largest banks, which earned 40 percent of their net profits outside the United States. They were called "multinationals," but 98 percent of their top executives were Americans. As a group, they now constituted the third-largest economy in the world, next to the United States and the Soviet Union. (556)

17. Sheppard cites many examples to prove his point. For instance, he cites novels from the nineteen-seventies (e.g. Anthony Prices' *Colonel Butler's Wolf* (1972); Simon Raven's *Places Where They Sing* (1970)) to show a conservative attitude in Britain regarding expanding education beyond the elite few to the many; the novels coincide with the expansion of "higher education in . . . mid-1960s" Britain. Raven's novel, in particular, exhibits faculty members who "are infantile, underhand, idle, gluttonous, self-serving, impotent, unprincipled, crude, foul-mouthed, drunken and cowardly" (Sheppard 20). Sheppard lists numerous other examples, but this illustrates the point.

18. On the problematic nature of F.R. Leavis' legacy, including notions of education through the English literary tradition, its elitist tendencies, and failure to deal with factors outside texts, see Eagleton (1983).

19. Consider, for instance, our fictional College on the Hill's tuition circa nineteen eighty-five as compared to two ivy league schools, Columbia and Princeton, at an even later date of nineteen eighty-seven; Columbia's tuition at that time was approximately $11,810, while Princeton's was around $12,550 ("Anxiety Over Tuition: A Controversy in Context" A16).
20. On light class loads for teachers at research universities see Patrick Colm Hogan's "Teaching and Research as Economic Problems" (1993).
21. While we do not have time to discuss it at length here, Agger makes some interesting comments about the "notoriously vague" guidelines for what constitutes proper publication. The "how much" and "where" question is never formally announced; it therefore makes it easy to discriminate in various ways. It is for this reason, remarks Agger, that numerous "women and minorities" who are "denied tenure increasingly sue their universities for wrongful dismissal based on sex and race discrimination, respectively. They must show that white males earning tenure at the same time had less illustrious publication and teaching records, a case relatively straightforward if not always legally successful" (Agger, *The Decline of Discourse* 124).
22. It is essential to note here Radway's own observation that such editorial freedom may ultimately be doomed; in fact, she qualifies her statement about relatively open editorial selection criteria, saying "the situation is changing rapidly," and then inserts an endnote indicating that BOMC. was purchased in nineteen-eighty-seven by Time Inc., who, after its purchase, initiated a vast "market research program" designed to totally overhaul the club's working structure.

   Such a broad based overhaul would most likely attempt to limit the editorial selection criteria Radway observes at the BOMC around nineteen-eighty-seven. This might well affect some of what I say in this section regarding DeLillo; however, as I hope the next few pages indicate, while this part of my argument relies on a contradiction between DeLillo's molar and molecular levels, the larger molar sphere in *White Noise* (i.e. character cohesion or relatively centered narrative point of view) carries the day. That is, its ubiquitous presence far outweighs the few molecular moments in the book.

NOTES TO CHAPTER FOUR

1. Though in his mention of Reed Jameson nowhere bothers to cite a work or even exemplary sentences supporting his point, I take it as reasonable to assert that his points refer to Reed's *Mumbo Jumbo* since it is one of the writer's most famous works and filled with numerous instances of "pastiche," a primary marker in Jameson's diagnosis of postmodernism.
2. I had lunch with Reed and two colleagues after he gave a talk at Community College of Philadelphia in April of 2002. Over lunch he stated much

the same objection regarding Jameson's narrow knowledge of African-American literary history. For this reason, among others, Reed believed it a mischaracterization to call his work "postmodern" in the Jamesonian sense.

3. For examples of Reed's numerous declarations, see his discussions with John O'Brien, Gaga (Mark S. Johnson), Peter Nazareth, and Shamoon Zamir in *Conversations with Ishmael Reed* (Dick and Singh 1995).
4. On satiric and comedic African masks, see, for instance, Drewal and Drewal's examination of Yoruba tribal masks (Drewal and Drewal 1990).
5. That the author consciously used another's (Lydia Maria Child's) work is affirmed in the "Conclusion" of *Clotel* (Zafar 133; Brown, *Clotel* 222)
6. Though this has not been discussed, the overarching structure of detection in *Mumbo Jumbo*—with LaBas as *black trickster detective*—similarly follows Brown in its thematic refiguring of both the traditionally racist detective genre and its caucasian hero, since it is the black HooDoo detective who solves the crime. For an interesting and insightful discussion of racism in the American detective novel—especially its hard-boiled varient—see Dennis Porter's *The Pursuit of Crime: Art and Ideology in Detective Fiction* (1981).
7. For an interesting discussion of the sermon's relation to blues and jazz see Huggins (1971).
8. On the issue of an Americanized remaking the self, see Madonna Marsden's "The American Myth of Success: Visions and Revisions" (1978).
9. While I would not necessarily agree with all of their claims and positions, much of the following criticism of Gates is indebted to earlier arguments offered by the following writers: Sandra Adell (1994) Joyce A. Joyce (1987), Norman Harris (1987), and Howard Felperin (1985).
10. In all fairness I should indicate that Gates is an intelligent thinker and is certainly aware of the impact skin color has on African-Americans in everyday life. In this respect there seems a certain disconnect between the scholar's literary critical thinking and his other beliefs.
11. My formulation here is greatly indebted to Patrick Hogan's reading of Edward Said's *Culture and Imperialism* (1993) in his book *Empire and Poetic Voice* (2004).
12. As Sandra Adell observes, "Gates claims that his work in *The Signifying Monkey* tries to accomplish . . . the identification and isolation of an 'authentic' Afro-American literary tradition grounded in the black vernacular" (120). He does this by employing the Signifying Monkey, whose ancestor is the (African) "Yoruba trickster figure, Esu-Elegbara" (Adell 130). The Signifying Monkey as trickster constitutes "a master trope 'in which are encoded several other peculiarly black rhetorical tropes'" and is "'he who dwells at the margins of discourse, ever punning, ever troping, ever embodying the ambiguities of langauge, [he] is our trope for repetition and revision, indeed our trope of chiasmus, repeating and reversing

simultaneously as he does in one deft discursive act'" (Adell 131; Gates, *The Signifying Monkey* qtd. in Adell 131). The history of African-American tradition is thus "a ritual of renaming, substitution, and analogue," in an effort to revise tradition (Adell 131)

Interestingly, Adell remarks that Gates' vision of troping at the "margins" is very much indebted to Houston Baker's earlier work (Baker 1984), and is in effect "playing off of—signifying on—Baker's spatial metaphor (and Derrida's *Margins of Philosophy*)" (131). The similarity of Gates to poststructuralists like Derrida is thus fairly obvious. We may also add to this similarity the fact that, as Adell indicates, Gates explicitly follows the lead of other poststructuralists; for example, he "superimposes his 'figures of signification' on Bloom's 'map of misprision' in a 'signifyin(g) riff'" (Adell 135; Gates, *The Signifying Monkey* 87) As an additional aside, Gates' other comments about the Signifying Monkey and his ancestor (Esu-Elegbara), are interesting, because he says that together they constitute a "'meta-discourse, a discourse about itself . . . '" (Gates qtd. in Adell 131). Of course, would not such a claim fly exactly in the face of the undecidability Gates so clearly seems to hold? That is, Gates wants to claim indeterminacy of African-American tradition; as he puts it, "our trope is chiasmus" (Gates, *The Signifying Monkey* 52; Adell 134). But he nevertheless recuperates chiasmus in what Adell terms a "Hegelian synthesis that yields *tradition*" (Adell 135; italics mine). The problem, according to Adell, is that Gates—to have tradition—must slide between a philosophical definition of "chiasmus" and a rhetorical definition—namely, between a Hegelian definition and a sort of deconstructive-rhetorical one. The philosophical definition sees chiasmus as "'a form of thought in which differences are installed, preserved, and overcome in one grounding unity of totality'" (Gasché qtd. in Adell 135). That is what Gates wants, if unconsciously. But a rhetorical-deconstructionist definition of "chiasmus"—something he also seems to use—prohibits the very "reversal and revision" that Gates needs to preserve his tradition because it—at least in varieties stretching from de Man to Derrida—is based on more than just "reversal and substitution" (Adell 135). This view—rightly or wrongly—sees the basic structures of all texts as indeterminable. As Adell puts it, there "no possibility for a hermeneutical dimension that would be capable of restoring truth of the text and its tradition"; in short, chiasmus "cannot serve as a figure of closure as does the concept of tradition" (Adell 135). Thus, we may say that Gates wants to have his chiasmus eat it too. Unfortunately, this will not do, at least not logically.

13. E. San Juan (1994) comments on the erasure of class by "postmodern liberals" like Gates (San Juan 66). In several sections of the paper in question San Juan responds to assertions Gates puts forth in his essay "'Beyond Culture Wars': Identities in Dialogue" (Gates 1993). San Juan's observations

merit quoting at length, since they reveal central and important problems with Gates' position regarding class, though they are somewhat beyond the scope of this section. As San Juan remarks,

> Gates . . . invokes the ideal of pluralism underpinned by tolerance and mastery of substantial knowledge gained from a liberal education of the kind trumpeted by Cardinal Newman. Immersed in a world "fissured by nationality, ethnicity, race, and gender" ["class" is revealingly omitted], Gates exhorts us "to transcend those divisions . . . through education that seeks to comprehend the diversity of human culture." Urging us to forge a "civic culture that respects both differences and commonalities," Gates puts a high premium on the postmodern virtue of hybridity, Dewey's pluralism, individuality, etc.—all these somehow immune from corruption by the centralized state, mass consumerism, and profit making. Ironically, while avoiding the traditional "universalistic humanism" of "melting pot" integrationists and "vulgar cultural nationalists" (like Leonard Jeffries), Gates succumbs to the pathos of the eclectic idealist so poignantly described by Frantz Fanon and George Jackson: he wishes that lived contradictions will go away by taking thought, by contemplating a dialogue among equals, by an encyclopedic inventory of differences. Granting that differences are all equal, what grounds this equivalence? Agreement to disagree—the obsession with open-mindedness—becomes a pretext for a sophisticated form of apologizing for the status quo. (66)

14. Though Kuenz never refers to Reed's work in her essay, I am nevertheless greatly indebted to her for much of what follows regarding Gates and the Harlem Renaissance.

15. The reference here is from Langston Hughes' essay in the *Nation* called "The Negro Artist and the Racial Mountain" in which he pleads for black readers to be "Negro enough to be different," as well as to identify with their "racial culture" (Hughes qtd. in Kuenz 198–199).

    On problems with the notion or metaphor of original "roots" see Patrick Colm Hogan's *Empire and Poetic Voice* (2004).

16. See especially Sandra Adell's exhaustive look at these issues in her book *Double Consciousness/Double Bind* (1994).

17. On the tendency to deny Marrant's narrative African-American status see John Sekora's "Black Message/White Envelope: Genre, Authenticity and Authority in the Antebellum Slave Narrative" (1987). I am indebted to Zafar for this reference.

18. As a important aside, two points need mentioning in this regard. First, Gates is a perfect case in point. To his credit Gates includes Marrant in African-American tradition (see *The Signifying Monkey* (1988)). But his vision of Marrant follows his poststructuralist hybrid formula and uses

Marrant's captivity genre in a way that preserves essential links between race and tradition. That is, Gates must see Marrant's engagement with the Cherokee as a trope representing the "black-white social dialogue" (Zafar 58). In specific, Gates views Marrant as starting the "Anglo African tradition" by employing an earlier text by "Ukawsaw Gronniosaw as a model to be revised" (Adell 133). But his use is problematic in the same way as indicated earlier in that by his own admission the shared nature of the "text of blackness"—its tradition—is found in "the process of revision that tropes and topoi undergo when they are seized by writers as they read each other's texts" (Adell 133). As already noted, Gates also believes such signifying is done by all texts, so the problem, again, is with the *specialness* of African-American tradition's signifying practice.

Moreover, the originary moment Gates isolates—namely, Marrant's revision of Ukawsaw Gronniosaw's text, which marks the beginning of "Anglo African tradition"—is further troubled by the logic of Gates' own argument. This is because he holds that such signifying should be "formal" in nature ("tradition, in part, turns upon this definition of texts read by an author and then Signified upon in some *formal* way" Gates, *The Signifying Monkey* 145; italics mine) (Adell 133). But, as Sandra Adell observes, such formal representation is exactly what is prohibited by Gates' own theory of playful and indeterminate signification, namely, its "condition of ambiguity" (Gates, *The Signifying Monkey* 45; qtd. Adell 133). This, of course, is related to the contradiction between Gates' own desire for closure—i.e. an identifiable tradition—and theoretical apparatus he wants to use (see endnote 12).

Second, for her part Rafia Zafar invokes Homi Bhabha's hybridity to explicate Marrant's text. Here, she interprets Marrant as a westerner whose encounter with the Cherokee embodies "western" (Christian-Protestant) and "nonwestern" (Cherokee) interaction (Zafar 59). In specific, she sees Marrant and other black practitioners of the captivity genre as "'Africans'" "writing American literature" (Zafar 6). But in so doing she also considers Marrant a Christian; thus, he (Marrant) is "both the agent of white, Protestant, colonizing power and the colonial subject adapting and mimicking the sign of the colonizer" (Zafar 59). Here, she follows Bhabha's claim that "the signifier of colonial mimcry [becomes] the affect of hybridity—at once a mode of appropriation and resistance" (Bhabha qtd. in Zafar 59). Zafar's reading of Marrant is insightful and very informative, but her use of hybridity, which she ties not only to Marrant's Christianity and blackness, but also to his—and other's—specifically African nature ("'Africans writing American literature'"), produces a rather vague identity category that prohibits placing Marrant or his texts within African-American tradition, whatever that might be. To her credit, Zafar sees that certain texts and authors are not easily accommodated into African-American tradition as it is currently constructed. But she nevertheless seems wedded to the idea of *tradition* itself. The difficulty of Zafar's own position viz a viz identity and tradition is evident in part of her book's title, which reads "*African-Americans* Write *American* Literature."

19. On the problems with autonomous meaning, as well as the role of definition and extension in creation of meaning see Patrick Colm Hogan's *The Politics of Interpretation: Ideology, Professionalism, and the Study of Literature* (1990).

20. I should say that this does some disservice to Hogan's argument in that it is much more detailed and addresses other ways in which linking race to tradition and culture are problematic (e.g. his investigation of the metaphorical reliance on "roots" in such linkage).

21. I believe all of this has a great deal to do with what writers like Thomas Frank have called "market populism" and others, like Fredric Jameson, have analyzed as "the rhetoric of the market" (Frank 2000; Jameson 1997). Thomas Frank, in his essay "Market Populism," talks about the emergence of this ideological trend in the nineteen nineties and its increasing power over peoples' minds. The following short passage outlines his basic point:

> From Dead heads to Nobel-laureate economists, from paleoconservatives to New Democrats, American leaders in the nineties came to believe that markets were a popular system, a far more democratic form of organization than (democratically elected governments). This is the central premise of what I call "market populism": that in addition to being mediums of exchange, markets are mediums of consent. With their mechanisms of supply and demand, poll and focus group, superstore and Internet, markets manage to express the popular will more articulately and meaningfully than do mere elections. By their very nature markets confer democratic legitimacy, markets bring down the pompous and the snooty, markets look out for the interests of the little guy, markets give us what we want. (14)

Part of this "market populism" is an ingenious, though surely poisonous, ideological discourse Fredric Jameson calls the "rhetoric of the market." For Jameson this rhetoric is a powerful and seductive ideological discourse serving to delegitimate "left discourse" while simultaneously affirming the natural legitimacy of the right's market discourse (Jameson, *Postmodernism* 1997): "My thesis in its strongest form," asserts Jameson,

> is that the rhetoric of the market has been a fundamental and central component of this ideological struggle, this struggle for the legitimation or delegitimation of left discourse. The surrender to various forms of market ideology—on the *left,* I mean, not to mention everybody else—has been imperceptible but alarmingly universal. Everyone is now willing to mumble, as though it were an inconsequential conces-

sion in passing to public opinion and current received wisdom (or shared communicational presuppositions) that no society can function efficiently without the market and that planning is obviously impossible. (263)

As a consequence this market ideology can therefore quite easily slide into the equally ideological claim that "'[t]he market is in human nature'" (Jameson, *Postmodernism* 263).

To relate these points back to Acker and the notion of "appearance" as constituting the essential ideological reality of postmodernity, we need only think of the way the market has been popularized in, for one, the television media. Here, one example will have to suffice for the general trend, though one could easily extend the list of such instances. As our one example we might consider the ubiquitous ads for internet stock trading firms. In these ads class has disappeared, replaced by images of egalitarian and democratic subjects punching away at keyboards, their classlessness signified by each subject's dress, spanning from that of construction worker to twenty-something hipster and aging yuppie. Regardless of the firm advertised, however, the message conveyed is always universal availability of access and social-economic mobility for all. This, of course, is a sham, all *image*, all *appearance*. But the ideological effects of image and appearance are far ranging, delegitimizing within viewing subjects other ways of viewing social relationships. As for the few televised images of the poor (e.g. in so called "third world" countries), market rhetoric reimages them (e.g. in mainstream news) as soon-to-be beneficiaries of globalized capitalism. More generally, such images are accompanied the ideological element of "prompted assent beliefs," namely, beliefs which people offer but have no "motivational force" behind them (Hogan, *The Politics of Interpretation* 26–27); that is, we have a public discourse which fosters claims regarding, among other things, "human rights," but in the rather innocuous form *promising no action:* "Human rights? . . . Of course, who doesn't believe in human rights."

It is because of all this that Acker believes "there is only appearance and disappearance, those who appear in the media and those people who have disappeared from the possibility of any sort of home."

22. For those unaware of Autonomia I offer Patrick Cuninghame's short summation of its importance and work:

The Italian new social movement of the mid to late 1970s, Autonomia (Autonomy), also known as Autonomia Operaia (Workers' Autonomy), represents a key collective actor in the history of late 20th century European protests and social conflict. Firstly, there is its role in the highly conflictual and relatively rapid transformation of Italy from a recently industrialised nation to a post-fordist, post-industrial society from the mid 1970s onwards; a process which is still very much ongoing with the gradual emergence of a Second Republic, within the broader context of European integration, from the political instability, regional imbalances and corruption scandals of the First Republic. Secondly, there is the light the experience of Autonomia has thrown on the question of changing nature of collective identity, political organisation and social contestation in urbanised, advanced capitalist societies. (1)

23. I think this criticism stands despite both Baudrillard's subsequent dismissal of Neo Geo in nineteen eighty-seven (Danto 2) and his even later assertion of "the total worthlessness of contemporary art" (Baudrillard qtd. in Ghaznavi and Stalder 1). In fact, the piece from which the later assertion is excerpted points not only to Baudrillard's inconsistency, but also to his ultra-right wing leanings. Later in that same piece Baudrillard claims, "the problematization of contemporary art can only come from a reactionary, irrational, or even *fascist* mode of thinking" (Baudrillard "A Conjuration of Imbeciles" qtd. in Ghaznavi and Stalder 1; italics mine).

24. For examples, see the collection of essays edited by Lentricchia (1996).

25. While I will not discuss it here, recent work by Paul Maltby also suggests that such characterization of DeLillo is problematic. In a recent and well support essay, Maltby (1996) examines a number of DeLillo's works (e.g. *The Names* (1982); *Libra* (1988); *White Noise* (1985)) and discerns within them not the trait of postmodern hyperreality, but rather the Romantic trait of the "visionary moment," which is a "flash of insight or sudden revelation which critically raises the level of spiritual or self-awareness of a fictional character" (Maltby 258). In fact, Maltby's essay finds exactly this flash of insight in DeLillo's work. The tendency is toward transcendence, or, put another way, to a deeper level of significance. Thus Maltby remarks that it "is typical of DeLillo's tendency to seek out transcendent moments in our postmodern lives that hint at possibilities for cultural regeneration" (261).

26. For a fascinating historical discussion of the philosophical turn away from reason and its relation to poststructuralism see Martin Jay's *Downcast Eyes: The Denigration of Vision in Twentieth Century French Thought* (1993).

27. In listing these numerous dates it would be unfair not to remark, as Steven Best and Douglas Kellner have, that Foucault "is a complex and eclectic thinker who draws from multiple sources and problematics . . ." (Best and Kellner 35). Among other things, this is evinced by the fact that while Foucault has had a tremendous affect on postmodern/poststructural theory, he was at one time a structuralist. At the same time, the claims regarding subjectivity in his earlier and later works would still seem to affirm my appraisal.

28. Rosenfeld's book, *Imagining Hitler* (1985), never explicitly mentions the term "postmodernism," but his investigation of novels representing Hitler

and Nazism explores works one might loosely term "historiographic metafiction," much of which draws upon poststructural theory. Indeed, many of the novels he investigates are shameless in their use and mixture of history and fiction. Moreover, Rosenfeld explores Hitler as a pop cultural phenomenon more generally, and in this respect the waning of the historically real Hitler. Thus, I feel justified in making this claim.

Bibliography

Aaron, Daniel. "How to Read Don DeLillo." Lentricchia 67–81.
Abrahams, Roger. *Deep Down in the Jungle . . . :Negro Narrative Folklore from the Streets of Philadelphia*. Chicago: Aldin, 1970.
Abrams, M. H. *A Glossary of Literary Terms*. New York: HBJ, 1993.
Acker, Kathy. *The Adult Life of Toulouse Lautrec by Henri Toulouse Lautrec*. Originally published by TVRT Press. New York: New York, 1978. Republished in *Portrait of an Eye*. New York: Grove, 1998. 185–311.
———. "Beth Jackson Interviews Kathy Acker" *Eyeline*. 3.1 (1996): 12 April 2001 <http://acker.the hub.com.au/ackerjack.html>.
———. *Blood and Guts in High School*. New York: Grove, 1984.
———. *Bodies of Work: Essays*. New York and London: Serpent's Tail, 1997.
———. "Conversation with Kathy Acker." *Apparatus and Memory*. 8.5 (1999): 15 May 2001 <http://proxy.arts.uci.edu/%7Enideffer/_SPEED_/1.1/acker.html>.
———. *Hannibal Lecter, My Father*. New York: Semiotext(e), 1991.
———. "Kathy Acker Interview with Karl Schmieder." *Narope*. 8.5 (1991): 11 Aug. 2001<http://www.ilato.org/kathy1.html>.
———. "The Path of Abjection: An Interview with Kathy Acker." *Some Other Frequency: Interviews with Innovative American Authors*. Ed. Larry McCaffery. Philadelphia: U of Pennsylvania P, 1996.15–35.
Adell, Sandra. *Double-Consciousness/Double Bind: Theoretical Issues in Twentieth-Century Black Literature*. Urbana and Chicago: U of Illinois P, 1994.
Agger, Ben. *Fast Capitalism: A Critical Theory of Significance*. Urbana and Chicago: U of Illinois P, 1989.
———. *The Decline of Discourse: Reading, Writing and Resistance in Postmodern Capitalism*. London and New York: Falmer, 1990.
———. *The Discourse of Domination: From the Frankfurt School to Postmodernism*. Evanston: Northwestern UP, 1992.
Althusser, Louis. "Ideology and Ideological State Apparatuses." *Lenin and Philosophy*. Trans. Ben Brewster. New York: Monthly Review, 1971.127–186.

"Anxiety Over Tuition: A Controversy in Context." *Chronicle of Higher Education* 43.38 (1987): A10-A17.
Baker, Houston A. *Blues, Ideology, and Afro-American Literature: A Vernacular Theory.* Chicago: U of Chicago P, 1984.
Bakhtin, Mikhail. *The Dialogic Imagination: Four Essays.* Trans. Caryl Emerson, and Michael Holquist. Austin: U of Texas P, 1988.
Bal, Mieke. *Narratology: Introduction to the Theory of Narrative.* Toronto: U of Toronto P, 1997.
Baraka, Imamu Amiri. "Afro-American Literature and Class Struggle." *Black American Literature Forum* 14 (1980): 6–37.
———. *Home: Social Essays.* New York: William Morrow, 1966.
———. "Black Art." *Selected Poetry of Amiri Baraka/Le Roi Jones.* New York: William Morrow, 1969. 106–107.
Barthes, Roland. "The Death of the Author." *Image, Music, Text.* Trans. Stephen Heath. New York: Hill, 1977. 31–43.
———. *Le Plaisir du texte.* Paris: Editions du Seuil, 1973.
———. *S/Z.* Trans. Richard Miller. New York: Hill, 1974.
Baudrillard, Jean. "The Ecstasy of Communication." Foster, ed. 126–134.
———. *In the Shadow of the Silent Majorities, or, The End of the Social and Other Essays.* Trans. Paul Foss, John Johnston, and Paul Patton. New York: Semiotext(e), 1983.
———. *Jean Baudrillard: Selected Writings.* Ed. Mark Poster. Stanford: Stanford UP, 1988.
Beck, Rudolf, Hidegard Kuester, and Martin Kuester, eds. *Terminologie der Literaturwissenschaft: Ein Handbuch für das Anglistikstudium.* Trans. Martin Kuester. Ismaning: Hueber, 1998.
Belsey, Catherine. "Constructing the Subject: deconstructing the text." *Feminisms: An Anthology of Literary Theory and Criticism.* Eds. Robin Warhol and Diane Price Herndl. Rutgers: Rutgers UP, 1997. 657–673.
Benjamin, Walter. *Illuminations.* Trans. Harry Zohn. New York: Schocken, 1969.
———. *Charles Baudelaire: A Lyric Poet in the Era of High Capitalism.* Trans. Harry Zone. London: NLB, 1973.
———. "The Author as Producer." *The Essential Frankfurt School Reader.* Ed. Andrew Arato and Eike Gebhardt. Oxford: Basil Blackwell, 1978. 254–269.
Benstock, Shari. *Textualizing the Feminine.* Norman and London: U of Oklahoma P, 1991.
Benveniste, Emile. *Problems in General Linguistics.* Coral Gables: U of Miami P, 1971.
Best, Steven, and Douglas Kellner. *Postmodern Theory: Critical Interrogations.* New York: Guilford, 1991.
Bevan, David, ed. *University Fiction.* Amsterdam: Rodopi, 1990.
Boime, Albert. *The French Commune: Imagining Paris after War and Revolution.* Princeton: Princeton UP, 1996.

Bordo, Susan. *Flight to Objectivity: Essays on Cartesianism and Culture.* Albany: SUNY Press, 1987.
Borges, Jorge Luis. *Labyrinths: Selected Stories and Other Writings.* Eds. Donald A. Yates and James E. Irby. New York: New Directions, 1964.
Bourdieu, Pierre. *Distinction: A Social Critique of the Judgement of Taste.* Trans. Richard Nice. Cambridge: Harvard UP, 1984.
Bowie, Malcolm. *Lacan.* Cambridge: Harvard UP, 1991.
Bradbury, Malcolm. *Eating People is Wrong.* Harmondsworth: Penguin, 1962.
———. *Stepping Westward.* Boston: Houghton Mifflin, 1966.
———. *The History Man.* London: Arrow Books, 1975.
———. "Campus Fiction." Bevan 49–55.
Breger, Louis. *Freud: Darkness in the Midst of Vision.* New York: John Wiley & Sons, 2000.
Briton, Derek. "Marketspeak: The Rhetoric of Restructuring and Its Implications for Adult and Higher Education." *Studies in the Education of Adults* 28:1 (April 1996): 19–33.
Brown, Terry. "Longing to Long: Kathy Acker and the Politics of Pain." *Literature Interpretation Theory (LIT)* 2:3 (1991): 167–177.
Brown, William Wells. *Clotel: or The Presidents Daughter.* New York: Random House,1990.
———. *Escape; or, A Leap to Freedom. The Roots of African-American Drama: An Anthology of Early Plays, 1858–1938.* Ed. Leo Hamalian and James Hatch. Detroit: Wayne State UP, 1991. 42–99.
Buck-Morss, Susan. *The Dialectics of Seeing: Walter Benjamin and the Arcades Project.* Cambridge: MIT Press, 1997.
Burke, Kenneth. *The Philosophy of Literary Form.* New York: Vintage, 1957.
Butler, Judith. *Gender Trouble: Feminism and the Subversion of Identity.* New York and London: Routledge, 1990.
Canary, Robert, and Henry Kozicki eds. *The Writing of History.* Madison: U of Wisconsin P, 1978.
Cannon, JoAnn. "The Reader as Detective." *Modern Language Studies.* 10 (Fall 1980): 41–50.
Carby, Hazel. "White Woman Listen! Black Feminism and the Boundaries of Sisterhood." Center for Contemporary Cultural Studies. 212–229.
Carroll, Anne. "Art, Literature, and the Harlem Renaissance: The Messages of God's *God's Trombones.*" *College Literature.* 29:3 (Summer 2002). 59–78.
Centre for Contemporary Cultural Studies, ed. *The Empire Strikes Back: Race and Racism in 70s Britain.* London: Centre for Contemporary Cultural Studies, 1982.
Chabot, C. Barry. "The Problem of the Postmodern." *Zeitgeist in Babel: The Postmodern Controversy.* Ed. Ingeborg Hoesterey. Bloomington and Indianapolis: Indiana UP, 1991. 22–39.
Chandler, Raymond. *The Notebooks of Raymond Chandler.* New York: Ecco, 1976.

———. *The Big Sleep.* New York: Vintage, 1992.
Chesnutt, Charles. *The Conjure Woman.* Ridgewood: Gregg, 1968.
Child, Lydia Maria. *Fact and Fiction: A Collection of Stories.* New York: C. S. Francis & Co., 1846.
Chomsky, Noam, and Edward Herman. *Manufacturing Consent: The Political Economy of the Mass Media.* New York: Pantheon, 1988.
Chomsky, Noam. "Bewildering the Herd: An Interview with Noam Chomsky." *The Humanist* Nov./Dec.1990:1–15.
Christianson, Scott. "A Heap of Broken Images: Hardboiled Detective Fiction and the Discourse(s) of Modernity." Walker and Frazer 33–58.
Cixous, Hélène. "Castration or Decapitation?" *Signs* 7:1 (Autumn 1981): 41–55.
Cixous, Hélène. "The Laugh of the Medusa." *New French Feminisms: An Anthology.* Ed. Isabelle de Courtivron and Elaine Marks. New York: Schocken, 1981. 255–256.
Clawson, Calvin. *Mathematical Mysteries: The Beauty and Magic of Numbers.* New York: Plenum, 1996.
Clayton, Jay, and Eric Rothstein eds. *Influence and Intertextuality in Literary Theory.* Madison: U of Wisconsin P, 1991.
Cohn, Dorrit. *Transparent Minds: Narrative Modes for Presenting Consciousness.* Princeton: Princeton UP, 1978.
Conley, Verena Andermatt. *Hélène Cixous: Writing the Feminine.* Lincoln: U of Nebraska P, 1984.
Connor, Steven. *Postmodernist Culture.* London: Blackwell, 1997.
Connery, Brian. "Inside Jokes: Familiarity and Contempt in Academic Satire." Bevan 123–137.
Coward, Rosalind, and John Ellis. *Language and Materialism: Developments in Semiology and the Theory of the Subject.* London and Boston: Routledge & Kegan Paul, 1977.
Cowart, David. *Don DeLillo: The Physics of Language.* Athens: University of Georgia Press, 2002.
Culler, Jonathan. *Structuralist Poetics: Structuralism, Linguistics, and the Study of Literature.* Ithaca: Cornell UP, 1975.
———. *On Deconstruction: Theory and Criticism after Structuralism.* Ithaca: Cornell UP, 1982. Cuninghame, Patrick. "The Future at Our Backs: Autonomia and Autonomous Social Movements in Italy in the 1970s."1 June 2001 <http:ktrumain.lancs.ac.uk/CSEC/nsc . . . /4e8a15e4d43857b8802567210071365b?Open Document>.
Danto, Arthur. "The Hyper-Intellectual." *New Republic* 10 Sept. 1990: 39–41.
Davis, Mike. *City of Quartz: Excavating the Future in Los Angeles.* New York: Vintage, 1992.
———. *Prisoners of the American Dream: Politics and Economy in the History of the U. S. Working Class.* London and New York: Verso, 1986.
DeLillo, Don. *Libra.* New York: Penguin, 1988.

———. *White Noise.* New York: Penguin, 1985.
Deleuze, Gilles, and Félix Guattari. *Anti-Oedipus: Capitalism and Schizophrenia.* Trans. Robert Hurley, et al. New York: Viking, 1977.
Deren, Maya. *Divine Horsemen: The Living Gods of Haiti.* New York: Thames and Hudson, 1953. Reprinted edition Kingston: McPherson & Company, 1984.
Derrida, Jacques. *Of Grammatology.* Trans. Gayatri Chakravorty Spivak. Baltimore: Johns Hopkins UP, 1976.
———. *Writing and Difference.* Trans. Alan Bass. Chicago: U of Chicago P, 1978.
———. "The Law of Genre." *Glyph 7.* Baltimore and London, Johns Hopkins UP 1980. 201–215.
———. *Margins of Philosophy.* Trans. Alan Sheridan. Chicago: U of Chicago P, 1982.
Dews, Peter. *Logics of Disintegration: Post-Structuralist Thought and the Claims of Critical Theory.* London and New York: Verso, 1987.
Dexter, Colin. *Last Bus to Woodstock.* London: Macmillan, 1975.
Dick, Bruce, and Amritjit Singh, eds. *Conversations with Ishmael Reed.* Jackson: UP of Mississippi, 1995.
Dickson-Carr, Darryl. *African American Satire: The Sacredly Profane Novel.* Columbia: U of Missouri P, 2001.
Domini, John. "Ishmael Reed: A Conversation with John Domini." Dick and Singh 128–143.
Doyle, Arthur Conan. *A Study in Scarlet.* New York: Penguin, 1981.
Drewal, Henry John, and Maragret Thompson Drewal. *Gelde: Art and Female Power among the Yoruba.* Bloomington: Indiana UP, 1990.
Dubey, Madhu. *Signs and Cities: Black Literary Postmodernism.* Chicago: U of Chicago P, 2003.
duCille, Anne. *The Coupling of Convention: Sex, Text, and Tradition in Black Women's Fiction.* New York: Oxford UP, 1993.
Eagleton, Terry. *Ideology: An Introduction.* London: Verso, 1991.
———. *Literary Theory: An Introduction.* Minneapolis: U of Minnesota P, 1983.
———. *The Illusions of Postmodernism.* Oxford: Blackwell, 1996.
Ebinghair, H. R., et al. *Numbers.* New York and Berlin: Verlag, 1990.
Elshtain, Jean Bethke. "Our Town Reconsidered: Reflections on the Small Town in American Literature." Yanarella and Lee Sigelman 115–136.
Engel, Monroe, ed. *Uses of Literature: Harvard English Studies 4.* Cambridge: Harvard UP, 1973.
"Ephémride Anarchiste." 3 Aug. 2001 <http://perso.club-internet.fr/ytak/mars1.html/#5>.
Epstein, Barbara. "Why Postmodernism is No Progressive." *Free Inquiry* 19:2 (Spring 1999): 43–53.
Ewen, Stuart, and Elizabeth Ewen. *Channels of Desire: Mass Images and the Shaping of American Consciousness.* New York: McGraw-Hill, 1982.
Felperin, Howard. *Beyond Deconstruction: The Uses and Abuses of Literary Theory.* Oxford: Oxford UP, 1985.

Ferris, Paul. *Dr. Freud: A Life*. Washington, D.C.: Counterpoint, 1997.
Feuer, Jane. "Genre Study and Television." *Channels of Discourse: Television and Contemporary Criticism*. Ed. Robert Allen. Chapel Hill and London: U of North Carolina P, 1987. 113–133.
Fish, Stanley. *Is There a Text In this Class? The Authority of Interpretive Communities*. Cambridge: Harvard UP, 1980.
Fleming, Ian. *Doctor No*. New York: Berkley Books, 1958.
Foster, Hal, ed. *The Anti-Aesthetic: Essays on Postmodern Culture*. Washington: Bay, 1983.
Foster, Hal. *Recodings: Art, Spectacle, Cultural Politics*. Washington: Bay, 1985.
Foucault, Michel. *The Archeology of Knowledge*. Trans. A.M. Sheridan Smith. London: Tavistock, 1972.
———. *Language, Counter-Memory, Practice*. Trans. Donald Bouchard and Sherry Simon. Ed. Donald Bouchard. . Ithaca: Cornell UP, 1977.
———. *The Order of Things: An Archaeology of the Human Sciences*. New York: Vintage, 1973.
———. *Power/Knowledge: Selected Interviews and Other Writings* 1972–1977. Ed. Colin Gordon. New York: Pantheon, 1980.
———. "What is an Author." *The Foucault Reader*. Ed. Paul Rabinow. New York: Pantheon, 1984. 101–120.
Fox, Robert Elliot. *Consciousness Sorcerers: The Black Postmodernist Fiction of LeRoi Jones/Amiri Barak, Ishmael Reed, and Samuel R. Delany*. New York and London: Greenwood, 1987.
Fraiman, Susan. *Cool Men and the Second Sex*. New York: Columbia UP, 2003.
Frank, Thomas. *The Conquest of Cool*. Chicago and London: U of Chicago P, 1997.
———. "The Rise of Market Populism: America's New Secular Religion." *Nation* 30 Oct. 2000: 40–43.
Freud, Sigmund. *Civilization and Its Discontents*. Trans. James Strachey. New York: W. W. Norton, 1961.
———. *The Interpretation of Dreams*. Trans. James Strachey. New York: Basic Books, 1965.
———. *Moses and Monotheism. The Standard Edition of the Complete Psychological Works of Sigmund Freud Vol. 23*. Ed. and trans. James Strachey. London: Hogarth, 1939. 23–110.
Frey, Julia. *Toulouse Lautrec: A Life*. New York: Viking, 1994.
Friedman, Ellen. "'Now Eat Your Mind': An Introduction to the Works of Kathy Acker." *Breaking the Sequence: Women's Experimental Fiction*. Ed. Ellen Friedman and Miriam Fuchs. Princeton: Princeton UP, 1989. 37–49.
———. "A Conversation with Kathy Acker." *The Review of Contemporary Fiction* 9:3 (Fall 1989): 12–22.
Frow, John. "The Last Things Before the Last: Notes on *White Noise*." Lentricchia 175–191.
Frye, Northrop. *Anatomy of Criticism: Four Essays*. Princeton: Princeton UP, 1957.

Gaga (Mark S. Johnson). "Interview with Ishmael Reed." Dick and Singh 51–58.
Ghaznavi, Corinna, and Felix Stalder. "Baudrillard: Contemporary Art is Worthless." 16 Aug. 2001 <http://felix.openflows.org/html/baudrillard.html.>
Gates, Henry Louis, Jr. . "Beyond the Culture Wars: Identities in Dialogue." *Profession* 93. Ed. Phyllis Franklin. New York: Modern Language Association, 1993. 6–11.
———. "The Blackness of Blackness: A Critique of the Sign and the Signifying Monkey." *Black Literature and Theory.* Ed. Henry Louis Gates, Jr. . New York: Methuen, 1984. 285–321.
———. *The Signifying Monkey: A Theory of African-American Literary Criticism.* New York: Oxford UP, 1988.
Giddens, Anthony. *Modernity and Self-Identity: Self and Society in the Late Modern Age.* Stanford: Stanford UP, 1991.
Giovanni, Nikki. "The True Import of Present Dialogue: Black vs. Negro." *The Black Poets.* Ed. Dudley Randall. New York: Bantam, 1971. 318–319.
Glassner, Barry. *The Culture of Fear.* New York: Basic Books, 1999.
Gover, Robert. "An Interview with Ishmael Reed." *Black American Literature Forum* 12 (1978): 16.
Grodin, M and C. Lindlof, eds. *Constructing the Self in a Mediated World.* New York: Sage, 1996.
Grudin, Robert. *Book: A Novel.* New York: Random House, 1992.
Gubar, Susan. "What Ails Feminist Criticism?" *Critical Inquiry* 24:4 (1998): 878–902.
Gullickson, Guy. *Unruly Women of Paris: Images of the Paris Commune.* Ithaca: Cornell UP, 1986.
Habermas, Jürgen. *Legitimation Crisis.* Trans. Thomas McCarthy. Boston: Beacon, 1975.
———. "Modernity versus Postmodernity." *New German Critique* (Winter 1981): 3–14.
———. *The Structural Transformation of the Public Sphere.* Ed. Tom McCarthy. Cambridge: MIT Press, 1987.
Harding, Sandra, and Merill B. Hintikka, eds. *Discovering Reality: Feminist Perspectives on Epistemology, Metaphysics, Methodology, and Philosophy of Science.* Boston: D. Reidel, 1983.
Harper, Philip Brian. *Are We Not Men?: Masculine Anxiety and the Problem of African-American Identity.* Oxford: Oxford UP, 1998.
———. "The Problem with Silence and Exclusiveness in the African American Literary Community." *African American Literary Theory: A Reader.* Ed. Winston Napier. New York: New York UP, 2001. 456–574.
Harris, Norman. "Who's Zoomin Who: The New Black Literary Formalism." *Journal of the Midwest Modern Language Association* 20:1 (1987): 37–45.
Harvey, David. *The Condition of Postmodernity: An Inquiry into the Origins of Cultural Change.* Oxford: Blackwell, 1990.
Hayles, Katherine. "Postmodern Parataxis: Embodied Texts, Weightless Information." *American Literary History* 2:3 (Fall 1990): 394–421.

Held, David. *Introduction to Critical Theory: Horkheimer to Habermas.* Berkley: UC Press, 1980.
Henry, Joseph. "A MELUS Interview: Ishmael Reed." Dick and Singh 205–218.
Hill, Hamilton. "Black Humor and the Mass Audience." *American Humor: Essays Presented to John C. Gerber.* Ed. O. M. Brack. Scottsdale: Arete Publications, 1977. 1–11.
Hill, Reginald. *An Advancement of Learning.* London: William Collins, 1971.
Hogan, Patrick Colm. *The Culture of Conformism: Understanding Social Consent* Durham and London: Duke UP, 2001.
———. *Empire and Poetic Voice: Cognitive and Cultural Studies of Literary Tradition and Colonialism.* Albany: SUNY Press, 2004.
———. *Philosophical Approaches to the Study of Literature.* Gainesville: UP of Florida, 2000.
———. *The Politics of Interpretation: Ideology, Professionalism, and the Study of Literature.* New York and Oxford: Oxford UP, 1990.
———. "Structure and Ambiguity in the Symbolic Order: Some Prolegomena to the Understanding and Criticism of Lacan." *Criticism and Lacan: On Language, Structure, and the Unconscious.* Eds. Patrick Colm Hogan and Lalita Pandit. Athens and London: U of Georgia P, 1990. 3–30.
———. "Teaching and Research as Economic Problems." *Education and Society* 11:1 (1993): 11–25.
Hogue, Lawrence. *Discourse and the Other: The Production of the Afro-American Text.* Durham: Duke UP, 1986.
———. "Postmodernism, Traditional Cultural Forms, and the African American Narrative: Major's *Reflex,* Morrison's *Jazz,* and Reed's *Mumbo Jumbo.*" *Novel* Spring/Summer (2002): 169–192.
Homer, Sean. *Fredric Jameson: Marxism, Hermeneutics, Postmodernism.* New York: Routledge, 1998.
hooks, bell. *Ain't I a Woman: Black Women and Feminism.* Cambridge: South End, 1981.
Horkheimer, Max, and Theodor W. Adorno. *Dialectic of Enlightenment.* Trans. John Cumming. New York: Herder, 1972.
Hornstein, Lillian Herlands, et al., eds. *The Reader's Companion to World Literature.* New York: Mentor, 1956.
Hoy, David Cozens, ed. *Foucault: A Critical Reader.* Cambridge: Basil Blackwell, 1986.
Huggins, Nathan Irvin. *Harlem Renaissance.* Oxford: Oxford UP, 1971.
Hulley, Kathleen. "Transgressing Genre." *Intertextuality and Contemporary American Fiction.* Ed. Robert Davis, and Patrick O'Donnell. Baltimore and London: Johns Hopkins UP, 1989. 171–190.
Hurston, Zora Neale. *Tell My Horse.* Philadelphia: Lippincott, 1938.
Hutcheon, Linda. *Irony's Edge: The Theory and Politics of Irony.* London and New York: Routledge, 1995.

———. *A Poetics of Postmodernism: History, Theory, Fiction.* New York and London: Routledge, 1988.
———. "The Politics of Postmodernism: Parody and History." *Cultural Critique* 5:3 (1986/1987): 179–207.
Huyssen, Andreas. *After the Great Divide: Modernism, Mass Culture, and Postmodernism.* Bloomington and Indianapolis: Indiana UP, 1986.
Irigaray, Luce. "This Sex Which Is Not One." de Courtivron and Marks 99–106.
Iser, Wolfgang. *The Act of Reading: A Theory of Aesthetic Response.* Baltimore: Johns Hopkins UP, 1978.
Jameson, Fredric. *Fables of Aggression: Wyndham Lewis, the Modernist as Fascist.* Berkley: U of California P, 1979.
———. *The Political Unconscious: Narrative as a Socially Symbolic Act.* Ithaca and New York: Cornell UP, 1981.
———. "Postmodernism and Consumer Society." Foster, ed. 111–125.
———. *Postmodernism, Or, The Cultural Logic of Late Capitalism.* Durham: Duke UP, 1997.
Jay, Martin. *Downcast Eyes: The Denigration of Vision in Twentieth Century French Thought.* Berkley: U of California P, 1993.
Jesse, Sharon. "Laughter and Identity in Ishmael Reed's Mumbo Jumbo." *Melus* 21:4 (Winter 1996): 127–129.
Jarrett, Michael. *Drifting on a Read: Jazz as a Model for Writing.* New York: H.B.J., 1999.
Johnson, Abby Arthur, and Ronald Mayberry Johnson. *Propaganda and Aesthetics: The Literary Politics of African-American Magazines in the Twentieth Century* Amherst: U of Massachusetts P, 1979.
Johnson, James Weldon. *God's Trombones.* New York: Viking, 1927.
Jones, Ernest. *The Life and Work of Sigmund Freud.* Vol. 1. New York: Basic Books, 1953. 3 vols.
Joyce, Joyce A. "'Who the Cap Fit': Unconsciousness and Unconscionableness in the Criticism of Houston A. Baker, Jr., and Henry Louis Gates, Jr. ." *New Literary History* 18:2 (1987) 371–383.
———. *Warriors, Conjurers and Priests: Defining African-centered Literary Criticism.* Chicago: Third World Press, 1994.
Jung, C. G. . *Memories, Dreams, Reflections.* Trans. Richard and Clara Winston. New York: Pantheon Books, 1963.
Kavadlo, Jesse. *Don DeLillo: Balance at the Edge of Belief.* New York: Peter Lang, 2004.
Kofman, Sarah. *The Enigma of Woman: Woman in Freud's Writings.* Trans. Catherine Porter. Ithaca: Cornell UP, 1985.
John Kramer. "The American College Mystery." Bevan 3–21.
John E Kramer Jr., and John E. Kramer III. *College Mystery Novels: An Annotated Bibliography, Including a Guide to Professorial Series-Character Sleuths.* New York: Garland Publishing, 1983.

Kramer, Victor, and Robert Russ, eds. *Harlem Renaissance Re-examined*. Troy: Whitston Publishing, 1997.
Kristeva, Julia. *Desire in Language: A Semiotic Approach to Literature and Art*. Ed. and Intro. Leon Roudiez. New York: Columbia UP, 1980.
———. "La Femme, ce n'est jamai ça.'" *Tel Quel* 59 (Automne): 19–24.
———. *Revolution in Poetic Language*. Trans. Margaret Waller. New York: Columbia UP, 1984.
Kuenz, Jane. "*Black No More:* George Schuyler and The Politics of 'Racial Culture.'" Kramer and Russ 197–211.
Lacan, Jacques. *Ecrits: A Selection*. Trans. and ed. Alan Sheridan. London and New York: Norton, 1977.
Latham, Rob. "Collage as Critique and Invention in the Fiction of William S. Burroughs and Kathy Acker." *Journal of the Fantastic in the Arts* 5:19 1993: 46–57.
LeClair, Tom. *In the Loop: Don DeLillo and the Systems Novel*. Urbana and Chicago U of Illinois P, 1987.
Lentricchia, Frank, ed. *Introducing Don DeLillo*. Durham and London: Duke UP, 1996.
Lentricchia, Frank. "The American Writer as Bad Citizen." Lentricchia 1–6.
———. "*Libra* as Postmodern Critique." Lentricchia 193–215.
Lingus, Alphonso. "The Will to Power." *The New Nietzsche*. Ed. David B. Allison. Cambridge and London: M.I.T. Press, 1985. 37–63.
Lodge, David. *Changing Places: A Tale of Two Campuses*. New York: Viking, 1978.
———. *Small World: An Academic Romance*. New York: Warner Books, 1986.
Lovitt, Carl. "Controlling Discourse in Detective Fiction, or Caring Very Much Who Killed Roger Ackroyd." Walker and Frazer 1990. 68–85.
Ludwig, Sämi. "Dialogic Possession in Ishmael Reed's Mumbo Jumbo: Bakhtin, Voodoo, and the Materiality of Multicultural Discourse." Sollors and Maria Dietrich 325–363.
———. *Concrete Language: Intercultural Communication in Maxine Hong Kingston's The Woman Warrior and Ishmael Reed's Mumbo Jumbo*. NewYork: Peter Lang, 1996.
———. "Ishmael Reed's Inductive Narratology of Detection." *African American Review*. 32:3 (1998): 435–444.
Luhrmann, Baz. *Moulin Rouge*. Dir. Baz Luhrmann. Twentieth-Century Fox, 2001.
Lyotard, Jean-François. *The Postmodern Condition: A Report on Knowledge*. Trans. Geoff Bennington, and Brian Massumi. Manchester: Manchester UP, 1984.
Macherey, Pierre. *A Theory of Literary Production*. Trans. Geoffrey Wall. London and New York: Routledge, 1978.
Mainwaring, Marion. *Murder at Midyears*. London: Macmillan, 1953.
Maltby, Paul. "The Romantic Metaphysics of Don DeLillo." *Contemporary Literature* 27:2 (1996): 258–277.
Marcuse, Herbert. *Counterrevolution and Revolt*. Boston: Beacon, 1972.

——. *Eros and Civilization: A Philosophical Inquiry into Freud.* Boston: Beacon, 1974.
——. *The One Dimensional Man.* Boston: Beacon, 1964.
Marrant, John. *A Narrative of the Lord's Wonderful Dealings with John Marrant.* Knoxville: U of Tennessee P, 1973.
——. *A Sermon Preached on the 24th day of June 1789, being the festival of St. John the Baptist.* Boston: The Bible and Heart, 1789.
Marsden, Madonna. "The American Myth of Success: Visions and Revisions." *The Popular Culture Reader.* Eds. Jack Nachbar, Deborah Weiser, and John Wright. Bowling Green: Bowling Green UP, 1978. 37–50.
Martin, Christine. "The New University Novel: A Mirror Not Just of Academe." *Conference of College Teachers of English Studies.* 53:2 (1988): 52–59.
McCaffery, Larry, ed. *Storming the Reality Studio: A Casebook of Cyperpunk and Postmodern Fiction.* Durham: Duke UP, 1992.
McCarthy, Mary. *The Groves of Academe.* New York: H.B.J, 1952.
McGee, Patrick. *Ishmael Reed and the Ends of Race.* New York: St. Martins Press, 1997.
McLeod, A. L. "The Poetry of Claude McKay." *Masterpieces of African-American Literature.* Ed. Frank Magill. New York: Harper Collins, 1992. 426–430.
Meece, Elizabeth, and Alice Parker, eds. *The Difference Within: Feminism and Critical Theory.* Amsterdam: John Benjamin, 1989.
Miller, Richard. "Social and Political Theory: Class, State, and Revolution." *The Cambridge Companion to Marx.* Ed. Terrell Carver. Cambridge: Cambridge UP, 1991.
Milner, John. *Art, War and Revolution in France 1870–1871: Myth, Reportage and Reality.* New Haven: Yale UP, 2000.
Mohanty, Chandra Talpade. "Under Western Eyes: Feminist Scholarship and Colonial Discourses." *Contemporary Postcolonial Theory: A Reader.* Ed. Mongia Padmini. London: Routledge, 1996. 168–189.
Morgan, Cherre, and Gloria Anzaldúúa, eds. *This Bridge Called My Back: Writings by Radical Women of Color.* New York: Macmillan, 1981.
Moss, Walter. "Alexander II and His Times." 19 Aug. 2001 <http://www.emich.edu/public/history/moss/atpt3.htm>.
——. *Russia in the Age of Alexander II, Tolstoy and Dostoevsky.* London: Anthem, 2002.
Nabokov, Vladimir. *Pnin.* New York: Doubleday, 1957.
Nazareth, Peter. "An Interview with Ishmael Reed." Dick and Singh 181–195.
Nietzsche, Friedrich. *Friedrich Nietzsche: Werke in Vier Bänden.* Band IV Salzburg: Bergland-Buch, 1985. IV Bänden.
Nketia, J. H. Kwabena. "African Roots of Music in the Americas—An African View." *Jamaica Journal* 43.3: 15–29.
Noiriel, Gérard. *Workers in French Society in the 19th and 20th Centuries.* New York: Berg, 1990.

Norris, Christopher. *Derrida*. Cambridge: Harvard UP, 1987.
Nover, Peter, ed. *The Great Good Place?: A Collection of Essays on American and British College Mystery Novels*. Frankfurt: Lang, 1999.
O'Carroll, Aileen. "The Paris Commune." 22 May 2001 <http://flag.blackened.net/revolt/talks/paris.html>.
O'Connor, William Van. "Parody as Criticism." *College English* 25: 4 (1964): 241–248.
Oren, Michael. "The Umbra Poets' Workshop, 1962–1965: Some Socio-Literary Puzzles." Eds. Joe Weixlmann and Chester Fontenot. *Studiesin Black American Literature Vol. II: Belief vs. Theory in Black American Literary Criticism*. Greenwood: Penkevill Publishing, 1986. 177–223.
Osteen, Mark. *American Magic and Dread*. Philadelphia: University of Pennsylvania Press, 2000.
Parini, Jay. "The *Fictional Campus: Sex, Power, and Despair*." The Chronicle of Higher Education 49.32 (2000): B12-B17.
Parker, Robert. *The Godwulf Manuscript*. London: Andre Deutsch, 1974.
Pelikan, Jaroslav. *Christianity and Classical Culture: The Metamorphosis of Natural Theology in the Christian Encounter with Hellenism*. New Have and London: Yale UP, 1993.
Pitchford, Nicola. *Tactical Readings: Feminist Postmodernism in the Novels of Kathy Acker and Angela Carter*. Cranbury and London: Bucknell UP, 2002.
Poe, Edgar Allan. "The Purloined Letter." *The Compact Bedford Introduction to Literature*. Ed. Michael Meyer. Boston and New York: St. Martins, 2000. 468–480.
Poovey, Mary. "The Twenty-First-Century University and the Market: What Price Economic Viability." *Differences* 12:1 (Spring 2001): 1–6.
Porter, Dennis. *The Pursuit of Crime: Art and Ideology in Detective Fiction*. New Haven and London: Yale UP, 1981.
Powers, Richard Gid. *Secrecy & Power*. New York: Macmillan, 1988.
Pusey, Michael. *Jürgen Habermas*. London and New York: Tavistock, 1987.
Radway, Janice. "The Book of the Month Club and the General Reader." *Reading in America: Literature and Social History*. Ed. Cathy Davidson. Baltimore: Johns Hopkins UP, 1989. 258–284.
Reed, Ishmael. *Airing Dirty Laundry*. New York: Addison-Wesley, 1993.
———."An Interview with Ishmael Reed by Reginald Martin." *Review of Contemporary Fiction* 4:2 (1984): 63–72.
———. *Mumbo Jumbo*. New York: Atheneum, 1972.
———. Personal Interview. 15 Apr. 2002.
Ridley, F. F. . *Revolutionary Syndicalism in France: The Direct Action of its Time*. Cambridge: Cambridge UP, 1970.
Riis, Thomas. *More Than Just Minstrel Shows: The Rise of Black Musical Theatre at the Turn of the Century*. Brooklyn: Brooklyn College of CUNY, 1992.
Robbe-Grillet, Alain. *For a New Novel: Essays on Fiction*. Trans. Richard Howard. New York: Grove, 1965.

Rosenfeld, Alvin. *Imagining Hitler.* Bloomington: Indiana UP, 1985.
Roudiez, Leon. Introduction. *Desire in Language: A Semiotic Approach to Literature and Art.* By Julia Kristeva. New York: Columbia UP, 1980. 1–20.
Saakana, Amon Saba. "Culture, Concept, Aesthetics: The Phenomenon of the African Musica Universe in Western Musical Culture." *African American Review* 29:2 (1995) : 329–341.
Said, Edward. *Culture and Imperialism.* New York: Random House, 1993.
Sampson, George. *The Concise Cambridge History of English Literature.* Cambridge and NewYork: Cambridge UP, 1946.
San Juan, Jr., E. "Problematizing Multiculturalism and the 'Common Culture.'" *Melus* 19:2 (Summer 1994): 59–85.
Sarup, Madan. *Identity, Culture and the Postmodern World.* Athens: U of Georgia P, 1996.
Saul, John Ralston. *Voltaire's Bastards: The Dictatorship of Reason and the West.* New York: Vintage, 1992.
Schell, Jonathan. "Cognitive Torture." *Nation* 14 July 2003: 8.
Schellenberger, John. "University Fiction and the University Crisis." *Critical Quarterly* 24:3 (Autumn 1982): 45–48.
Scholes, Robert. *Structuralism in Literature: An Introduction.* New Haven and London: Yale UP, 1974.
Schulte-Sasse, Jochen. Forward. *Theory of the Avant-Garde.* By Peter Bürger. Trans. Michael Shaw. Minneapolis: U of Minnesota P, 1984. vii-xivii.
Sekora, John."Black Message/White Envelope: Genre, Authenticity and Authority in the Antebellum Slave Narrative." *Callaloo* 10:3 (Summer 1987): 482–515.
Sheppard, Richard. "From Narragonia to Elysium: Some Preliminary Reflections on the Fictional Image of the Academic." Bevan 11–48.
Sheppard, Walt. "When State Magicians Fail: An Interview with Ishmael Reed." Dick and Singh 3–13.
Shumway, David *Michel Foucault.* Charlottesville and London: UP of Virginia, 1989.
Silverman, Kaja. *The Subject of Semiotics.* New York and Oxford: Oxford UP, 1983.
Simpson, David. "Raymond Williams: Feeling for Structures, Voicing 'History.'" *Cultural Materialism: On Raymond Williams.* Ed. Christopher Prendergast. Minneapolis: U of Minnesota P, 1995. 29–50.
Slaughter, Sheila, and Larry Leslie. *Academic Capitalism: Politics, Policies, and the Entrepreneurial University.* Baltimore: Johns Hopkins UP, 1997.
Slavitt, David. *Cold Comfort.* New York: Methuen, 1980.
Smart, Barry. *Michel Foucault.* London and New York: Tavistock, 1985.
Snead, James. "European pedigres/African contagions: nationality, narrative, and communality in Tutuola, Achebe, and Reed." *Nation and Narration.* Ed. Homi Bhabha. New York and London: Routledge, 1990.
Sollors, Werner, and Maria Diedrich, eds. *The Black Columbiad: Defining Moments in African American Literature and Culture.* Cambridge: Harvard UP, 1994.

Spivak, Gayatri Chakravorti. "A Response to 'The Difference Within: Feminism and Critical Theory.'" Meese and Parker 214–235.
———. *The Post-Colonial Critic: Interviews, Strategies, Dialogues*. Ed. Sarah Harasym. New York: Routledge, 1990.
———. *Outside in the Teaching Machine*. New York: Routledge, 1993.
Stearns, Peter. *Revolutionary Syndicalism and French Labor: A Cause without Rebels*. New Brunswick: Rutgers UP, 1971.
Swope, Richard. "Crossing Western Space, or the HooDoo Detective on the Boundary in Ishmael Reed's *Mumbo Jumbo*." *African American Review* 36:4 (2002): 611–628.
Tani, Stefano. *The Doomed Detective: The Contribution of the Detective Novel to Postmodern American and Italian Fiction*. Carbondale and Edwardsville: Southern Illinois UP, 1984.
"Underworld Media Watch." 11 Aug. 2002 <http//perival.com/delillo/underworld_media.html>.
Walker, Ronald, and June Frazer, eds. *The Cunning Craft*. Macomb: Western Illinois UP, 1990.
White, Hayden. *Metahistory: The Historical Imagination in Nineteenth-Century Europe*. Baltimore and London: Johns Hopkins UP, 1973.
———. "The Value of Narrativity in the Representation of Reality." *Narratology*. Eds. Susana Onega and José Angel Garcia. London and New York: Longman, 1996. 273–285.
"White Rabbit." *Law & Order*. Produced by Dick Wolf. N.B.C. WNBC, Philadelphia. 19 Oct. 1994.
Wiggershaus, Rolf. *The Frankfurt School: Its History, Theories, and Political Significance*. Trans. Michael Robertson. Cambridge: MIT Press, 1994.
Williams, Raymond. *Keywords: A Vocabulary of Culture and Society*. New York: 1983.
———. *Marxism and Literature*. Oxford and New York: Oxford UP, 1977.
Wilson, Keith. "Academic Fictions and the Place of Liberal Studies: A Leavis Inheritance." Bevan 57–73.
Wollen, Peter. "Don't be Afraid to Copy it Out." *L.R.B.* 20 (Feb. 1998): 37–41.
Wright, Elizabeth, ed. *Feminism and Psychoanalysis: A Critical Dictionary*. Oxford: Basil Blackwell, 1992.
Yanarella, Ernest, and Lee Sigelman eds. *Political Mythology and Popular Fiction*. New York: Greenwood, 1989.
Yellen, Jean Fagen. *The Intricate Knot: Black Figures in American Literature, 1776–1863*. New York: New York UP, 1972.
Young, Al. "Interview: Ishmael Reed." Dick and Singh 41–50.
Zafar, Rafia. *We Wear the Mask: African Americans Write American Literature, 1760–1870*. New York: Columbia UP, 1997.
Zinn, Howard. *A People's History of the United States: 1492-Present*. New York: Harper Perennial, 1995.

Index

A
Abrams, M. H., 17–18
Academic publishing, 147–150
Academic specialization, 134–135, 155
Academic writing, 114, 134, 149–150
Acculturation, 68, 74, 115
Acker, Kathy; *see also Adult Life of Toulouse Lautrec by Henri Toulouse Lautrec* (Acker)
    class and law, 88–89
    cultural phallogocentrism, 8–9, 72
    guerrilla warfare through fiction/language, 191
    "I" and ideological position, 69–70, 79, 81–82
    identification of narrators, 184
    literary genres, 68–71
    personal history of, 7–8, 98, 100
    postmodern text/writing strategies, 183–192
    reason, gender, patriarchy, and capitalism, 8, 68
    social and economic conditions, 186
    text, self, and gender, 72–85
    unified subject/text, 69
Adell, Sandra, 177–178
Adorno, Theodore, 130, 153, 190, 193
Adult Life of Toulouse Lautrec by Henri Toulouse Lautrec (Acker), 2, 5, 7, 113
    binary male/female reversal, 82, 100
    character bound/external narrator, 83–84, 109–110
    deconstructing detective narrative, 85–100
    detective genre vs. traditional narrative, 72–74, 90–92
    gender hierarchy, 79–81, 87
    gender relations and capitalism, 84–85, 104, 108
    historical narratives, use/abuse of, 100–112
    identification problem, 78, 81
    identity, masculinization of, 98
    lisible (readable) text, 72–74, 77, 86, 90, 97
    parody/blank parody, 185
    paternal metaphor/law of the father, 88
    pornography genre, 83, 104
    profanity and language, 89, 96
    reader's critical participation, 75
    reality effect disruption, 94–96
    referential character confrontation, 80
    scriptable (writable) detective tale, 86
    women, marginalized, oppressed, as other, 8, 70–72, 101–103, 111
African-American identity, 5, 7, 15–17, 35, 175–176, 179
African-American literary tradition, 12–13, 164, 169, 174–182
Agger, Ben, 132–134, 146–148
Althusser, Louis, 6, 68, 87
"American College Mystery, The" (Kramer), 118
American HooDoo, 42, 169
American myths, 173

Anarchism/anarchist movement, 106–108
Anti-humanism in university, 126
Anti-Oedipus (Guattari), 189
Aristotle, 99
Art, 185, 188–189, 192
Asson ceremony, 54–55
Astin, Alexander, 144–145
Atonism, 20, 25–27, 33–35, 45, 51, 61
Author/authorship, 3–6, 15–17, 21, 45
   author function, 167
   cultural identity and, 21, 36
   ideological functions of, 36–37
   literary "houngan," 48–49
   unitary authorship, 15
   Voodoo loa possession, 50
   western monotheistic tradition, 46
Autonomy, 129–130, 188

B
Baker, Houston, 37–40, 168
Bakunin, Mikhail, 108
Bal, Mieke, 9, 80, 84, 96–97, 110
Bambara, Toni Cade, 6
Baraka, Amiri, 6, 37–40, 47, 60, 168
Barthes, Roland, 2, 73–74, 86, 89, 93–94
Baudrillard, Jean, 2–3, 5, 12–13, 115, 152, 187–190, 199
Beck, Rudolf, 1
Belsey, Catherine, 10, 69–70, 73–74
Benjamin, Walter, 17, 44
Best, Steven, 152, 189, 202
Bhabha, Homi, 177, 179–180
Big Sleep, The (Chandler), 93, 95
Bildungsroman, 125
Black Literature in America (Baker), 38, 173
Black Literature and Literary Theory (Gates), 164
Blanqui, Auguste, 108–109
Bloom, Allan, 133
Book: A Novel (Grudin), 116, 118, 125
Book of the Month Club (BOMC), 11, 13, 114, 155, 166, 195, 198
"Book-of-the-Month Club and the General Reader, The" (Radway), 122, 156–157
Bordo, Susan, 98–100
Bowie, Malcolm, 88
Bradbury, Malcolm, 116, 126
Brecht, B., 8, 17, 44
Briton, Derek, 200
Brown, William Wells, 170–171
Burke, Kenneth, 159–161

C
Canetti, Elias, 154
Capital (Marx), 186
Capitalism, 5, 8, 67, 85, 106, 127, 129, 153, 201
Capitalist exploitation, 72, 85, 102–103, 184
Censorship, 37
Chabot, C. Barry, 198
Chandler, Raymond, 93, 95, 97
Changing Places (Lodge), 116
Chaucer, 125
Chesnutt, Charles, 169–170
Childs, Lydia Maria, 170–171
Christianity/Christian icons, 42, 45, 51
Christie, Agatha, 87–90
Civilization and Its Discontents (Freud), 32
Class struggle, 111, 189
Clotel; or, The President's Daughter (Brown), 170
College novel/mystery, 115, 118, 134, 194
Commercialism, 10
Commodification, 142
Commodity, 103
Community (communal), 17, 47–49, 54, 65–66, 87, 115, 126–127, 150, 171–173, 182
Conjure (Reed), 38, 46, 63, 170
Conjure Woman, The (Chesnutt), 169
Conner, Steven, 187
"Constructing the Subject: deconstructing the text" (Belsey), 10
Consumer culture/identity, 10, 153, 197
Consumerism, 5, 10, 134, 142, 151–154, 193
Cooking as authoring trope, 63–66
Corporatized university, 126–130
Cowley, Malcolm, 24
"Critical Languages" (Akers), 187, 189
Culler, Jonathan, 77, 94
Cultural differences, 3, 11, 30

Index

Cultural identity
abandonment of past, 24
African-American Diaspora, 56
authorship/authority and, 21
common cultural ownership, 182
contemporary media and, 22
history and, 19
purchasable identity, 151–153
Cultural nationalism, 38

D
Dadaism, 44
Dance as authoring trope, 61–63
Deconstruction, 85–86, 187–190, 192, 199
Deleuze, Gilles, 13, 188–189
DeLillo, Don, 2–5, 10–11, 13, 111, 113–114; *see also White Noise* (DeLillo)
college novel/mystery sub-genre, 10
consumerism, 5, 10, 196
as postmodern writer, 192–202
readership audience for, 114–115, 192
Deren, Maya, 6, 16, 20–21, 41–42, 54–55, 65
Derrida, Jacques, 2–3, 6–9, 21, 50, 67, 71–72, 98, 164, 167, 183–184, 199
Descartes, R., 98–100
Detection, 8
Detective fiction/genre, 7, 68, 72–73, 76, 85–87, 183–184
"textes de désir," 93
Dialectic of Enlightenment (Adorno), 190
"Différance," 21, 174
Discipline, 134, 147–149
Discourse/discursive formations, 50, 87
Discursive community, 114–115, 133–134, 146, 195
Dissemination, 6, 50, 167
Divine Horsemen: The Living Gods of Haiti, The (Deren), 6, 16
Domini, John, 169
Douglas, Aaron, 171
Doyle, Arthur Conan, 88, 95, 97
Drifting on a Read: Jazz as a Model for Writing (Jarrett), 18
Dubois, W.E.B., 177

E
Eagleton, Terry, 74, 160, 199, 202
Eco, Umberto, 35–36
Economic conditions, 186
Écriture, 89
Education, market-driven model of, 130–131
Enlightenment, 2, 24, 131
Epstein, Barbara, 202
Ethics, 3, 5
Ethnicity, 176, 181
Ewen, Elizabeth, 186
Ewen, Stuart, 186
Exile's Return (Cowley), 24

F
Fast Capitalism (Agger), 134
Feminine consciousness, 99–100
Feminist theory, 70–71, 118
Fielding, Henry, 75–77, 86, 185
Fleming, Ian, 125
Focalization, 84
Foster, Hal, 188
Foucault, Michel, 2–3, 6, 13, 36–37, 50, 67, 101, 110–111, 148, 164, 167, 188, 199
Fragmentation of contemporary life, 11
Frankfurt School, 190, 200
Frazer, James, 27–29, 32, 42
Freud, Sigmund, 16, 28–32, 42, 86, 104
Fromm, E., 190
Frow, John, 143, 154
Frye, Northrop, 170

G
Gaddis, William, 158
Gallo, Charles, 105–109, 185
Gates, Henry Louis, 12–13, 164–165, 173–180
Gayle, Addison, 37–40
Gender hierarchy, 79–81, 85, 87
Gender oppression, 7, 72
Gender relations, 85, 104
Global capitalism, 129
God's Trombones (Johnson), 171–172
Golden Bough, The (Frazer), 27, 42
Grand narrative (master narrative), 167

Groves of Academe, The (McCarthy), 116
Grudin, Robert, 116, 118, 125
Guattari, Félix, 13, 188–189

H

Habermas, Jürgen, 2, 11, 127, 129–130, 133
Haitian Voodoo, 41–42
Halley, Peter, 188
Harlem Renaissance, 19, 25, 34, 54, 61, 168, 171, 176–177
Harlem Renaissance (Huggins), 24
Harvey, David, 102–103
Heath, Stephen, 89
Hegel, G.W.F., 107
Hermeneutic code, 73, 86, 92, 116–117, 194
Historical figures, images of, 80
Historical narrative, 68, 80, 100–101
History Man, The (Bradbury), 126
Hogan, Patrick Colm, 13, 114, 147, 175–177, 180–182, 202
Horkheimer, Max, 130, 153, 190, 193
Hornstein, L. H., 75
Huggins, Nathan, 24–25
Hughes, Langston, 177
Hutcheon, Linda, 32, 100–101, 115
Huyssen, Andreas, 2

I

Identity, 8–9, 15–16, 40, 72, 98–99, 180–181
Ideological State Apparatuses, 6–7, 68, 115
Ideology, 37, 69, 86, 134, 190, 197–189
Improvisation, 6, 56–57, 59, 63–64, 172
Interdiscursivity (interdiscursive), 68, 75, 86, 105, 110–111, 183
Interpellation, 68
Interpretation of Dreams (Freud), 29
Intertextuality, 3, 5–6, 9, 29, 41, 43–44, 68, 75, 105, 183
Iser, Wolfgang, 74
Islam, 33, 35–36, 39
Iteration, 94, 96–97, 184

J

Jameson, Fredric, 11–13, 16, 44–45, 68, 87, 105, 122, 164–169, 182–183, 185, 193–195, 197

Jarrett, Michael, 18, 42
Jazz tradition, 6, 15–16, 30, 32, 34, 44, 54–56, 59, 62
Johnson, James Weldon, 171–172
Johnson, Joe, 38–39
Jones, Ernest, 29
Joyce, Joyce, 58
Jung, C. G., 28–32

K

Karenga, Ron, 6
Keller, Evelyn Fox, 98–99
Kellner, Douglas, 152, 189, 202
Keynes, John Maynard, 102
Kofman, Sarah, 104
Koons, Jeffrey, 189
Kramer, John, 118
Kristeva, Julia, 2–3, 6, 8–9, 44, 183
Kropotkin, Peter, 108
Kuenz, Jane, 176
Kuester, Hildegard, 1
Kuester, Mark, 1

L

Lacan, Jacques, 2–3, 9, 67, 69–71, 79–80, 82, 84, 86, 88, 183
Last Days of Louisiana Red, The (Reed), 37–38
Law of the Father (Name-of-the-Father), 88
"Law of Genre/Gender," 71–72, 184
Lawson, Thomas, 188
Leavis, F. R., 132
Legitimization crisis, 11, 87, 128
Lentricchia, Frank, 113–114
Leslie, Larry, 129–130
Liberal arts mission, 131–132, 150
Linear narrative, 184
Lisible (readable) text, 72–77, 85–86, 93, 184
Literary culture, 133
Literary genres, 68–71, 86, 115
"Literature as Equipment for Living" (Burke), 159–161
Lodge, David, 116
Logocentrism, 8, 71–72
Lovitt, Carl, 89
Luhrmann, Baz, 105

Index

Lyons, John, 124
Lyotard, Jean Françoise, 2–3, 164, 167, 199

M

McCarthy, Mary, 116
Macherey, Pierre, 69, 73, 96
Major, Clarence, 6
Maltby, Paul, 192
Marcuse, Herbert, 7, 100, 190
Marketspeak, 200
Marrant, John, 178
Martin, Gyde Christine, 126
Martin, Reginald, 40
Marx, Karl, 108, 186
Marxism, 38, 60, 70, 89, 134
Masculine scientific/rational mind, 98
Mass media, 22, 42–43, 115, 186
Memories, Dreams, and Reflections (Jung), 31
Metanarratives, 199
Micronarratives, 3, 122–124
Modernism, 2, 198
Modernity, 200
Monotheism, 20, 33, 45
Moulin Rouge (film), 105, 192
Mumbo Jumbo (Reed), 2, 4–5, 23, 113
   abandonment of cultural past, 24
   African-American identity, 5, 7, 15–16, 19, 35, 37
   alternative history, 20–21
   anthropological and psychological narratives, 42–43
   atonism in, 33–35
   authorship, authority, and cultural identity, 7, 21, 27, 33–34, 40
   black jazz tradition, 6, 34
   Christian vs. voodoo worship, 22
   Christian/religious conception in, 20–21
   cooking as authoring trope, 63–66
   critical/constructive satire of, 17–19
   dance as authoring trope, 61–63
   denigration of the bodily, 26–28
   Freud, Jung, and the black tide of mud, 29–32
   Gates and Jameson critiques of, 164–169, 174
   intertextal moments, 29, 31
   jazz player as trope, 53–61
   manichean concept of "demon," 29
   monotheistic/dispersed authorship, 45–53
   reversal of priorities of race, 52
   "Situation Reports (SRs)," 43–44, 59
   syncretic vision of authorship, 40–45, 59
   technological and social developments, 24
   voodoo tradition, 6, 16, 23
Murders in the Rue Morgue, The (Poe), 88
Mutualism, 108

N

Nabokov, Vladimir, 118
Name of the Rose, The (Eco), 35
Narrative contracts, 76, 93–94
Narrative rhythm, 96
Narrative techniques, 3, 9, 45
   focalization, 84
   historical narrative, 68
   identification of narrators, 184
   iteration, 94, 96–97
   lisible (readable) text, 72–77, 85–86, 93, 184
   metanarratives, 199
   realistic narratives, 69, 183
Narratology, 83
Narratology: Introduction to the Theory of Narrative (Bal), 9
Nature, 20, 22, 28, 45, 99
Neo Geo movement, 188
"Neo-HooDoo" aesthetic, 6, 17, 19, 50–51, 63
"Neo-HooDoo Manifesto" (Reed), 46, 50–53, 57, 63–64
New Black Aesthetic, 7, 24–25, 35, 37–39
New Historicism, 4, 6–7, 32
Nietzsche, F. W., 190
Nketia, J. H. Kwabena, 63
Non-identity, 12

O

Occultism, 31
"Octoroons, The" (Child), 170
"Oedipalization of the subject," 67
One Dimensional Man (Marcuse), 190
Oppression of women and poor, 5, 7–8

P

Paris Commune, 85, 107–109, 184–185, 191–192
Parker, Charlie, 53–55, 57
Pastiche, 16–17, 165–166, 185, 195
Paternal metaphor, 88
Patriarchy, 5, 8, 67, 85, 184
Pelikan, Jaroslav, 27
Perovskaya, Sophia, 111, 185
Petronius, 18
Phallocentrism, 8, 71–72, 98
Phallogocentrism, 8–9, 72, 100, 184
Plato, 99
Platonic rhetoric, 26
Pnin (Vladimir), 118
Poe, Edgar Allan, 88, 90
Political agency, 10
Politics (political), 2–5, 8, 12–13, 85, 102, 109, 188–189
Polytheism, 27, 45–46
Poovey, Mary, 128–129, 131, 151
Popular culture, 152
Pornography genre, 83
Porter, Dennis, 68, 72–74, 87, 90, 93
Possession, 29, 41, 47–48, 50, 53, 59
Postmodernism, 12–13, 15, 32, 113, 174, 183, 185, 200–201
  blank parody of, 44
  character and categorical legitimacy of, 1
  deconstruction and, 187
  defined, 1, 44, 198
  literature and history, 101
  postmodern art, 188–189
  postmodern culture, 114, 152, 166
  practices and theories of, 163
"Postmodernism and Consumer Society" (Jameson), 165–166
Postmodernism, or, The Cultural Logic of Late Capitalism (Jameson), 165–166
Poststructural postmodernism, 2–3, 13, 16, 44, 168, 174, 200
Poststructuralism, 1–2, 32, 50
  postmodernism and, 1–2
  textual activism and, 183–192
  tradition and, 180
Pratt, Mary Louise, 179
"Principle of thrift," 36–37
Proairetic code, 73, 116
Progress, 24
Proudhon, Pierre-Joseph, 107–108
Psychoanalysis, 9, 70
Psychologism, 70
Public sphere, discourse in, 133–135
Publishers, 147–148
"Purloined Letter, The" (Poe), 90
Pynchon, Thomas, 158

Q

Qu'est-ce que la propriéte? (Hegel), 107

R

Radical reflexivity, 2–3
Radway, Janice, 11, 114, 122, 156–157, 159
Rationality, 22
Readers, 3–5, 113, 155–161
Reading public, 133
Realism (realist text), 73–74, 193
Reason, 8, 130–131
Reed, Ishmael, 2–4, 12, 38, 111, 114; *see also Mumbo Jumbo* (Reed)
  African-American literary legacy, 168–172
  anti-racism of, 4
  authority, authorship, and identity, 12, 16, 47–48
  authorship as political critique, 6
  critique of ethnocentric white history, 4
  employment of "I," 46
  Gates vs. Jameson critiques of, 164–169, 174
  intertextuality of, 5
  literary "houngan," 48–50, 52
  New Black Aesthetic, 37–38
  political commitment of, 15
  satire, critical and constructive functions, 17–18
  as traditional postmodernist, 164–183
  Umbra poetry group, 38
  use of syncretic tradition, 42
  writing tropes of, 48, 53
Reflections on Gender and Science (Keller), 98
Rigaud, Milo, 16, 52–53
Rose, Jacqueline, 71
Rosenfeld, Alvin, 199

Index

S

S/Z (Barthes), 73
Saakana, Amon Saba, 62–63
Salle, David, 188
Satire, 17–18, 42
Satyricon (Petronius), 18
Schell, Jonathan, 201–202
Schellenberger, John, 155
Schematism, 131–132, 148
Scholes, Robert, 94
Schulte-Sasse, Jochen, 191
Scriptible (writable) text, 86, 184
Secrets of Voodoo (Rigaud), 16
Self-reflexiveness, 2
Serviteur-houngan, 53–55
Sheppard, Richard, 124–125, 131
Shepperd, Walt, 169
Shrovetide in Old New Orleans (Reed), 16, 55
Signifying Monkey: A Theory of African American Literary Criticism, The (Gates), 164–165, 173, 177
Silverman, Kaja, 67
Simulacrum, 152
Simulations, 5, 152, 187
Slaughter, Sheila, 129–130
Small World (Lodge), 116
Social relations, 67–68, 74
Sollers, Philippe, 76
Sovereign person, 190
Steinbach, Heim, 188–189
Stepping Westward (Bradbury), 116
Sterns, Peter, 107
Structuralism, 75, 77
Study in Scarlet, A (Doyle), 95
Subjectivity, 199
Surrealism, 44
Syncretism (syncretic), 16–17, 40–41, 168, 182

T

Technological developments, 157
Text, 3–5
Textes de désir, 93
Textuality, 2–3, 134, 189
Tom Jones (Fielding), 75–76
Transculturation, 179
Truth, 3

U

Umbra poetry group, 38
Underworld (DeLillo), 114
Unitary authorship, 15, 38–39, 48, 53, 164
Unity, 15, 71–72, 98, 101, 122, 164, 194
Unity of action, 76
University novel (college novel), 115, 118, 134, 194
University in public life, 10, 115, 131

V

Vaissman, Meyer, 188
Voloshinov, V. N., 89
Voodoo, 6, 15, 41, 44–46, 50, 54
Voudoun, 41, 53

W

Washington, Booker T., 38
Way of the New World, The (Gayle), 38
We Wear the Mask: African Americans Write American Literature, 1760–1870 (Zafar), 178
"What is an Author" (Foucault), 36
White Noise (DeLillo), 2, 10, 13
   academic prestige and income, 144–147
   accessibility to, 10–11, 113
   autonomy and commercial research, 129–130
   as Book of the Month Club selection, 122, 155–161, 195
   chancellor as corrupt bureaucrat, 126–127, 131
   characterizations in, 118
   as college novel/mystery, 116–126
   commodification of popular culture/cultural phenomena, 140–142
   consumerism and purchasable identity, 151–154
   corporatized university, 126–130
   disciplinary specialization, 134–135
   education, market-driven model of, 130–131
   elitism and cultural reproduction, 144–149, 152
   hermeneutic code, 116–117
   liberal arts mission, 131–132, 150

molar unities/molecular elements, 122–124, 157, 194–195
nature of contemporary life, 11
professor, literary traditions of, 124–125
readers and hopes of liberation, 155–161
reason and capitalist education, 130–151
social-political critique, 193
university's crisis in mission, 10

Williams, Raymond, 160
Writable (*le scriptible*), 74

Y
Yellow journalism, 22
Young, Al, 169

Z
Zafar, Rafia, 178–179

For Product Safety Concerns and Information please contact our EU
representative GPSR@taylorandfrancis.com
Taylor & Francis Verlag GmbH, Kaufingerstraße 24, 80331 München, Germany

www.ingramcontent.com/pod-product-compliance
Lightning Source LLC
Chambersburg PA
CBHW062131300426
44115CB00012BA/1886